King Hezekiah of Judah

King Hezekiah of Judah

True History—His True Story!

FRANCESCO CARGNEL

RESOURCE *Publications* • Eugene, Oregon

KING HEZEKIAH OF JUDAH
True History—His True Story!

Copyright © 2024 Francesco Cargnel. All rights reserved. Except for brief quotations in critical publications or reviews, no part of this book may be reproduced in any manner without prior written permission from the publisher. Write: Permissions, Wipf and Stock Publishers, 199 W. 8th Ave., Suite 3, Eugene, OR 97401.

Resource Publications
An Imprint of Wipf and Stock Publishers
199 W. 8th Ave., Suite 3
Eugene, OR 97401

www.wipfandstock.com

PAPERBACK ISBN: 979-8-3852-0595-0
HARDCOVER ISBN: 979-8-3852-0596-7
EBOOK ISBN: 979-8-3852-0597-4

Picture on the cover and figure 22: Ouria Tadmor, © Dr. Eilat Mazar

Unless otherwise indicated, all Scripture quotations are taken from the New King James Version®. Copyright © 1982 by Thomas Nelson. Used by permission. All rights reserved.

Scripture quotations from The Authorized (King James) Version. Rights in the Authorized Version in the United Kingdom are vested in the Crown. Reproduced by permission of the Crown's patentee, Cambridge University Press

Scripture quotations are taken from the New Revised Standard Version Updated Edition. Copyright © 2021 National Council of Churches of Christ in the United States of America. Used by permission. All rights reserved worldwide.

Contents

1	**Introduction**	
2	**The Life of King Hezekiah in the Biblical Overview**	1
2.1	The Name Hezekiah	1
2.2	The Geopolitical Situation	2
2.3	The Chronology of the Kings	6
2.4	The Complete Biblical Report	13
2.5	The Sequence of Events in the Chronological Order	31
3	**The Life of Hezekiah from Different Points of View**	45
3.1	Childhood and Youth	46
3.2	The Reformer	51
3.3	The Architect	56
3.4	The Foreign Affairs Expert	61
3.5	The Warlord	63
3.6	The Terminally Ill	66
3.7	The Praying Man	70
3.8	The Psalmist	76
3.9	The Proverbs Collector	77
3.10	The Doubter	80
3.11	The Fallen	85
3.12	The Father	94
3.13	The Miracles—God Intervenes	104
3.14	The Letters	124
3.15	Hezekiah and the Prophets	128
3.16	The Bronze Serpent . . . Then as Now . . .	129
3.17	The Hezekiah Tunnel	146
3.18	The Pregnant Woman Who Cannot Give Birth . . .	148
3.19	The Post-War Period	150
4	**The Life of Hezekiah in a Historical Context**	153
4.1	The Problem of the Transition from Jotham to Ahaz	153
4.2	Timeline of Hezekiah's Life in a Historical Context	171
4.3	Extrabiblical Testimonies	176
4.4	Where Even the Absence of Records Is a Testimony	193
5	**Afterword of the Author**	197

1

Introduction

A wise Christian missionary couple, whose names unfortunately have not been handed down, once said,

> It is always about finding the **living** Word of God (Jesus Christ) in the **written** Word of God (the Bible) . . .

> *In the beginning was the Word, and the Word was with God, and the Word was God. He was in the beginning with God. All things were made through Him, and without Him nothing was made that was made. In Him was life, and the life was the light of men. And the light shines in the darkness, and the darkness did not comprehend it.* (John 1:1–5)

> *And the Word became flesh and dwelt among us, and we beheld His glory, the glory as of the only begotten of the Father, full of grace and truth.* (John 1:14)

In this book, we will embark on a long, sometimes arduous, but very rewarding and highly interesting journey into the word of God. We will look at the life of a man who is mentioned in detail in the Bible in three different books. This man lived over 2,700 years ago and was one of the twenty kings of Judah. His name is Hezekiah. This king, with the exception of King Solomon, is mentioned in the Bible more than all the other kings of Israel and Judah before or after his reign. Nevertheless, there is comparatively little extrabiblical or biblical literature or writings about King Hezekiah. What is the reason for this? Unfortunately, as soon as one takes a closer look at the subject, difficulties immediately arise in dating the dates of Hezekiah's life as well as in the order, presentation, and interpretation of his life events. To make matters worse, this information in the Bible is spread over three different books with various emphases in the respective reports. In this work, we will try to face the difficulties, address them openly, and resolve them. The reader is promised that it will certainly be worthwhile to take this journey with us. Astonishing insights are waiting for us, legendary insights into the time, into the word of God, into the thoughts of God, his actions with Hezekiah, and hopefully just as deep insights for us and our present life. We will see that the written word of God becomes a living word. We will see how the life of this man, a king of Judah, which lasted only fifty-four years, will affect us and how it will speak to our hearts. We will feel how the living word will meet us from the written word. After studying this book, we will possibly question and readjust our path of life with God. Therefore, every potential reader is already warned at this point, should you wish to read on: the study of this book, even if it "sneaks up on you" a bit semi-scientifically at the beginning, could have consequences for your life!

The present work is structured in such a way that in the following chapter the reader is first presented with an overall view of the life of Hezekiah, including the historical and geopolitical framework, and then in chapter 3 with a special focus on various individual facets. In doing so, we would also like to try to interpret the word of God, to interpret the events and apply them to our lives, before the last chapter once again brings together a lot of biblical and extrabiblical information in an overview. At the end the author addresses the reader personally with an epilogue.

The passages in the Bible that report directly about Hezekiah can be found in the following books and sections:

2 Kings	Chs. 18–20
2 Chronicles	Chs. 29–32
Isaiah	Chs. 36–39

If we want to quote or refer to passages in the word of God, we will use the following notation.

Examples:

2 Kings, chapter 18, verse 4 shall be:	**2 Kgs 18:4**
2 Chronicles, chapter 29, verses 1–3 shall be:	**2 Chr 29:1–3**
Isaiah, chapter 37, verses 2–5 shall be:	**Isa 37:2–5**

In the same way, we want to use this common notation for the other books of the Bible when we quote from them. So, for example, the Gospel of Matthew would be "Matt," the second book of Samuel "2 Sam," etc.

Our main sources about the life of Hezekiah are these three books of the Bible mentioned above. Extrabiblical and apocryphal sources will not be discussed in chapter 2, but we will include them in chapters 3 and 4, if they can provide reliable additional information.

We would like to ask you now to read and study the three sections of the Bible mentioned above intensively.

We also encourage you to always have a Bible at hand to study this book and to read the passages indicated in it.

Let us have a quick look at some background information on these three books of the Bible:

The books 1 and 2 Kings as well as 1 and 2 Chronicles are actually each a whole book and were only divided up in much later centuries in order to ensure a better manageability of the papyrus scrolls used at that time, which were otherwise quite long. This is only because the Septuagint (Old Greek translation of the Old Testament from about 250 BC) and the Vulgate (Latin translation of the Old and New Testaments from about AD 382–393) were used to produce translations that were simply much longer than the Hebrew scrolls. In Hebrew, as is well-known, the vowels are omitted in the script. In the Vulgate and Septuagint, as usual, they wrote including the vowels, so that the scrolls of these translations simply became much longer. Therefore, the scrolls were divided over the particularly long scrolls for better handling. That is why we have 1 and 2 Kings and 1 and 2 Chronicles today. A division of the scrolls based on content or other motives is not known and cannot be assumed.

The authors of Kings and Chronicles are not named in them and are not really known. In the Jewish tradition the prophet Ezra is assumed to be the author of the Chronicles, but this cannot be proven beyond doubt.

The Kings books tell more of the complete history of the kings of the Northern Kingdom of Israel and the Southern Kingdom of Judah beginning from the last days of King David until Zedekiah, the last king of

Judah, with emphasis on royal and prophetic elements. In contrast, the chronicles focus exclusively on the events in the Southern Kingdom of Judah (not a single king of the Northern Kingdom of Israel is mentioned) with clear emphasis on priestly and theological elements. The release of Jehoiachin in Babylonian captivity in the thirty-seventh year of his imprisonment is the last event recorded in 2 Kings (2 Kgs 25:27–30). King Jehoiachin of Judah was arrested in 597 BC during the first campaign of the Babylonians against Judah. Thus his release must have been 560 BC (= 597 − 37). The return of the Jews from the Babylonian captivity after the destruction of Jerusalem by Nebuchadnezzar took place in 538 BC. Since the Kings books no longer report on this, the Kings books must have been written or at least completed in Babylon between these two events (Jehoiachin's release and the return from the Babylonian exile), i.e. between 560 and 538 BC and presumably still in Babylon.

In 2 Chronicles we find in chapter 2 the very detailed family tree of the line of David, in which after King Jehoiachin seven more generations are listed before the family tree ends. If we calculate the duration of one generation to be about thirty years (i.e. a total of about two hundred years, because 7 × 30 = 210), we arrive at the year 400 BC (i.e. two hundred years after Jehoiachin's capture in 597 BC) as the presumed approximate time period for the writing of the Chronicles.

At first glance, it is originally very surprising that both the Kings books and the Chronicles deal so intensively with the fate of King Jehoiachin, who reigned for only three months but then spent thirty-seven years in Babylonian captivity. This special attention becomes clear, however, immediately after one notices that the Davidic line of kings runs through Jehoiachin—up to Jesus Christ (Matt 1:11–12), which of course one could not know at that time. In addition, Jehoiachin also fulfills the prophecy to Hezekiah that sons who descend from him will be taken to Babylon (2 Kgs 20:18).

The book of Isaiah was written by the prophet Isaiah. Any other assumptions are in our opinion inaccurate and result only from unfounded doubts about the reliability and divine inspiration of the word of God, which of course includes the possibility of true prophetic predictions. Otherwise, in our view, there is neither sufficient biblical nor extrabiblical evidence against Isaiah's sole authorship. On the contrary, all extrabiblical findings, such as the 24 feet long Isaiah scroll found in the Qumran caves on the northwestern shore of the Dead Sea in 1947, dated 200 BC and completely preserved, speak clearly for one authorship, wholeness, and unity of the book. The Septuagint, after all, already from the third century BC as well knows only one book of Isaiah. In addition, the Bible itself and especially Jesus Christ in the New Testament always quote from only <u>one</u> book of Isaiah. Concerning the contents, it is interesting that Isaiah in the altogether sixty-six chapters of his book only in chapters 36–39 comprehensively presents historical events, and mostly about King Hezekiah. The other chapters of Isaiah's book are mainly devoted to prophetic topics. The chronologically last historical event, about which Isaiah reports, is the death of Sennacherib in 681 BC (Isa 37:38), so that the book must have been written or at least completed after that. However, it cannot have been many years later, because Isaiah was already very old, and because he was even a prophet under Hezekiah's great-grandfather Azariah (Uzziah). According to Jewish tradition in the Talmud and other Jewish sources, Isaiah hid from Hezekiah's son, Manasseh, in the hollow trunk of a cedar tree but was discovered there and then sawed through together with the tree by Manasseh's order (cf. also Heb 11:37). Since Isaiah himself no longer reports anything about the reign of Hezekiah's son, Manasseh, it can be assumed that his book was completed around 680 BC. Thus, we can date our three sources approximately in their time of writing and also put them in a chronological order:

- Isaiah   approx. 680 BC   (author: the prophet Isaiah)
- 2 Kings   approx. 560–538 BC   (author: unknown)
- 2 Chronicles   approx. 400 BC   (author: unknown, Ezra?)

Moreover, we want to make it clear to ourselves that Isaiah is indeed an <u>eyewitness</u> of the events!

After studying this book, the reader will probably be very surprised at how many details the Bible reveals to us about the life of King Hezekiah.

2

The Life of Hezekiah in the Biblical Overview

The Name Hezekiah

It is generally known that the names of the acting persons in those days often had a deeper meaning. Therefore, we will take a closer look at the name *Hezekiah*. In Hebrew the name exists in the short form הִזְקִיָּה *ḥizqîjāh* and the long form וּהִזְקִיָּהוּ *ḥizqîjāhû* which means either "My strength is YHWH" or "YHWH has made me strong." In 2 Kgs 20:10 as well as in 2 Chronicles we find the form וּהְיָקְזְחִי *jəḥizqîjāhû*, which one very similarly can translate "YHWH makes me strong."

This also includes the short form הְיָקְזְחִי *jəḥizqîjāh* (Hos 1:1; Mic 1:1; Ezra 2:16). In the Assyrian inscriptions, the writing *Ha-za-qi-ia-(ú)* is found for king Hezekiah, as well as in an Assyrian purchase contract from 603 BC. On the latest spectacular find of an original royal seal (see chapter 4), which Hezekiah possibly even held in his own hands, the ancient Hebrew writing והיקזח *ḥzqjhw* is found, which is identically attested on impressions of seals of royal officials who call themselves "servants of Hezekiah."

The Septuagint, the ancient Greek translation of the Old Testament from about 250 BC, gives the name with Εζεκιας, and the Vulgate as the Latin translation of the Old and New Testament from about AD 382–393 gives *Ezechias*. Nowadays we write *Hezekiah* in English translations and in the German-speaking world we find *Hiskija*, which probably comes closest to the original form, while the French *Ézéchias* rather reminds us very much of the Latin spelling of the Vulgate from the AD fourth century.

When we look at the course of Hezekiah's life, especially at his two most difficult situations, namely the time of his fatal illness and the time of the siege by the Assyrians, we may note with admiration that Hezekiah relied on the strength and power of God in both of these almost hopeless situations, and therefore quite rightly received his name in prophetic foresight. His name became the foundation of his life.

We may learn **God made Hezekiah strong! Hezekiah relied on the strength of God!**

And what a wonderful testimony the word of God gives here about Hezekiah:

> He trusted in the Lord God of Israel, so that after him was none like him among all the kings of Judah, nor who were before him. For he held fast to the Lord; he did not depart from following Him. (2 Kgs 18:5–6a)

The Geopolitical Situation

The political situation in the time of Hezekiah is relatively complicated.

The original kingdom of Israel had already been divided for two hundred years into a Northern Kingdom called *Israel* and a Southern Kingdom called *Judah* due to disputes about the rightful successor of King Solomon—not only in our times there are divisions (2 Kgs 12). Both empires were self-sufficient states with different royal dynasties. The capital of the Northern Kingdom was Samaria; the capital of the Southern Kingdom was Jerusalem. Of the total of twelve tribes of Israel, the tribes of Judah and Benjamin belonged to the Southern Kingdom, the remaining ten tribes to the Northern Kingdom.

The political and military power dominating the then known world was the Assyrian Empire located in the northeast of Israel, which we now call the *New Assyrian Empire,* in distinction to less influential former Assyrian dominions. We can date it to about 911 BC until its decline around 611 BC, when the newly emerging world power Babylon *(New Babylonian Empire)* overpowered the Assyrian Empire.

The *Egyptian Empire* in the southwest also still played an important role during the lifetime of Hezekiah but had already passed its zenith and had lost its power of expansion. After Hezekiah's death and still during the lifetime of his son Manasseh, the Assyrians under their king

Assurbanipal would even conquer and destroy the rich and powerful Egyptian metropolis Thebes in 664 BC.

The *Philistines* living in the adjoining northwest on the shores of the Mediterranean traditionally gave rise to disputes and were mostly not very friendly. Adjacent to it in the north was still the land of *Aram* with its capital Damascus in present day called Syria.

During the reign of Hezekiah's father, *Ahaz,* the then king of Israel *Pekah* allied himself with the Arameans under their king *Rezin* and led a campaign against Judah, which was successful at first, but was then broken off and did not reach Jerusalem. The consequences for the Aramaeans and also for the Northern Kingdom of Israel were devastating. For although the threat of Aram and Israel was now averted, King Ahaz then, through a catastrophically short-sighted political misjudgment and against the explicit advice of the prophet Isaiah (2 Kgs 16:7–9), persuaded the Assyrians under Tiglath-Pileser III to take up arms against Aram and Israel. As a result, Aram was almost completely wiped out in 732 BC and the Northern Kingdom of Israel was successively lost to the Assyrians, city by city, within a few years until finally the capital Samaria fell in 722 BC, thus sealing the final end of the Northern Kingdom of Israel.

After the abduction of the inhabitants of the Northern Realm by the Assyrians, which according to Assyrian sources took place in several waves from 722/721 BC under Sargon II until about 670 BC under Esarhaddon or his son Assurbanipal 669 BC (Ezra 4:10), these ten tribes of Israel are considered lost until today.

Interestingly enough, from the time Ahaz took over the royal rule (735 BC) until the completed forced resettlement of the Hebrew inhabitants of the Northern Kingdom with its capital Samaria (approx. 670 BC), it was almost exactly sixty-five years (735 – 670 = 65), which fulfilled the prophecy of Isaiah to Ahaz, according to which Ephraim "will no longer be a people in sixty-five years" (Isa 7:8). Subsequently, the Assyrians settled various other ethnic groups in the cities of the former Northern Empire, from which the Samaritan people (the name Samaria is still in here) was formed in the further course of history, which we encounter several times in the New Testament during the lifetime of Jesus (see also in detail 2 Kgs 17:24–41).

Due to these developments and the clumsy short-sighted actions of King Ahaz, the Assyrian threat was now directly on the borders of Judah...

The Bible then mentions in Isa 20:1 that Sargon II took the Philistine city of Ashdod; he did not appear in person for this but sent the tartan, his commander in chief. We do not know the trigger or reason for this, but the Assyrian records confirm this event and date it to the year 712 BC. That is, already in the time of the reign of Hezekiah.

FIGURE 1

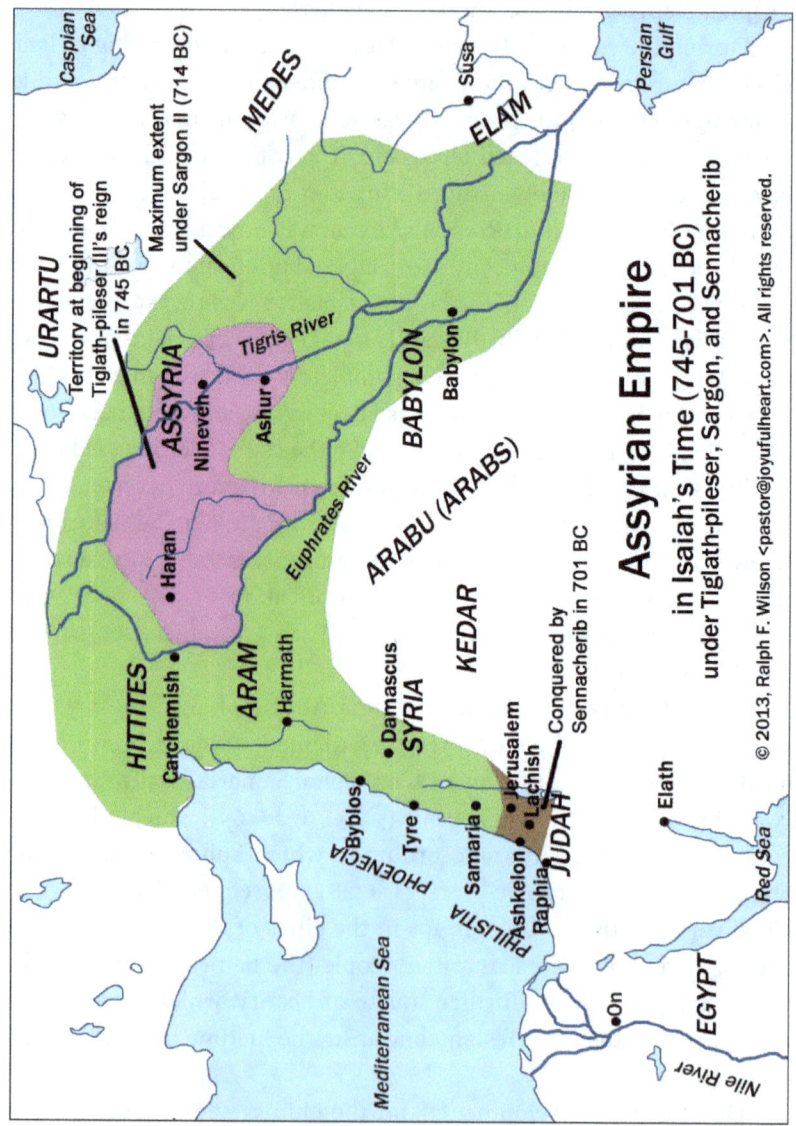

FIGURE 2

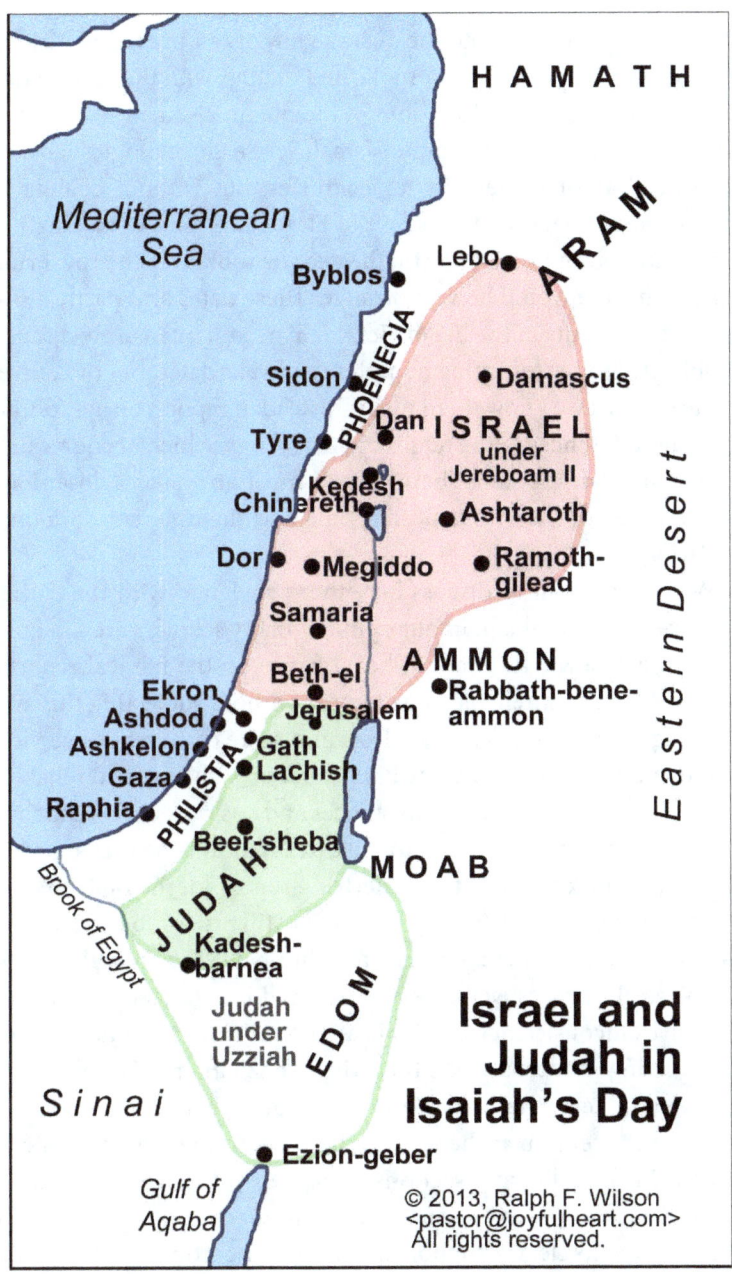

The Chronology of the Kings

Before we can now enter into the overall view of our protagonist's life, we have to deal with a somewhat complicated matter: with the chronology of the kings of the Southern Kingdom of Judah and also a little bit with the kings of the Northern Kingdom of Israel. These chronologies have been controversial among scientists for centuries, but without dealing with them, we cannot begin the narrative of Hezekiah's life. A presentation of his life story without date of birth, the year he took over the royal rule or the end of his life would be very strange. These dates and partly also the dates of other events in the life of Hezekiah are still intensively discussed. The bible gives an astonishing abundance of year dates, but of course no absolute dates as we know them today. Instead, it reports on age, duration of rule, and references to the reigns of other kings, which of course do not have absolute dates as well. Therefore, we must now take a closer look at the chronology of the events of that time and the different opinions on their dating.

We do not want to discuss here the "problems" with the dating of the life events of Hezekiah. In our opinion, many scholars are too quickly fixed on their view ("this cannot be") or give up the biblical report too lightly as allegedly unreliable or as a myth, without subjecting this apparent finding to a more detailed analysis in a more comprehensive view. If one takes an unbiased look at the biblical reports, the assured reliable extrabiblical sources, and the circumstances and customs of this epoch with a basic attitude that, in addition to the extrabiblical texts that are considered reliable, also considers the underlying reports of the Bible to be reliable in the first instance (for they have so far still proved to be so), one can certainly achieve a coherent result that eliminates the alleged problems, harmonizes all sources with one another, and is consistent in itself. This also resolves inconsistencies in biblical-critical dating attempts, as many of these dating models assume that King Ahaz fathered Hezekiah at the age of nine or ten. The reader himself judges what he considers more probable, a conception at the age of nine years or the sequence of events presented in the following sections with their underlying assumptions. Fortunately, there are also scientists who approach these questions without bias and who clearly support a dating and chronology harmonized between the extrabiblical and biblical accounts. The breakthrough came with the work of Edwin R. Thiele: *The Mysterious Numbers of the Hebrew Kings* (in three editions 1951, 1964, 1983). Initially met with resistance at the time, the chronology on which it is based has since established itself after further (Bible-compliant!) clarification and is in the process of becoming generally accepted. Thiele's chronology is now regarded as the solution to the task of harmonizing the biblical year dates with the extrabiblical references, a task that for centuries seemed impossible. Let Edwin R. Thiele speak for himself at the end of the preface of the third edition of his groundbreaking work and let us guess how he was able to achieve this success:

> *It is my hope that this presentation will serve to bring confidence in the biblical numbers of the Hebrew Kings, in God who placed them on their thrones, and in the principles of righteousness. He expected them to uphold. This confidence, now so woefully lacking, is our primary need in our troubled and perplexed times. If we would restore confidence in God, we must restore confidence in the Bible—confidence that comes through an intelligent trust.*[1]

In the following, we would like to limit ourselves to presenting a realistic and consistent sequence of all events and to reconcile the biblical and secure extrabiblical reports. We do not quite follow the year dates of Thiele's chronology, but have made slight modifications, which in our opinion are more logical and fit into the overall context more harmoniously and without contradiction. Before we dedicate ourselves to this chronology, we must, for a better overall understanding, jointly acquire some useful information about that time.

The Accession Year

With the data about the durations of rule in the old writings to be considered, we must always take into account a possible small inaccuracy that is difficult to resolve. This is due to the fact that in the historiography of these times, the first months of a new king's assumption of office until the end of the calendar year of his assumption of office were often (but not always) counted not as the first but as the zeroth year of the regency. This period is called the accession year. Only the full following year was then counted as the first year of the new king's regency. Because we do not know exactly when the authors of the old writings set accession years and when they did not, the consequence is that we actually

---

1. Edwin R. Thiele, *The Mysterious Numbers of the Hebrew Kings* (Grand Rapids: Zondervan, 1983), 24.

always have a possible inaccuracy of up to one year in the details of the reigns. The matter is further complicated by the fact that, apparently in the historiography of the Southern Kingdom of Judah, an accession year was frequently set, whereas in the Northern Kingdom of Israel it was rather less frequent. It becomes even more difficult because the two empires in the meantime probably at least once in their historiography have changed the principles in the application of an accession year. We do not want to create unnecessary confusion at this point. It is only important to note that we must always keep in mind this uncertainty of up to one year when considering the duration of the reigns and the dates derived from them. This book wants to deal with the events in the life of King Hezekiah. It tries to put these events into a comprehensible temporal context, to underpin the credibility of the biblical text with the help of the temporal data found there and to tell the story of Hezekiah on this basis. The chronology presented in the later course, although now widely and increasingly supported by many scholars, has no scientific claim. It only makes clear that the story can be told relatively easily and that all biblical information and confirmed extrabiblical dates fit together harmoniously. Scientists sometimes go even further and try to determine these dates precisely to months or even weeks, but we want to be content with an accuracy of +/− one year. In our opinion, this should be completely sufficient to support the reliability of the biblical data and to give our narrative a coherent timeframe.

Coregencies

A very important construction in the Hebrew royal dynasties, and perhaps not sufficiently appreciated in the past especially by Bible-critical scholars, was the so-called "coregencies."

The possible reasons for coregency are still understandable from today's point of view:

a. The king could no longer continue his official business.

For example, by disease: Azariah (Uzziah) became leprous around 750 BC and had to go into a separate quarantine. In this quarantine he lived on (about ten years) and kept the title of king, although his successor—in this case his son Jotham—had already taken over the official duties. Therefore, from 750 BC there were two ruling kings until Azariah (Uzziah) died and Jotham ruled alone from then on.

b. <u>The king was in captivity or in exile.</u>

Example: King Amaziah was defeated and captured by King Joash of the Northern Kingdom of Israel. His son Azariah (Uzziah) had to take over the official business. After Amaziah's release and return to Jerusalem, he had to flee to Lachish, but fell victim to a conspiracy there some time later (2 Kgs 14; 2 Chr 25).

c. <u>The king wanted to settle his succession without bloodshed and without disputes even before his own death and to prepare the successor for the tasks of a king.</u>

Hezekiah himself did this, for example, by making his son Manasseh coregent at the age of twelve. He did this in wise foresight exactly five years after the siege of Jerusalem by Sennacherib and also five years after his recovery from the deadly disease, which had prolonged his life by another fifteen years. More precisely, Hezekiah was one of the few people who knew the exact date when they would die. It is all the more logical that he took timely measures to regulate his succession. In this case, five years after the events of siege and sickness, i.e., ten years before the date of death known to him, he took the precaution to introduce his son Manasseh into the official duties by appointment into the coregency in a sufficient period of time and to train him in these duties (by the way, exactly when Manasseh became twelve years old—more on this later).

In fact, for the most diverse reasons, coregencies can be applied or, with a certain probability, assumed up to eight times for the kings of Judah and up to four times for the royal dynasties of the Northern Kingdom of Israel. During a life as a king, two periods of coregency were even possible: one at the beginning of the royal existence, when the father-king appoints the son as coregent, and then at the end of his royal existence, when the then aging, weakened, or sick former son-king himself appoints his son as successor and brings him into coregency.

Why is all this important?

The whole depiction around the coregencies shows that there have been some periods of time in which periods of rule have overlapped. This makes it much easier to fit the biblical information on the durations of rule into the dating of the extrabiblical sources. We will now conclude this topic by defining the two terms that are important in this context and remember them for the further course of the discussion. By differentiating between these two terms, we will attempt to present the section of the chronology of the kings of Judah that is relevant for our purposes without contradiction and in a harmonized manner between biblical and extrabiblical testimonies, and to embed the life story of Hezekiah in it.

Coregency

This is the period of time in which a designated successor king (always the son) is either voluntarily taken into coregency by the currently reigning father-king or involuntarily, because the acting king is currently unable to rule or only partially able to rule due to external circumstances such as illness or captivity. We do not know how the division of official duties was then carried out. It is obvious, however, that the father-king still had the final authority in the essential questions.

Autocracy

This is the period in which a king reigns without a coregent, for example, when the father king dies and the successor king, who may have been allowed to coreign for some time, becomes the sole ruler.

Let us take the example of Manasseh again: Hezekiah appoints his son Manasseh at the age of twelve years and five years after the attack of Sennacherib on Judah (702–701 BC)—i.e., in about 697 BC—as coregent, until Hezekiah dies ten years later—in 687 BC. Manasseh was thus coruler from 697 until 687 BC, when he attained sole rule through the death of his father.

It seems to be so that the reports in 2 Kings and 2 Chronicles and the year and age indications and durations of a royal rule contained therein sometimes refer to the assumption of a coregency and sometimes only to the assumption of sole rule. It can be assumed that the writers of 2 Kings and 2 Chronicles had their reasons for this, which we can perhaps partly guess today, but do not really know.

Later, when we finally take into account the title of this chapter and will tell the whole story, we want to add in the overall view of the events, where necessary, whether a dating in the report just refers, in our view, to a co- or sole reign. We will see that by this simple measure the pieces of the puzzle come together, and a coherent chronology is created. This chronology will then fit smoothly and harmoniously into the extrabiblical dates with their fixed anchor points, which have been judged to be reliable and which we will discuss in the following section.

By the way, a very nice indication for the subject of coregency can be found in the apocryphal book the Ascension of Isaiah, which dates from the first century BC. Although it is not part of the biblical canon, it describes how King Hezekiah "calls" his son Manasseh into the reign. More about this in chapter 4.

Coregencies did indeed exist; they are not a modern invention of contemporary biblical lunatics who desperately try to justify the biblical text, but simply reality.

Fixed Anchor Points in the Chronology

In the book of 2 Kings, each new royal rule in the Southern Kingdom of Judah is introduced with a similar scheme, which looks something like this:

"In the **xth** year of **Name 1**, king of Israel, **Name 2** became king, the son of **Name 3**, king of Judah. And **Name 2** was **xx** years old when he became king, and he reigned **yy** years; and the name of his mother was **Name 4**. And he did what was (**right / evil**) in the eyes of the LORD."

So, we find in this scheme:

(1) The temporal reference to the parallel ruling king in the Northern Kingdom of Israel
(2) The name of the new king of Judah and the relation to his father
(3) The age of the new king of Judah when he took over his royal rule

(4) The duration of his reign in years (for Jehoahaz and Jehoiachin in months)

(5) The name of his mother (and sometimes also the name of her father)

(6) A summary assessment of his regency—right or evil

Here (1)—i.e., the temporal reference to the parallel ruling king in Israel—was no longer possible after the fall of the Northern Kingdom under Hoshea in 722 BC. As is to be expected, (1) does not occur thereafter either and is omitted as a further dating aid, this incidentally precisely during the lifetime of Hezekiah.

For the kings of the Northern Kingdom there is a very similar scheme, and then of course with a temporal reference to the king in the Southern Kingdom of Judah, who is currently ruling in parallel. However, neither the age of the new king when he took office nor the name of his mother is mentioned in this scheme, which we therefore find only for the kings of Judah.

There is a whole series of Assyrian, Babylonian, and other nonbiblical texts, some of which allow quite reliable dating of events in the royal books and chronicles of the Bible. This was made possible in particular by simultaneously recorded astronomical events such as solar or lunar eclipses, which can now be dated exactly mathematically with the help of computers.

We want to take the three events that are most essential for our time frame and define them as "fixed anchor points" of our chronology. This means that the biblical chronology—or our interpretation of it—must also meet these year dates more or less reliably—in other words, it must be possible to "calibrate" it. A permissible inaccuracy should not exceed one year (the acession year).

A. 724-722 BC—Siege/Capture of Samaria (Shalmaneser V / Sargon II)

B. 702-701 BC—Campaign against Judah and siege of Jerusalem (Sennacherib)

C. 588-587 BC—Siege and destruction of Jerusalem (Nebuchadnezzar)

The challenge of the following depictions must therefore be to tell the biblical story of the kings of Judah—let us begin around 821 BC with Hezekiah's great-great-grandfather Amaziah—in a chronological sequence. This chronological sequence must be provided with dates that correspond to all biblical statements and must be brought into harmony with all secured extrabiblical dates.

We will later find that in this way we even gain completely new insights and impressions that can enrich the existing knowledge and offer attempts at explanation that are very interesting. These newer insights are also able to eliminate difficulties that have not yet been completely resolved or to offer coherent explanations. As an example, we would like to mention here the "problem" with the son of the king named Maaseiah, who was killed by an Israelite soldier in a battle of the Syrian-Ephraimitic war between Judah, Aram, and Israel. We want to resolve this apparent inconsistency in the biblical text, for example. More details will follow later in chapter 4.

The Complete Biblical Report

We will now attempt to tell the story from a certain point in time, beginning with Hezekiah's great-great-grandfather Amaziah, until the end of Jerusalem in 587 BC under Zedekiah, the last king of Judah, in a summary without any claim to completeness. We want to pause at our protagonist King Hezekiah and take a closer look at the course of his life. The following narrative combines the information from 2 Kings, 2 Chronicles, and Isaiah 36–39 into a continuous report, whereby no contradictions between the three books could be found. The three biblical reports differ only in the depths of detail and focus of the presentation of individual events. For better readability and comprehensibility, we deliberately want to leave out references to the respective biblical passages to a large extent, but we explicitly assure that we will not add anything (apart from dates that correspond to our suggestion of chronology) that is not really mentioned in the biblical report in this way. Nor do we wish to add any information that can be obtained from nonbiblical sources at this point, but *in the following chapter, we will restrict ourselves in our overall view of the events to information from the biblical reports.* As announced before, we will then, where necessary, make distinctions between sole and coregencies. We want to put these in parentheses and additionally mark them in *italics*, so that you can see that we have added them. After studying the whole of the following narrative, each of us should first judge for himself whether, from his point of view, it could have happened this way or whether it shows inconsistencies or improbabilities. In a second step, we would like to check all contents and their dates (which we now try to do as far as possible in real year dates) against all biblical and extrabiblical reports.

We emphasize once again that in the following account of the events we will initially refer *only to the biblical reports*. Where it seemed advisable to us, we have added a little information, which is then also indicated in *italics*. We do not want to look at the kings before Amaziah, since they lived long before Hezekiah, who is the subject of this work. We enter into the history of Hezekiah's great-great-grandfather . . .

Hezekiah's great-great-grandfather **Amaziah**, the son of the then king Joash, was born in 821 BC by his mother Jehoaddan. At the age of twenty-five years, he took over the (*sole*) rule over Judah in 796 BC. He did what was evil in the eyes of the LORD. In a warlike conflict with the Northern Kingdom of Israel, he was defeated and captured by the then ruling king of Israel, also named Joash (like Amaziah's father). In 792 BC, his son **Azariah (Uzziah)** was therefore appointed (*coruling*) king at the age of sixteen. Amaziah eventually returned from captivity to Jerusalem, but then had to go into hiding in Lachish because of a conspiracy against him. Nevertheless, he fell victim to this conspiracy in 767 BC after a total reign of twenty-nine years at the age of fifty-four.

Hezekiah's great-grandfather **Azariah (Uzziah)** thus became (*sole*) ruler over Judah in 767 BC—in the twenty-seventh year of King Jeroboam II, the king of the Northern Kingdom of Israel. Azariah (Uzziah) was born in 808 BC by his mother Jecholiah and remained king for a total of fifty-two years after taking over the (*co*)regency in 792 BC until his death in 740 BC. Azariah (Uzziah) did what was right in the eyes of the LORD. The name Azariah (Uzziah) is written in such a peculiar way because this king is always called "Azariah" in the second book of Kings and for reasons unknown to us in 2 Chronicles always "Uzziah." That is why it was agreed to call him Azariah (Uzziah). Nevertheless, it is always one and the same person. Azariah (Uzziah) became sixty-eight-years old, of which he had to live the last ten years in isolation (quarantine). He was militarily very successful, as the report in 2 Chr 26:1–15 impressively describes. The latest war technology apparently also contributed to this: "And in Jerusalem he made artistically conceived machines that were to stand on the towers and corners of walls to shoot arrows and large stones" (2 Chr 26:15a). The same verse sums up how famous and mighty he had become through his faithfulness to God and through his wonderful help: "And his name went forth even to afar. For miraculously he was helped until he was very powerful" (2 Chr 26:15b). Then success and fame obviously got to his head (2 Chr 26:16), because one day he entered the temple without authorization and wanted to offer incense sacrifices himself instead of the only authorized priests. When the horrified priests tried to dissuade him from his self-important plan in front of the incense altar, Azariah (Uzziah) became angry with the priests already holding the incense pan in his hand. At that moment he was beaten by God with *leprosy*, which broke out on his forehead. Afterwards he left the scene in a terrified hurry. This event took place in the year 750 BC. Subsequently, Azariah (Uzziah) had to go into seclusion, where he lived in a specially prepared building outside the walls of Jerusalem until his death. As a result, his son **Jotham** had to take over the official duties in the same year 750 BC at the age of twenty-five and became (*co*)ruler. During the reign of Azariah (Uzziah) an exceptionally large earthquake apparently occurred (Zech 14:5).

Hezekiah's grandfather **Jotham** was born in 775 BC by his mother Jerusha and in 750 BC—in the second year of the reign of king Pekah (751 to 731 BC) of the Northern Kingdom—he took over the (*co*)regency at the age of twenty-five years because of his father's leprosy. Jotham did what was right in the eyes of the LORD. After the death of his father in 740 BC, he took over the (*sole*) reign over Judah. After taking over his (*co*)rule, Jotham was king for a total of sixteen years, until 735 BC when his son **Ahaz** was appointed (*co*)ruler of Judah. Three years later Jotham died in 732 BC at the age of only forty-three years.

Hezekiah's father **Ahaz** became—in 735 BC, the seventeenth year of the reign of king Pekah (751–731 BC) of the Northern Kingdom—at the age of twenty years (*co*)ruler over Judah, until he took over the (*sole*) rule three years later in 732 BC after the death of his father. Ahaz first saw the light of day in 755 BC, the name of his mother is not mentioned for unknown reasons. Ahaz did what was evil in the eyes of the LORD.

Ahaz practiced an almost fanatical idolatry, which led to God's fateful turning away from Judah. He even offered some of his sons as human sacrifices and carried all idolatry "under every green tree" (2 Chr 28:4) in Judah. Ahaz suffered some considerable military defeats against the Northern Kingdom of Israel, which was allied with Aram (today's Syria), and against the Philistines and also the Edomites. The more disgrace and defeats he accumulated as king, the greater became his disloyalty to God and his insatiable urge to idolatry. The inglorious climax was the measure to completely empty the house of God, the temple, of all utensils, to close it from the outside and to forbid any temple service. Instead, altars for foreign gods were built everywhere in Judah. In the defeats in the battles against Aram and against the Northern Kingdom of Israel, among others, the son of the king named Maaseiah, the house prince and his prime minister, as well as 120,000 warriors of his army, were killed. In addition, another two hundred thousand prisoners were taken away to Samaria, although they were allowed to return immediately to Judah after the intervention of the prophet Oded, who lived there. In addition to all the defeats and the open hostility against God, Ahaz also made a fatal mistake, in that he, against the fervent advice of the prophet Isaiah, bought the Assyrians under Tiglath-Pileser III through considerable payments of gold and silver (2 Kgs 16:8) to ally himself with him and take up arms against Aram and Israel. The Assyrians subsequently destroyed Aram including the capital Damascus. The defeats did not make Ahaz turn back, but rather drove him even more to challenge God, so that he even decided to worship the gods of Aram, since they had obviously helped to defeat him and Judah first. Therefore, Ahaz had an idol altar, which he had seen during the visit of Tiglath-Pileser III in Damascus, which had been defeated by the Assyrians, rebuilt and set up in the temple in Jerusalem. However, the Assyrians did not stop in Damascus, but then gradually penetrated into the Northern Kingdom of Israel (*Israel was an ally of Aram*), surrounded its capital Samaria, and stood directly on the borders of Judah. The already tense geopolitical situation had thus dramatically worsened for Judah.

In the meantime, in 741 BC, **Ahaz's** son **Hezekiah** was born to his mother Abijah. In 728 BC—the third year of the reign of King Hoshea (*731 to 722 BC*) of the Northern Kingdom—King Ahaz's son **Hezekiah** was appointed (*co*)ruler over Judah at the age of twelve or thirteen years.

In 724 BC—the seventh year of the reign of King Hoshea of the Northern Kingdom—the new king of Assyria Shalmaneser V (*726–722 BC*) raised against Samaria and began his siege. This was the twelfth year (*including the three years of coregency under his father Jotham*) of the reign of King Ahaz and it was the fourth year of the (*co*)reign of Hezekiah.

In the year 722 BC—in the ninth year of the reign of King Hoshea of the Northern Kingdom—Samaria was then taken, and the removal of the ten tribes of the Northern Kingdom by the "King of Assur" began *(in the meantime, Sargon II had become King of Assyria instead of Shalmaneser V)*. This was the sixth year of the *(co)*reign of Hezekiah (728 − 6 = 722 correctly derived ➔ **anchor point A** from page 12).

Ahaz ruled *(after the death of his father in 732 BC) for a* total of sixteen years until he died in 716 BC at the age of only thirty-nine years. It is remarkable that the people and apparently also his son Hezekiah, who followed him, refused because of his horrible idolatry to bury Ahaz in the king's tomb to which he was actually entitled (2 Chr 28:27).

Hezekiah now became *(sole)* ruler over Judah through the death of his father in 716 BC at the age of twenty-five (2 Kgs 18:2).

Spiritual Reforms

Immediately after the funeral service for his father and his own coronation ceremonies, Hezekiah began "right in the first year of his government, in the first month" (2 Chr 29:3) with drastic spiritual reforms. He introduced extensive measures to eradicate all forms of idolatry. Both the idols of Baal and Asherah were destroyed, as well as any other cultic memorial stones. The "high places" on which the people had worshiped God according to their own desires and not according to the Mosaic principles pleasing to God were smashed to pieces, as was the famous bronze serpent that had been lifted after Moses had it made at the end of the forty-year desert journey at the behest of God to save the people from the poisonous serpents (Gen 21:5–9). In the meantime, it was called "Nehushtan" ("the Bronzes") and had also been elevated to a cult object to be worshiped.

Simultaneously with the cleansing of all idolatry, Hezekiah launched a comprehensive action to restore the temple and temple services. The temple was unlocked again, within sixteen (2 × 8, the 8 is the biblical number of the new beginning) days it underwent a radical cleansing from the desecrations under Hezekiah's father, Ahaz, and the equipment that had been taken away or destroyed was brought back there, repaired, or rebuilt again. Afterwards Hezekiah and the priests prepared a great Passover, which had to be postponed for another month, because the cleansing of the priests and the purges from the idols were not yet completed. Hezekiah and the priests sent invitations to all people in the whole land of Judah, but also to the rest of the Hebrews in the whole Northern

Kingdom of Israel, who had been spared from the Assyrian abduction, for this upcoming Passover (*"from Beersheba to Dan"* = *from the very south of Judah to the very north of Israel*), together with the heartfelt request to celebrate this feast jointly and to repent together from the faithless ways of the last decades against God the LORD. The "runners" sent out went from town to town and delivered this invitation from the king (*one must imagine it as a kind of relay race, in which one runner took the king's message from one town to another, passed it on to the next runner, who then ran again to the next town, etc. After the message was delivered, the runners returned to their respective home cities. The beginning was made by men from the king's bodyguard*). With a few exceptions, however, Hezekiah's invitation was rejected or even ridiculed in the cities of the Northern Kingdom of Israel. From the tribes of Judah and Benjamin, on the other hand, came a large crowd.

The Passover began on the fourteenth day of the second month (715 BC). Since many of those present had not been able to sanctify and purify themselves sufficiently to celebrate the Passover properly, Hezekiah personally prayed to God and asked for forgiveness and purification for everyone who came and whose heart was set on seeking God. And the LORD heard Hezekiah's prayer and the people were purified so that they could all celebrate the feast with a joyful heart. They celebrated the feast of unleavened bread that followed the Passover for seven days with such fervor and joy in the LORD that they jointly decided to extend it for another seven days, which caused Hezekiah and the rulers to donate a large number of sheep and bulls for it.

> *The whole assembly of Judah rejoiced, also the priests and Levites, all the assembly that came from Israel, the sojourners who came from the land of Israel, and those who dwelt in Judah. So there was great joy in Jerusalem, for since the time of Solomon the son of David, king of Israel, there had been nothing like this in Jerusalem. Then the priests, the Levites, arose and blessed the people, and their voice was heard; and their prayer came up to His holy dwelling place, to heaven.* (2 Chr 30:25–27)

After the end of these moving and spiritually renewing celebrations in Jerusalem, many of those present went to the other cities of the tribes of Judah, Benjamin (= *Southern Kingdom*) and even Ephraim and Manasseh (= *Northern Kingdom*), in order to destroy the idols and places of worship there as well. And only when they had finished this did they return home to where they had come from.

After these certainly unique comprehensive spiritual renewing celebrations, Hezekiah immediately set about establishing a regular temple service. He determined the twenty-four departments necessary for this and from his own property he gave animals for the daily, weekly, monthly, and annual sacrifices. He asked his people to give the tenth part of their income, and the people followed his wish joyfully and in great numbers, so that the collection of the offerings lasted from the third to the seventh month—that is, over four months. The priests and Levites found so much abundance that Hezekiah had to have pantries built in which what the priests and Levites did not consume themselves could be brought in and stored. And Hezekiah hired selected men who were responsible for ensuring that the priests and Levites were regularly and correctly distributed the portions due to them. The idols were destroyed, the temple was purified, its doors and gates were repaired, the whole people had asked God for forgiveness and were purified, the priests and Levites were reinstated, and their provision was assured. Thus, the regular temple service could begin again and be maintained permanently.

> *And he [Hezekiah] did what was good and right and true before the Lord his God. And in every work that he began in the service of the house of God, in the law and in the commandment, to seek his God, he did it with all his heart. So he prospered.* (2 Chr 31:20b–21)

Major Construction Activities and Economic Growth (2 Chr 32:27–30)

In the years that followed, Hezekiah was able to bring about considerable economic growth, which resulted in the establishment of many new towns, the pantries and stables filled up, and Hezekiah himself acquired considerable assets.

Victories against the Philistines (2 Kgs 8:8)

Hezekiah was also able to put an end to the disastrous work of his father in military matters. Thus, he succeeded in regaining the territories lost to the Philistines under Ahaz (2 Chr 28:18), inflicting considerable defeats on the Philistines and pushing them back to the Mediterranean as far as Gaza.

Resistance against Assur
(2 Kgs 18:7b)

Likewise, Hezekiah began to rebel against the threat and oppression of the Assyrians brought about by the clumsy actions of his father. He refused to obey the king of Assyria at a moment that seemed to be favorable to him (*and thus of course also the tribute payments*).

Threat by Assur, Beginning of the Campaign of Sennacherib against Judah
(2 Chr 32:1)

In the fourteenth year of the (*sole*) reign of king Hezekiah, i.e., about 702 BC (716 − 14 = 702 <u>correctly derived</u> ➜ **anchor point B** from page 12), the Assyrians under their new king Sennacherib (705–681 BC) therefore started a retaliation campaign against "all fortified cities" in Judah, which soon achieved success.

Defense Fortification
(2 Chr 32:2–7)

As the unstoppable Assyrian army advanced, Hezekiah began to prepare the defense of Jerusalem. The city walls were strengthened and renewed, watchtowers and defense towers were built on them. An additional outer wall was raised around Jerusalem and a defensive wall was built. Weapons were made in large numbers; an army was formed and "military captains" were deployed. Hezekiah knew that the water supply was of vital importance, both for the besieged city and for the besieging army. He therefore decided to block all water sources around Jerusalem, except for the Gihon spring, so that the expected besiegers would not find water to supply them. The water from the Gihon spring was led through an underground tunnel (see chapter 3) directly into the Siloah Pond in Jerusalem, which was to be built in a hurry and was not visible from the surface. In this way Hezekiah had guaranteed a permanent supply of fresh water for Jerusalem and at the same time left as little water as possible for the besiegers who were coming to settle there.

In a speech Hezekiah swore the inhabitants of Jerusalem to the forthcoming events and appealed not to fear, "for the king of Assyria has an arm of flesh, but with us is our God, the LORD!" (2 Chr 32:8). And the people relied on his words.

Illness, Recovery, and Miracles
(2 Kgs 20:1–11; 2 Chr 32:24; Isa 38)

"In those days" Hezekiah became ill, he had got an ulcer, and the prophet Isaiah had to announce to him that he was going to die and therefore should settle legacies and succession (*Manasseh was only about 7-8 years old then*). Hezekiah turned to the LORD in his need in prayer, reminding him that he had lived in faithfulness to him and with an undivided heart. Thereby Hezekiah wept a lot (*where is such a thing reported in the ancient scriptures about a great ruler?*). Isaiah was still on his way home and had not come very far, when God spoke to him that he should return and announce to Hezekiah that he had heard his prayer and seen his tears and that he would be healed. On the third day Hezekiah would go up to the temple in health and he, the LORD, would add another fifteen years of life to it, saving him and Jerusalem from the hand of the king of Assyria and protecting the city. Isaiah brought Hezekiah this good news and ordered him to spread a fig cake on the boil. Hezekiah asked for a sign to confirm that God would do all this. Isaiah presented Hezekiah with the choice of whether, as a sign from God to confirm his promises, the sundial of Ahaz should move ten "steps" forward or backward.

Since Hezekiah found backward movement even more impossible than forward movement, he chose the latter. Isaiah then prayed to God, asking for the sign for Hezekiah that the sundial should go back ten steps, and so it happened immediately and for all to see. In the following three days Hezekiah became healthy. Out of deep gratitude, Hezekiah wrote a beautiful psalm of thanksgiving and praise (Isa 38:9–20).

Visit from Babel and Threat of Court
(2 Kgs 20:12–19; 2 Chr 32:25–31; Isa 39)

"In those times" (*703/702—but probably rather 702 BC*) Merodach-Baladan (*Assyrian: Marduk-apla-iddina II*), the king of Babel (*very probably already from his Chaldean retreat at the Persian Gulf*) sent a legation with gifts and a letter to Hezekiah. The news of Hezekiah's recovery combined with the miraculous backward movement of the sundial had reached Babylon very quickly (*this was the official occasion, but most likely the actual reason for the visit was the attempt to form an anti-Assyrian alliance with Hezekiah and the kingdom of Judah*). Hezekiah was apparently very pleased with the legation from Babylon and showed his guests openly all his possessions, all treasures, the storerooms, war material—simply everything. There was nothing in all his house and in all his dominion that Hezekiah did not show them (Isa 39:2b).

Asked by the prophet Isaiah, Hezekiah freely admitted this. Isaiah must then proclaim to him the word of the LORD that all, all the property of Hezekiah and all that has been accumulated over the centuries by the kings of Israel would one day be looted to Babylon without exception. There would be nothing left of it. Moreover, in the future some of the male descendants of Hezekiah from different generations would be taken to Babel and would have to serve as court officials at the palace of the king of Babel. Hezekiah recognized his arrogance and pride, he accepted the word of the LORD, but then concluded for himself in a comforting way that at least during his lifetime there would be peace and security. (*If at some point the Babylonians were to carry off the treasures of Judah and the descendants of Hezekiah, this could not have been done by the advancing Assyrians.*)

Sennacherib Lays Siege to Lachish, Tribute Paid by Hezekiah
(2 Chr 32:9; 2 Kgs 18:14–16)

In the months that followed, the Assyrian army, led by its king, Sennacherib, advanced to the strategically important city of Lachish and laid siege to it. Hezekiah was no longer able to help himself in this seemingly hopeless situation and sent word to Sennacherib that he had acted unjustly against Assyria and would agree to any form of tribute payment, provided that Sennacherib stopped his military punitive action against Judah. Sennacherib initially accepted this and demanded a huge tribute payment from Hezekiah of eight hundred talents silver and thirty talents gold. One talent is about seventy-seven pounds, so we are talking about over twenty-eight tons of silver and one ton of gold. Hezekiah agreed despite these substantial sums and fulfilled Sennacherib's demand. To do so, he had to take all silver from the royal treasure chambers and in addition, he even had to have the golden door wings of the temple demolished (2 Kgs 18:14–16). Sennacherib gratefully accepted the tribute payment and then took Lachish 701 BC nevertheless completely.

Sennacherib Sends Surrender Call to Jerusalem (2 Kgs 18:13–37; 19:1–37; 2 Chr 32:1–23; Isa 36, 37)

After the capture of Lachish, Sennacherib sent three of his high-ranking men together with a large part of his army as a delegation to Jerusalem. These three envoys were the Tartan (commander-in-chief of the army, cf. Isa 20:1), the Rabsaris (Supreme Court official, cf. Jer 39:3), and the Rabshakeh (supreme dignitary). The Rabshakeh, obviously the chief spokesman of these three high Assyrian officials because of his knowledge of foreign languages, tried to persuade King Hezekiah to surrender (2 Kgs 18:19–25). The Rabshakeh, whose name is not mentioned, spoke fluent Hebrew and Aramaic. He called out to King Hezekiah in Hebrew, but Hezekiah sent out three officials named Eliakim (the palace chief), Shebna (the royal scribe), and Joah (an advisor to Hezekiah).

Then the Rabshakeh, using all the rules of the art of propaganda, began his speech, which served the sole purpose of intimidating the people present, showing them the hopelessness of their situation and undermining their fighting spirit.

The first part of the speech of the Rabshakeh has the following content:

He asks the people to ask Hezekiah, their king, a question directly from Sennacherib, the great king of Assyria: "*In whom do you, Hezekiah, now actually trust?*"

With this question he intends the following:

1. He gives the people himself two possible answers to this question, together with an explanation why this must be doomed to failure:

a. To Egypt? Hezekiah trusts in Egypt? History has shown that an alliance with Egypt is always directed against oneself in the end.

b. To the LORD your God? Hezekiah trusts in God? But did not Hezekiah have his altars on the heights destroyed? *(The Rabshakeh was obviously very well informed, but did not understand why Hezekiah had ordered this at that time, namely to end the false service.)*

2. He proposes a provocative bet: The Assyrians would voluntarily provide Hezekiah's army with two thousand horses if Hezekiah only provided the necessary riders *(which Hezekiah could not provide, of course)*.

3. He then also serves up the barefaced lie that Sennacherib had received the divine task from God the LORD to go against Judah and destroy it.

Hezekiah's officials then asked the Rabshakeh to speak to them in the Aramaic (Syrian) language instead of Hebrew, because the people on the city wall listened and could understand everything. The Rabshakeh took note of this, but continued his speech even more scornfully, even louder, and still in Hebrew, now even addressing the people on the city wall directly.

<u>The second part of the Rabshakeh's speech is now directed straightly against trust in God and has the following content:</u>

1. Hezekiah should not deceive the people and that he could not save them from the hand of Sennacherib.

2. King Hezekiah shall no longer put the people off to the LORD, neither can the LORD save Jerusalem.

3. Instead, Jerusalem should surrender and the people in it will survive, continue to live under very good conditions in another country.

4. Never before have any of the gods of the lands that the Assyrians have already invaded been able to save these peoples from the Assyrians, so why should the god of the people of Judah be able to do this? He then lists a few cities as examples, the last one being Samaria, and asks again whether his gods could have saved Samaria from the Assyrians. *(Samaria, the capital of the Northern Kingdom*

of Israel, had been captured and destroyed twenty-one *years earlier in 722 BC, after a three-year siege by the Assyrians.)*

But nobody answered the Rabshakeh, because Hezekiah had ordered it that way. Everyone was silent, no one spoke a word. Hezekiah's officials returned to Hezekiah and told him what had happened. After Hezekiah had learned what Sennacherib had told him through the Rabshakeh, he tore his clothes (*at that time an expression of deepest emotion, for example, in great sadness, despair, and outrage, see Gen 37:29, where Joseph can no longer find his son Jacob*), went to the temple, and recited to God the LORD the scornful words of Sennacherib, which had been transmitted by the Rabshakeh, in prayer.

Then he sent two of his three officials, who had to listen to the Rabshakeh outside the city wall, namely Eliakim, the palace chief, and Shebna, the scribe, together with the elders of the priests (*not mentioned by name*) wrapped in sackcloth *(an expression of deepest humility)* to the prophet Isaiah. They asked Isaiah to pray to God in the name of King Hezekiah and to ask him to punish the king of Assyria for the scornful and God-despising words he had spoken through the Rabshakeh. Isaiah told them that the LORD God had answered and that they need not fear him, because he wanted to let Sennacherib hear a rumor that he would set out again toward Assyria and perish there by the sword. And indeed, the Rabshakeh learned shortly afterwards that Sennacherib had set out with his part of the army from Lachish to Libnah *(about ten miles to the northwest)*, in order to provide Tirhakah, the king of Cush *(Ethiopia, southern Egypt)* with his army, who supposedly advanced there to help Judah and Hezekiah. Thereupon the Rabshakeh returned to Sennacherib on the spot. Arriving there, he immediately sent messengers with another message to Hezekiah, this time in the form of a letter.

The letter of the Rabshakeh has the following content:

1. Hezekiah should not be deceived by God
2. May Hezekiah remember how the Assyrians dealt with all the other lands they conquered. Why should Judah of all countries be saved?
3. He once again lists a whole series of cities (*even more than before in his speech in front of the city wall*) as examples, all of which were destroyed by the armies of Assyria, and he states that their gods

could not help them either. Why should the god of Judah be able to do this?

Hezekiah received the letter, read it, and went with it to the temple in Jerusalem, where he spread it out before God and prayed from the depths of his soul for help. We would like to recite this prayer of Hezekiah here completely:

> And Hezekiah received the letter from the hand of the messengers, and read it; and Hezekiah went up to the house of the Lord, and spread it before the Lord. Then Hezekiah prayed before the Lord, and said: "O Lord God of Israel, the One who dwells between the cherubim, You are God, You alone, of all the kingdoms of the earth. You have made heaven and earth. Incline Your ear, O Lord, and hear; open Your eyes, O Lord, and see; and hear the words of Sennacherib, which he has sent to reproach the living God. Truly, Lord, the kings of Assyria have laid waste the nations and their lands, and have cast their gods into the fire; for they were not gods, but the work of men's hands-wood and stone. Therefore they destroyed them. Now therefore, O Lord our God, I pray, save us from his hand, that all the kingdoms of the earth may know that You are the Lord God, You alone." (2 Kgs 19:14–19; Isa 37:15–20)

Soon after, the prophet Isaiah sent his king Hezekiah the answer of God. *(The complete answer of God comprises fourteen verses in the Holy Scriptures. We would like to reproduce here only the last verses with God's counsel.)*

> Therefore [because he has mocked God], thus says the LORD concerning the king of Assyria: "He shall not come into this city, nor shoot an arrow there, nor come before it with shield, nor build a siege mound against it."
>
> "By the way that he came, by the same shall he return; and he shall not come into this city," says the LORD. "For I will defend this city, to save it for my own sake and for my servant David's sake."
> (2 Kgs 19:32–34; Isa 37:33–35)

Rescue from the Siege

The following night the unbelievable happened, an angel sent by God killed 185,000 men in the Assyrian camp within this one night. In the early morning they were all found dead, the circumvallation around

Jerusalem was littered with the bodies of Assyrian warriors. Thereupon, Sennacherib and his remaining troops left at once and returned "covered with shame" to his capital Nineveh (see Pss 13; 76:4–6).

The Time After

After these events, God gave the people of Judah a time of quiet and peaceful years (2 Chr 32:22b–23), in which the country and the people could slowly blossom again after the war. During this time, many Jews offered gifts to God in gratitude for salvation from the Assyrians. King Hezekiah was meanwhile highly respected among all nations for his successful resistance against Sennacherib, and gifts and treasures were brought to him in recognition. This peaceful state lasted until Hezekiah died in 687 BC at the age of fifty-four years, exactly fifteen years after God healed him from his terminal illness in an answer to prayer and gave him fifteen more years of life (702 – 15 = 687). Thus, Hezekiah's son Manasseh, after he had already been appointed (*co*)regent by Hezekiah in 697 BC, took over the (*sole*) rule over Judah in 687 BC.

Sennacherib's Death:

The judgment of God, pronounced by the prophet Isaiah that Sennacherib would die by the sword in his own land (Isa 37:7), was then fulfilled a few years later (*according to the Assyrian sources, which confirm the biblical prophecy in 681 BC*) when he was killed by the sword in the temple of the Assyrian god Nisroch by his sons Adrammelech and Sharezer. (*After a short fight for the crown, the two had to flee to the country of Urartu, today's Armenia.*) His son Esarhaddon then succeeded Sennacherib to the Assyrian throne.

Hezekiah's son Manasseh was born in 709 BC through his mother Hephzibah. In 697 BC he was elevated by his father Hezekiah to the position of (*co*)regent at the age of twelve, *knowing that he had only ten years to live*. After Hezekiah's death, he came to (*sole*) rule in 687 BC. Manasseh did what was evil in the eyes of the LORD. Now having become the (*sole*) ruler over Judah, Hezekiah's son Manasseh turned all the good that his father had done into the complete opposite. He reestablished all imaginable idolatry, which had been abolished in his father's time; he began to sacrifice his own sons like his grandfather ("let them go through the fire"

[2 Kgs 21:6]). He practiced fortune telling and black magic, conjured up dead spirits, and had the temple service stopped again, even setting up idols in the temple itself. He shed a great deal of innocent blood and led all Judah into sin. Manasseh's actions enraged God so much that he sealed the fate of Jerusalem and had his prophets (*probably Isaiah*) announce that he would put the "measuring cord of Samaria" (*the capital of the Northern Kingdom of Israel, which had been destroyed several decades earlier in 722 BC*) on Jerusalem and "wipe it out" and "cast it out" (2 Kgs 21:13) Manasseh's abominations became so bad that the LORD God had Manasseh taken away to Babylon in bronze shackles by the king of Assyria (*most likely Assurbanipal—the Assyrian records mention that Manasseh paid tribute to Esarhaddon and then to his son Assurbanipal*) for reasons not handed down. There in captivity, the desperate Manasseh repented of his gruesome and pagan deeds and begged God for forgiveness. He allowed him to return from captivity to Jerusalem. (*This probably happened sometime between 652 and 648 BC. Manasseh had not been taken to the Assyrian capital Nineveh, but to Babylon [2 Chr 33:11], where Assurbanipal's brother Shamash-shumu-ukin was appointed king over Babylon at that time. In 652 BC, however, a fratricidal war broke out between the two, which was documented in great detail and ended in 648 BC with the victory of Assurbanipal and the death of Shamash-shumu-ukin. It is very possible that Manasseh was released quite quickly because of the fratricidal war that broke out.*) With the realization that his prayers were answered, Manasseh finally realized that the LORD God is the true God. Manasseh now returned to Jerusalem as a believer in God. There he laboriously tried to undo all the idolatry that he had established and cultivated in the decades of his previous reign. He had the temple cleaned and restored the temple service, and he also became very active in the fortification of Jerusalem and the other cities of Judah, as well as in the building of an intact army and army leadership.

The positive phase towards the end of his life was *about ten years*, while Manasseh had been committing his abominations and seducing Judah to sin and idolatry for *about thirty-five years* before. In addition, there were the first *ten years as codominant* under his father Hezekiah, during which Manasseh could have taken his father as a positive example for his own reign. So Manasseh ruled for a total of fifty-five years (*ten/thirty-five/ten*) until he died in 642 BC at the age of sixty-seven and his son Amon took over the (*sole*) reign at the age of twenty-two. Amon unfortunately followed the bad examples of his father. Manasseh was buried in the garden of his house, so just like his grandfather Ahaz, he was not buried in a king's tomb. In spite of the conversion at the end of his life, the Holy Scripture also judges Manasseh: "And he did that which was evil in the eyes of the LORD" (2 Kgs 21:2).

We list the following reigns only for the sake of completeness, in order to date the destruction of Jerusalem by Nebuchadnezzar and to confirm our chronology up to this event. For our historical framework of the life of Hezekiah, these kings play no role. Incidentally, there is overwhelming extrabiblical material for their dates, which fully supports all biblical reports and statements.

Amon reigned only two years, then **Josiah** reigned thirty-one years, then **Jehoahaz** even only three months, then **Jehoiakim** eleven years, then **Jehoiachin** again only three months, then **Zedekiah**, the last king of Judah, another eleven years.

The regency span of all kings after the death of Hezekiah's son Manasseh in 642 BC is therefore (2 + 31 + 11 + 11 years and 2 x 3 months) fifty-five years and six months in total. This leads completely correctly (642 − 55 = 587) to the year 587 BC, the year of the destruction of Jerusalem by the Babylonian king Nebuchadnezzar, the end of the kings of Judah, and thus step-by-step through all the individual year dates of the above-mentioned royal reigns, to the ➔ correctly derived **anchor point C. from page 12.**

The Bible itself also gives very precise and direct information about the fall and destruction of Jerusalem by the Babylonians and dates this, according to 2 Kgs 25:8 and Jer 52:12, to the nineteenth year of Nebuchadnezzar's reign, even more precisely to the fifth day of the seventh month. According to the quite reliable Assyrian sources, Nebuchadnezzar began his reign in 605 BC. From the exact specification of day and month as well as the formulation "in the nineteenth year" it follows that this nineteenth year was not yet completed, and thus we determine from the Assyrian specification for the year of Nebuchadnezzar's inauguration (605) minus the biblical specification of the previous reign in full years (19 − 1 = 18) again correctly (605 − 18 = 587) the year 587 BC. Here, too, there are controversial discussions among scholars as to whether 587 or 586 BC was the correct year of the destruction of Jerusalem by the Babylonians. But we do not want to discuss that in this book, it is irrelevant for the consideration of the history of Hezekiah. We have come to the conclusion that 587 BC is the correct date.

We find it extremely remarkable that the divine prophecy to Hezekiah, delivered by the prophet Isaiah, that one day all the treasures of Jerusalem would be stolen from Jerusalem by the Babylonians, was completely fulfilled by the destruction of Jerusalem in 587 BC by Nebuchadnezzar **exactly one hundred years** after the death of Hezekiah 687 BC. We will go into this in more detail later.

With the destruction of Jerusalem in 587 BC and the subsequent removal of the people of Judah into Babylonian captivity, the era of the kings of Israel finally ended and a circle was completed.

Starting Over

The LORD God called Abraham out of the city of Ur in Chaldea and brought him into the land of Canaan to make a nation out of him. Centuries later, Abraham's descendants (Jacob, Joseph, and his brothers), due to various internal and external circumstances, end up in Egypt, where they grow as a people, but end up in slavery. Under Moses, 430 years later (Exod 12:49), the people, who had grown considerably in the meantime, were led out of Egyptian enslavement and back to the land of Canaan, which they then took possession of under Joshua. Centuries later, the people of Israel yearn for a kingdom that begins with Saul and reaches over David and his son Solomon, but then already leads to a division of Israel around 931 BC because of the disputes over the succession of Solomon. The Northern Kingdom subsequently falls steadily away from God, not a single one of the kings ruling there until the downfall of its capital Samaria in 722 BC is considered good by the word of God. The ten tribes of the Northern Kingdom are lost forever with the removal by the Assyrians. The Southern Kingdom of Judah experiences many ups and downs with a downward basic tendency, whereby among the last kings it only goes downwards. Thus, also Jerusalem and Judah finally perish 135 years after the Northern Kingdom in the year 587 BC, and the wretched remnant that is left of the once radiant people of Israel now finds itself in captivity in Chaldea, in Babylon. There, where everything began with Abraham, a circle has been closed.

A few decades later, God made a new beginning with the people of the Jews.

So much for the biblical report in the overall view.

A detailed table with the chronology of the kings of Judah from Azariah (Uzziah) to Manasseh, including all references to dates from the Bible as well as further derivations and calculations, can be found in chapter 4.

The Sequence of Events in the Chronological Order

The reader may be surprised that we have reproduced the events in Hezekiah's life in a slightly different order than the sequence of the biblical accounts. In all three books relevant to us, the Bible reports the main events in varying degrees of detail, in the following order

2 Kgs 18–20:

1. **King Ḥezekiah—introduction and summary**
2. **Spiritual reforms**
3. **The Assyrian threat and the rescue from it / Sennacherib's death**
4. **The illness of Hezekiah and its healing ("in those days . . .")**
5. **The visit from Babel and prophecy to Hezekiah ("at that time . . .")**
6. **Hezekiah's death**

2 Chr 29–32:

1. **King Hezekiah—introduction and (short) summary**
2. **Spiritual reforms**
   a. Comprehensive abolition of idolatry
   b. Cleaning of the temple
   c. Celebration of the Passover
   d. Renewal of the temple service
   e. Supply for priests and Levites
3. **The Assyrian threat and the rescue from it / Sennacherib's death**
4. **Hezekiah's disease and healing (very short—"in those days . . .")**
5. **Hezekiah's wealth and the visit from Babel (very short)**
6. **Hezekiah's death**

Isa 36–39:

1. **The Assyrian threat and the rescue from it / Sennacherib's death**
2. **The illness of Hezekiah and its healing ("in those days...")**
3. **The visit from Babel and prophecy to Hezekiah ("at that time...")**

The Holy Scripture has obviously chosen a <u>thematic</u> order here, not a strictly chronological order. The accounts of the spiritual reforms, the Assyrian threat and salvation, Hezekiah's illness and its cure, and the visit from Babylon are the four main themes of the biblical account. Each one of these themes is told in its entirety, from the beginning to the end, without interruption or interpolation. A good example of this is the passage about the Assyrian invasion and the salvation from it. This section stretches from 702 BC to the death of Sennacherib in 681 BC. Hezekiah died six years earlier, in 687 BC, so that the following reports about his illness and the visit from Babylon could definitely not take place after that. The Bible simply reports the theme "Assyrian threat" from beginning to end and then begins with another theme ("in those days...") about Hezekiah's illness and his healing. The same with "at that time..." about the visit from Babylon. The two introductions "in those days..." and "at that time..." are a clear indication that the authors wanted to signal here a temporal parallelism with the other events.

In the summary of the biblical reports in the sections above, we have chosen a <u>chronological</u> sequence in the narration of events, which is logical from our point of view, as follows:

Chronological Sequence of Events

1. **King Hezekiah—introduction**
2. **Spiritual reforms**
   a. Comprehensive abolition of idolatry
   b. Cleaning of the temple
   c. Celebration of the Passover
   d. Renewal of the temple service
   e. Supply for priests and Levites
3. **Major construction activities and economic growth**
4. **Victories against the Philistines**

5. **Resistance to Assyrian oppression**
6. **The Assyrian threat and the rescue from it**
   a. Sennacherib begins his campaign against Judah
   b. Hezekiah fortifies Jerusalem and raises an army
   c. **The illness of Hezekiah and its healing ("in those days . . .")**
   d. **Visit from Babel, prophecy to Hezekiah ("at that time . . .")**
   e. Sennacherib penetrates to Lachish and besieges it
   f. Hezekiah pays tribute to Sennacherib
   g. Sennacherib takes Lachish and lays siege to Jerusalem
   h. Sennacherib sends the Rabshakeh with a request for surrender
   i. Salvation through the intervention of God
7. **Hezekiah's death**
8. **Sennacherib's death**

We would now like to justify the individual chronological classifications:

To (2) Spiritual Reforms

The Bible gives very clear information about the fact that Hezekiah, immediately upon assuming sole rule after the death of his father Ahaz, heralds the comprehensive spiritual renewal process. Hezekiah starts this process as quasi first official act "right in the first year of his reign, in the first month" (2 Kgs 29:3). Through this formulation and the later following explanation that the planned Passover could not take place on schedule and had to be postponed by one month to the fourteenth day of the next month (the Passover was actually always supposed to take place on the fourteenth day of the first month, "Nisan"), we can conclude quite well that Hezekiah very probably took over the throne from Ahaz towards the end of 716 BC. But the time until the fourteenth day of the first month of the following year (715 BC) was no longer sufficient for the abolition of the idols, the cleansing of the temple, which took sixteen days (2 x 8), and the nationwide invitations including a calculated travel time for the people. So it came about that the Passover was celebrated on the fourteenth day of the second month, "Ijjar." From this we can deduce that Hezekiah became the sole ruler of Judah towards the end of 716 BC, heralded the spiritual reforms, ordered the purifications, and as a result the Passover feast began on the fourteenth day of the second month 715 BC (2 Chr 30:15). The collections for the priests and Levites followed from the third to the seventh month of the same year (2 Chr 31:8)—i.e., until the middle of the year 715 BC. The construction of the storerooms and the organization of a regular supply for the priests and Levites may also have been completed in 715 BC.

For the sake of completeness, it should be mentioned here that the first month of the Jewish calendar, "Nisan," corresponds to our month April. For the Hebrews the year always began in spring. So we can now even give the date of the first Passover under the new king Hezekiah very accurately: it must then have been May 14, 715 BC.

To (3) Major Construction Activities and Economic Growth

According to 2 Chr 32:27–30 many new cities were built under Hezekiah and he himself could acquire a considerable fortune. All this speaks for a prosperous time of increased building activity and economic growth. Archaeological excavations have confirmed this. Some scientists try to explain this with an increased influx of refugees from the Northern Realm, which had fallen completely into the hands of the Assyrians with the fall of Samaria in 722 BC and from which there were now several waves of departures. It is obvious that the refugees tried to reach the Southern Kingdom of Judah in order to start a new life there. Therefore, it is more likely that this time of growth and wealth is to be classified chronologically here, not in the post-war period after the withdrawal of the Assyrians, in which Judah was completely conquered, destroyed in many places, and also robbed of its treasures. Therefore, this phase is to be dated here in the period 715–705 BC.

To 4) Victories against the Philistines

Under the less successful Ahaz some areas of Judah had been lost to the Philistines (2 Chr 28:18). According to 2 Kgs 18:8 Hezekiah was able to win them back, inflict considerable defeats on the Philistines and push them back to Gaza at the Mediterranean. The Assyrian records of King Sennacherib help us in this chronological classification. He describes in the report on his campaign against Judah that Hezekiah had the then ruler of Ekron (the most important city in Philistine), Padi, who was a vassal of the Assyrians, deposed and then arrested him in Jerusalem (*he was then released with Hezekiah's tribute payments to Sennacherib*). This can only be explained in a situation in which Hezekiah must have had considerable influence on the Philistines, namely after his victories against them and the extension of his influence to that point. The exchange of a pro-Assyrian-minded city prince in Ekron (*at that time the city with the largest oil production in the Orient*) for a non-pro-Assyrian-minded one can therefore only have taken place at the beginning of the growing resistance against Assyrian rule (see following section), that is, around 705/704 BC. The military successes against the Philistines must therefore have taken place before and thus also in the period <u>715–705 BC.</u>

To (5) Resistance against the Assyrian Oppression

Hezekiah had recognized the far-reaching negative effects of the pro-Assyrian course of his father, Ahaz, and now, out of a situation of strength (see the previous explanations) and presumably in agreement with the Egyptians (of which, however, he was warned by the prophet Isaiah), tried to shake off the Assyrian rule at a moment that seemed the most favorable to him (2 Kgs 18:7b). This seemingly favorable moment came when the very successful and feared Assyrian king Sargon II was unexpectedly ambushed and killed by a local prince named Gurdi during a campaign in Anatolia, and his son Sennacherib had to take over the reign. Some of the neighboring peoples, especially Babel, sensed a weak moment among the Assyrians due to this sudden change of leadership and began to rebel against Assur. Hezekiah also tried to use this supposed moment of weakness and also rebelled against Assyria's yoke. He probably stopped paying tribute payments—and obviously had the pro-Assyrian Padi deposed from Ekron. Sargon II died in 705 BC and Sennacherib became Assyrian king. It is therefore obvious that Hezekiah's resistance to Assyrian oppression flared up openly around <u>705/704 BC.</u>

To (6) The Assyrian Threat and the Rescue from It

In fact, Sennacherib did not have time at first to deal with the rebellious Judah. First, he launched his <u>first campaign</u> against the murderers of his father, but this was probably more symbolic in nature and without any significant strategic importance. Then, in his second campaign, he liberated the rebellious Babylonians under Merodach-Baladan, who had himself proclaimed king over Babylon again in 703 BC after 721–710 BC (when he was deposed by Sargon II). When Sennacherib finally succeeded in 703/702 BC in bringing down the rebels in his immediate neighborhood, he was able to devote himself to the recalcitrant king Hezekiah. Sennacherib immediately announced his third campaign, the punitive action against Judah.

a. Sennacherib Begins His Campaign against Judah

According to Assyrian records, Merodach-Baladan had himself proclaimed king of Babylon again in 703 BC—probably also calculating a weakness of the Assyrians. Merodach-Baladan had already reigned as king of Babylon in 721–710 BC and had already taken advantage of the death of an Assyrian ruler, namely that of Shalmaneser V in 722/721 BC. His brother Sargon II then followed. Merodach-Baladan managed the feat of holding out against Sargon II for several years, who defeated him in 710 BC, so that he had to retreat to inaccessible areas of the Persian Gulf. With the death of Sargon II, Merodach-Baladan then tried again to come to power in Babylon (what worked once might work again). In 703 BC he again declared himself king of Babylon, but could only hold out for nine months until he was deposed by Sennacherib in his second campaign. After that he retreated again to areas on the Persian Gulf. Now Sennacherib had stabilized his rule, pacified the insurgent regions in his immediate vicinity, and the way was clear for further conquests. This must have been either late in 703 or early in 702 BC. So Sennacherib then started his campaign towards Judah after some preparations in 702 BC.

b. Hezekiah Fortifies Jerusalem and Raises an Army

The fortification of Jerusalem described in 2 Chr 32:2–7 must have begun immediately after Hezekiah learned that Sennacherib started his campaign towards Judah. The described blockage of the water sources outside Jerusalem and the underground supply of the city from the covered Gihon spring through the Hezekiah Tunnel to the Siloah pond in Jerusalem must have been done in great haste, because the archaeological evidence and the inscription found in the tunnel prove it, that this achievement, unique for its time, was so time-sensitive that the excavation began from both directions at the same time, i.e., from the city and from the spring, in order to ensure the completion of the tunnel system and thus the vital water supply for the threatening siege by the Assyrians in time before their arrival (see chapter 3). If you dug from both directions, you were simply twice as fast. In this respect, it can be assumed that the fortification of Jerusalem and the tunnel project took place shortly after the beginning of Sennacherib's campaign against Judah—i.e., also <u>around 702 BC</u>.

c. The Illness of Hezekiah and Its Healing ("In Those Days...")

Here we now chronologically insert a passage, which in the Bible follows only after the reports about the Assyrian threat and the God-worked salvation, into the middle of the event. Why are we doing this? First of all, the relevant passages (2 Kgs 20:1-11; Isa 38) begin with the formulation "in those days," which already indicates a parallelism of events. The essential argument, however, is that God the LORD, in answering Hezekiah's prayer, not only promises him his healing, but also, without being asked (*Hezekiah's prayer was, after all, initially concerned only with his fatal illness*), promises to save and protect him and Jerusalem ("this city") from the hand of the king of Assyria (2 Kgs 20:6; Isa 38:6). This means that the Assyrian threat was already immanent, i.e., Sennacherib's campaign had begun and the arrival of the Assyrian army was only a matter of time. It is just as clear with God's promise to Hezekiah that the divinely wrought salvation from the siege of Jerusalem could not yet have taken place, otherwise God's promise would be meaningless. This proves that these events belong here in time, that is, before God's supernatural intervention against the Assyrian army. That the siege of Jerusalem itself could not have begun at all is made clear by the fact that otherwise the visit from Babel would not have been possible (see the following section).

So, since at the time of Hezekiah's illness the campaign of Sennacherib had already begun, but the Assyrian army had not yet arrived before Jerusalem, we can here relatively well determine the year <u>702 BC</u> with respect to Hezekiah's illness and the associated miracle at the sundial of Ahaz (for this dating see also the explanation in section e below)

d. Visit from Babel, Prophecy to Hezekiah ("At That Time...")

This event is also thematically classified in the Bible according to the Assyrian threat and also according to Hezekiah's illness and recovery. The following should be noted: the chronological classification behind Hezekiah's illness is self-evident, since his recovery was one of the reasons for the visit from Babel. The beginning of the passages (2 Kgs 20:12-19; Isa

39) with the formulation "at that time" again indicates a parallelism of events. We are convinced that the visit from Babel must also have taken place at the time of the ongoing campaign of Sennacherib in Judah, but before the beginning of the siege of Jerusalem. There is a whole series of sound arguments for this.

The Chronological Classification of Merodach-Baladan

As mentioned above, according to the Assyrian records, Merodach-Baladan also tried to profit from the death of the dreaded Assyrian king Sargon II. He sensed a phase of weakness of the Assyrians due to this change of leadership and declared himself king of Babylon for the second time in 703 BC. Sargon's son and heir to the throne Sennacherib obviously could not tolerate this and moved against Merodach-Baladan, who could thus enjoy his second royal rule over Babylon for only nine months. In 702–700 BC Merodach-Baladan again hid in the Persian Gulf before he had to go into exile in Elam (Persia), where he died in 694 BC. This makes it absolutely clear that Hezekiah and Merodach-Baladan at the same time, 703/702 BC have the same interests, namely to shake off the Assyrian threat.

The Bible refers to Merodach-Baladan as the king of Babel at the time of the visit of the legation. So, it can only be this period of time. The period of the first royal rule of Merodach-Baladan 721–710 BC simply does not fit into the temporal context. Since we assume, as explained in the previous section, that Sennacherib's campaign against Judah had already begun at the time of Hezekiah's illness and recovery, Sennacherib must have deposed Merodach-Baladan just before, after which this (altogether rather tough) fellow withdrew to the "sea areas," i.e., back to the Persian Gulf in Chaldea in southern Babylon, according to the Assyrian texts. Therefore, we can relatively well date the section on the legation from Babel by the Assyrian data to <u>702 BC</u> as well.

FIGURE 3

Portrait of Merodach-Baladan

Hezekiah's Treasures

Hezekiah, who had just recovered from a fatal illness through divine intervention, was obviously very pleased with the visit from Babel, as he found himself in a very difficult situation in the face of the approaching Assyrian army, and so he was certainly pleased with the encouragement and potential allies. In these high spirits he presented all his treasures, precious objects, war material and all kinds of other achievements and equipment to the envoys from Babel (2 Chr 32:27–29). This is a further indication that the Assyrian siege of Jerusalem was still to come, because after 2 Kgs 18:14–16 Hezekiah wanted to avert the imminent disaster by paying a very substantial tribute (this is also confirmed by the Assyrian campaign report of Sennacherib), for which he had to take all silver from the treasure chambers and even break off the golden doorposts of the temple. This account documents quite clearly that Hezekiah had to plunder his treasures to a considerable extent in order to meet Sennacherib's exorbitant demands. In other words, when the visit arrived from Babel, all the gold and silver must have been still in Jerusalem! The hypothesis that Hezekiah was able to accumulate a corresponding fortune in the years following his salvation from the siege and Sennacherib's withdrawal is not really plausible. Sennacherib "stopped by" once again in Babylon and Chaldea during his retreat from Jerusalem to Assyria in 701/700 BC, since the rebellion there had still not completely ceased, in order to at least bring this matter to a final end—and thus fulfills God's prediction that he would return on the way he had come (2 Kgs 19:33). After all, Sennacherib had begun his campaign against Judah from Babylon, after he drove Merodach-Baladan from the throne there. Merodach-Baladan, who was still quite tough, managed to escape into exile to Elam again in 700 BC. Even if Hezekiah had succeeded in restoring prosperity and wealth in a country devastated by war within a few years, this was certainly not the case until 700 BC, within only one year. After that, Merodach-Baladan did not play a role on the international scene, especially not as king of Babylon. Consequently, he could no longer send a delegation from Babel to Hezekiah. A few years later he died in exile in Elam (a mountainous region in the east of Chaldea, today's Persia/Iran) in 694 BC.

On the basis of these quite convincing indications, we must fix the legation of Merodach-Baladan and the biblical section on the visit from Babylon at a time when Sennacherib had already begun his campaign against Judah but had not yet reached Jerusalem. Nor had Hezekiah paid his tribute yet. Therefore, we can date the visit from Babel quite well to the year 702 BC.

a. Sennacherib Penetrates to Lachish and Besieges It

According to Sennacherib's records, he conquered forty-six fortified cities in Judah. Even if we should assume that he did not have to conquer all of them with great effort, but probably surrendered some of the cities immediately, this is still a considerable number. Moreover, according to his own statements, Sennacherib first had to conquer the Philistine city-state of Ashkelon, which was allied with Judah. All in all, these are clear indications that Sennacherib's campaign against Ashkelon and Judah, with the capture of forty-six cities, including the very well-documented, rather protracted siege and conquest of Lachish, which lasted for months, and the siege of Jerusalem can hardly be completely squeezed in within the year 701 BC. Much more realistic is the beginning of the Assyrian campaign in the course of 702 BC. However, since Sennacherib had not yet captured Lachish (according to 2 Chr 32:9 he was still laid siege against

THE LIFE OF HEZEKIAH IN THE BIBLICAL OVERVIEW   41

Lachish when he first called upon Hezekiah to surrender Jerusalem), the siege of Lachish cannot have <u>begun</u> until <u>the end of 702 BC.</u>

b. <u>Hezekiah Pays Tribute to Sennacherib</u>

The situation was increasingly hopeless for Hezekiah, so that he still tried to avert the downfall of Jerusalem (and perhaps also that of Lachish, which was about to be captured) after 2 Kgs 18:14–16 at the very last moment, by proposing to Sennacherib a tribute payment of any amount if he would only desist from Judah and end his campaign. Sennacherib fixed a gigantic sum, which Hezekiah could just about raise and sent to Sennacherib, together with Padi of Ekron, which had been fixed in Jerusalem until then. Since this probably happened shortly before the capture of Lachish, which according to Sennacherib's own campaign report took place in 701 BC after a siege of several months, we must also fix Hezekiah's tribute payment at the beginning of <u>701 BC.</u>

c. <u>Sennacherib Takes Lachish and Lays Siege to Jerusalem</u>

Sennacherib does not keep his promise, takes Lachish in spite of the tribute payment of Hezekiah in <u>701 BC</u>, made the city his new war base, and turned part of his army further to Jerusalem.

d. <u>Sennacherib Sends the Rabshakeh with a Request for Surrender</u>

According to 2 Kgs 18:17, he sends the Rabshakeh from Lachish with two other high-ranking Assyrian officials and a large part of his army to Jerusalem to call upon Hezekiah to surrender. The siege of Jerusalem began. This can also be clearly assigned to the year <u>701 BC.</u>

e. <u>Sennacherib Must March against the Egyptians before the City of Libnah</u>

After 2 Kgs 19:8–9, Sennacherib's attention is then diverted from Jerusalem for a while, since he obviously had to fend off a relief attack by the Egyptians allied with Hezekiah before the city of Libnah (not far from Lachish). *"Then the Rabshakeh returned and found the king of Assyria warring against Libnah, for he heard that he had departed from Lachish. And the king heard concerning Tirhakah king of Ethiopia, 'Look, he has come out to make war with you.'"*

f. Salvation through the Intervention of God

The siege of Jerusalem will have lasted only a few months. After the three senior Assyrian officials returned to Sennacherib but did not meet him in Lachish because he was involved in the skirmish with the Egyptians, there is another, this time written, request for surrender to Hezekiah. He presented the letter of the Rabshakeh to God in the temple and asked God to save Jerusalem. Hezekiah's prayer was answered and before the gates of Jerusalem 185,000 Assyrian soldiers died in one night, many of them brave heroes and princes and colonels of the army, after which Sennacherib immediately broke off the campaign and returned to Assyria "covered with shame" (via Chaldea, there was still the tough long-time troublemaker Merodach-Baladan to be dealt with; 2 Chr 32:20).

Also this must have happened in the year 701 BC. Merodach-Baladan must have then 700 BC escaped after the final defeat of the uprising against Sennacherib from the Persian Gulf into exile in the neighboring Elam, where he died in 694 BC.

To (7) The Postwar Period and Hezekiah's Death

This ends the narrative of all essential events. After 2 Chr 32:22b–23 there follow some more quiet years, in which Hezekiah and the people of Judah are highly respected in the neighboring countries because of their successful resistance against the Assyrians. Both is confirmed by the Roman-Greek historian Flavius Josephus (37–100 AD). According to our chronology of the kings (see chapter 2.4), but also by the simple calculation that Hezekiah had been given another fifteen years of life by God in 702 BC after being cured of his fatal illness, we find out that Hezekiah then died in 687 BC (702 − 15 = 687) at the age of fifty-four years.

To (8) Sennacherib's Death

From reliable Assyrian sources we know that Sennacherib was slain with the sword by two of his sons in a temple in Nineveh at the end of 681 BC (2 Kgs 19:36–37; 2 Chr 32:21). This is the last historical event recorded in the biblical accounts we are looking at regarding the history of the life of King Hezekiah.

Now we can create a timeline for the events in Hezekiah's life.

THE LIFE OF HEZEKIAH IN THE BIBLICAL OVERVIEW

Timetable of events:

1. **King Hezekiah**

Hezekiah's birth	741 BC
(Aram and the Northern Kingdom invaded Judah)	735–734 BC
(Damascus is conquered by the Assyrians)	732 BC
Beginning of the coregency	728 BC
(Samaria is besieged and conquered by the Assyrians)	724–722 BC
Beginning of the sole reign (death of Ahaz's father)	716 BC

2. **Spiritual reforms**

Comprehensive abolition of idolatry	716 BC
Cleansing of the temple	716 BC
Celebration of Passover (fourteenth day of the second month)	715 BC
Renewal of the temple service	715 BC
Supply for priests and Levites (third–seventh month)	715 BC

3. **Large construction activities, economic growth** — 715–705 BC

4. **Victories against the Philistines** — 715–705 BC

5. **Resistance to Assyrian oppression** — 705–703 BC

6. **The Assyrian threat and the rescue from it**

Sennacherib begins his campaign against Judah	702 BC
Hezekiah fortifies Jerusalem and raises an army	702 BC
The disease of Hezekiah and its cure	702 BC
The visit from Babel and the prophecy to Hezekiah	702 BC
Sennacherib penetrates to Lachish and besieges it	702–701 BC
Hezekiah pays tribute to Sennacherib	701 BC
Sennacherib takes Lachish, lays siege to Jerusalem	701 BC
Sennacherib's call to surrender by Rabshakeh	701 BC
Salvation through the intervention of God	701 BC
Sennacherib's departure and return (via Chaldea)	701 BC
(Merodach-Baladan must flee from Chaldea into exile)	700 BC

7. **Hezekiah's son Manasseh becomes coruler** — 697 BC

8. **Merodach-Baladan dies in exile in Elam** — 694 BC

9. **Hezekiah's death, Manasseh becomes sole ruler**   687 BC
10. **Sennacherib's death**   681 BC

We would like to emphasize at this point that with this chronology we are in no way questioning the authority of the Bible. The word of God does not report the events here in a strictly historical chronological order, as we have now arranged, but simply tells us about the events in a <u>thematic</u> sequence in excerpts selected according to their meaning. We have tried here to arrange these reports <u>chronologically</u>.

3

The Life of Hezekiah from Different Points of View

In the meantime, we have worked out some basics, such as the geopolitical situation in the time of Hezekiah. We also had to deal with the difficulties in the chronology of the kings, but we were able to solve them satisfactorily and set a coherent time frame in which we embedded Hezekiah's story. We then brought together the three biblical accounts with their different emphases into a single harmonized report, put the events presented into a logical chronological order with a comprehensible and coherent dating, and then justified this sequence. Now all the foundations have been laid for us to look at the events in detail.

After chapter 2 illustrated the life of King Hezekiah in a biblical overview, the following sections will deal with individual aspects of his life in much more detail. In addition to the biblical testimonies, we will now also draw on information from secure extrabiblical sources.

The greatest cut in Hezekiah's life is of course marked by the year 702/701 BC, when the seemingly invincible Assyrian army under its king Sennacherib marches against Judah and Jerusalem. Hezekiah then, on top of everything else, falls fatally ill with an ulcer, but by the grace of God he has been healed of it. Then the Assyrians, also by divine grace, without being able to conquer Jerusalem, must leave again. So all this happened until 701 BC and thus in <u>Hezekiah's fortieth year of life</u> (our chronology calculates his year of birth to be 741 BC)!

Excursus: The Forty, the Number of the Trial

The fortieth year of life has often marked an important turning point in the lives of people in the Bible. Let us only think of Moses as a famous example. The number forty is composed of the factors four and ten (4 x 10 = 40), which are also important in the biblical context.

The number four stands for human nature and the number ten for the responsibility of man (Ten Commandments, ten plagues, ten virgins, ten pounds entrusted, tithing . . .). The number three for the number of the Trinity and the divine perfection in combination with the number four then results in either the seven (3 + 4) or the twelve (3 x 4), both of which represent the unity between God and man. The forty, in turn, is the combination of the number of human nature (4) and the number of human responsibility (10), and in the biblical context it is always the number of trial!

Let us only think of Moses's forty days on Mount Sinai (Exod 32) until the people of Israel poured the golden calf, of Jesus's forty days in the desert, of the city of Nineveh, which was given forty days to repent (Jon 3:4–10), or let us think of the forty years of wandering in the desert by the people of Israel. Just like Moses at forty and later again at eighty (2 x 40) years, Hezekiah now also goes through his trials. At forty, he faces his greatest challenges and his greatest responsibility, both before his people and before God. But let us start the examinations with his childhood.

Childhood and Youth

The title of this chapter may at first seem surprising.

There are no direct biblical or extrabiblical accounts of Hezekiah's childhood and youth. Nevertheless, we know a little about his mother and we read in the Bible about the events in the time of his father Ahaz, which Hezekiah experienced to a great extent, and which certainly influenced him. Let's remember that Hezekiah became coruler of Judah at the age of twelve to thirteen years and only at the age of twenty-five did he become the sole ruler, i.e., all the years before he had to watch how his father Ahaz ruled with little success and fanatically clung to the idols.

Therefore, it is certainly worthwhile to look at what happened under Hezekiah's father, King Ahaz, since we may assume that Hezekiah experienced most of it at first hand as a child or youth. But let us first take a closer look at Hezekiah's parents...

Mother Abijah (2 Chr 29:1)

The name of Hezekiah's mother "Abijah" is also called "Abi" (2 Kgs 18:2) and means "My father is Jehovah." Abijah could be used as a female as well as a male first name (for example, the successor of King Rehoboam was also called Abijah and reigned 913–911 BC in Judah). It is striking that the name of the mother of the new king is never mentioned among the kings of the Northern Kingdom of Israel, but (almost) always among the kings of Judah. Sometimes even the father of the mother is mentioned, obviously if this had a meaning or if the father was possibly a well-known person. The father of Hezekiah's mother Abijah, i.e., Hezekiah's maternal grandfather, is actually mentioned, his name was Zechariah. The name Zechariah appears several times in the Bible. So, there are some candidates for Hezekiah's maternal grandfather. The well-known prophet Zechariah appears only two hundred years later and falls out immediately, a priestly advisor of King Azariah (Uzziah) (2 Chr 26:5) might have appeared too early to have begotten Abijah, so that she could become Ahaz's wife. The only interesting candidate who could have been the father of Abijah is King Zechariah (son of Jeroboam) of the Northern Kingdom. He reigned in Israel only a short six months in 753–752 BC before he was murdered by Shallum, who then succeeded him.

Hezekiah was born in 741 BC when his father Ahaz was about fifteen years old (early procreation was not uncommon in these regions and times), it is to be assumed that Abijah was also quite young when Hezekiah was conceived—let's suppose between sixteen and twenty years. So Abijah might have been born around 760–755 BC—this actually fits well with the assumed dates of life of King Zechariah of Israel. Whether this is really true and whether King Zechariah was Hezekiah's maternal grandfather must remain open, however. Although there was a phase in which Judah and Israel cultivated very friendly relations (even allies) and documented this through mutual family ties, this phase was actually several decades over at that time. Likewise, if Abijah's father was indeed Zechariah, the former and murdered king of Israel, one might expect that the Bible would have briefly mentioned this. Therefore, we cannot say with certainty who Hezekiah's maternal grandfather was, but at least there is a suspect . . .

The meaning of the name Abijah as "My father is Jehovah" tells us that Hezekiah's mother was apparently a believer and faithful to the LORD God. It is possible that his mother taught her son, the future king Hezekiah, intensively in faith and shaped him positively.

Father Ahaz (2 Kgs 18:1)

The name <u>Ahaz</u> is interesting because it is not a name in itself, but a shortened form of the name <u>Jehoahaz</u>, which carries the meaning of <u>Jehovah</u> and can be translated as "Jehovah has seized". One of the former kings of Israel ruled under this name in the Northern Kingdom from 814–798 BC. The shortened form of <u>Ahaz</u> without the prefixed <u>Jeho</u> (= Jehovah) is obviously an allusion to the absence of God in Ahaz's life.

We had already noticed that the mother of the new king was never mentioned in the naming of the kings of the Northern Kingdom, <u>but always in the naming of the kings of the Southern Kingdom</u>—with one exception: in fact, only in the case of Ahaz the naming of the mother is missing. The reasons for this are not known, but it is clear that such a conspicuous absence of something that is otherwise always present has some meaning, even in the later kings of Judah, who are mentioned only very briefly or had only a reign of a few months. It is virtually impossible to assume that in a royal dynasty the mother of an heir to the throne was not known. We can certainly rule out this reason for her absence. But what else could have been the reason for not naming Ahaz's mother? King Ahaz was certainly one of the most evil and worst kings of Judah. Maybe his grandson Manasseh was even worse, but he still converted to God in his old age and spent the last ten or so years of his life trying to make up for some of the mistakes he made. In this respect, we can indeed call Ahaz the most evil and worst king of Judah. He was therefore even denied a king's tomb (2 Chr 28:27). Perhaps the Holy Scripture wanted to spare the mother of Ahaz the shame of being recorded forever in the word of God as the mother of the most evil and worst king of Judah.

In the previous chapter we have already reported a great deal about the bad deeds of Ahaz, his bitter enmity with God and his fanatical idolatry that grew out of it. But let us take a look at what Hezekiah had to experience in his young years.

In the Age of Six to Seven Years (Approx. 735 BC)

Hezekiah experienced Ahaz's defeats against Aram allied with Israel. As a small boy he had to tremble along when the storm on Jerusalem was imminent, but then did not happen. In the various defeats, the king's son Maaseiah, the lord of the manor, the prime minister and 120,000 warriors died. In addition, two hundred thousand prisoners were taken away to Samaria, but they were released immediately after the intervention of the prophet Oded.

In the Age of Eight to Nine Years (Approx. 733-732 BC)

Ahaz, against the insistent advice of God (Isa 7:3-13), "bought" Assyria as an ally against Aram and Israel at high prices with gold and silver. The Assyrians under Tiglath-Pileser III stormed Damascus in 733/732 BC and destroyed it, perhaps killing Ahaz's father and Hezekiah's grandfather Jotham, who may have been a prisoner there since 735 BC. From Damascus, Ahaz brought back a new idolatry and the model of a new altar of sacrifice to idols, which he had reproduced and even had placed in Jerusalem in the middle of the temple.

In the Age of Twelve to Thirteen years (Approx. 728 BC)

Hezekiah was declared coregent by Ahaz. This was the earliest possible time, because at the age of twelve a child became *gadol* according to the Hebrew tradition, which means as much as being responsible for his own actions and deeds (see also Luke 2:42). Thus he was practically considered an adult. (By the way: In today's modern Hebrew *gadol* means interestingly something similar to "super cool!")

At first, there is no reason why Ahaz made his son Hezekiah coregent at the age of twelve. However, it is to be trusted in the so very malicious father that he wanted to draw his heir to the throne, who was obviously attached to the God of Israel, into his evil and pagan hands at the earliest possible time, namely when he was *gadol*—that is, when he was responsible for himself.

We know such behavior from history as well as from the present time. Bad people often try to draw as many other people as possible into their evil machinations.

At the Age of Nineteen Years (Approx. 722 BC):

Hezekiah had to witness in the previous year's how the Assyrian spirits, called up by his father, oppressed the kingdom of Judah more and more, demanded higher and higher tribute, and overran the Northern Kingdom of Israel (from which perhaps his maternal grandfather came) city by city, until after a three-year siege, which was certainly terrible for the city's inhabitants, they also took and destroyed Samaria, the capital of the Northern Kingdom, in 722 BC. He experiences the atrocities of the Assyrians, he learns about the deportations, the families torn apart, and he sees how the streams of refugees from the Northern Realm push into Judah.

In all these years he had to endure the evil machinations of his father, partly already as coregent in the coresponsibility. Likewise, while he was attached to the God of Israel, he had to watch his father worship the idols and brought every cult "under every green tree" in Judah. According to 2 Chr 28:3 he even had to witness the incomprehensible when his father, in a cultic intoxication, offered his younger brothers in the valley of Ben-Hinnom to some god (presumably Moloch—according to the reference in 2 Kgs 23:10) as burnt offerings.

Hezekiah will also have noticed how Ahaz did not listen to the prophet Isaiah and that this always proved to be disadvantageous in retrospect. Isaiah came from a royal family. His father Amoz was a younger son of Joash, the king of Judah (835–796 BC), the predecessor and father of Amaziah, the king with whom we have begun the story in chapter 2. King Amaziah was thus the uncle of Isaiah.

Thus, Isaiah, who lived in Jerusalem, always had relatively easy access to the respective ruling king due to his descent. As little as Hezekiah's father Ahaz listened to Isaiah, so much more did Hezekiah later, during his reign, seek the proximity of the prophet, seek his advice, ask him to speak with God, for prayer support—and he also trusted in what Isaiah told him in each case. It can be assumed that the trust and this intimate connection to the prophet was already established in Hezekiah's young years.

How much young Hezekiah disapproved of his father's rule can be seen in the violent and very immediate turnaround that Hezekiah heralded in many aspects as soon as his father died, and he became sole ruler. Already in the first month of his reign, he radically began to abolish idolatry and its sites and symbols and to reestablish the correct orders of worship of the God of Israel. Such a radical change of course at such short notice says a great deal about what the person who brought him about thought about his father as predecessor and his actions.

The Reformer

Hezekiah's spiritual reformation was all-encompassing, radical, and took place immediately after his father Ahaz died and Hezekiah's (*sole*) rule began. The reversal could not be any faster or more radical.

It is almost as if Hezekiah had literally just been waiting for this and had all the plans already up his sleeve, because without hesitation he immediately began to clean up and abolish the terrible idolatrous and God-hating living conditions that his father Ahaz had so frenetically introduced into Judah in a very consistent, very thoughtful, and very structured way. The fierceness of Hezekiah's reaction clearly reflected his profound aversion to his father's actions and his ungodly spiritual attitude, which had spread throughout Judah because of Ahaz. And Hezekiah's cleaning up was all the more thorough. In doing so, and this is the key to understanding his spiritual attitude and his deep faith and trust in God, he did not only take care of an outward tidying and cleansing, like the destruction of the idol altars and the Nehushtan or the repair and cleaning of the temple. No, Hezekiah was also and above all concerned with an inner, a spiritual cleansing. The whole people (even to Israel, the Northern Kingdom conquered by the Assyrians, he sent out invitations) should cleanse themselves and repent before God: to repent and admit to having been on the wrong and evil ways, to have been seduced by Ahaz. All should repent to God and confess this publicly—and from now on remain on Godly ways. Hezekiah was also quite pragmatic, because despite the speed of his actions after taking over sole rule, there was obviously not enough time to have everything prepared by the fourteenth day of the first month (*Nisan*) of the spiritual Jewish calendar (many had to travel a long way) so that all could have celebrated the Passover together and the people could have been purified. This date is actually irrevocably planned for the Passover. But now the Passover celebrations were simply postponed by one month to the fourteenth day of the second month. This is what you call pragmatism! Here it was obviously and understandably better to lead the people to spiritual conversion and purification as quickly as possible than to remain attached to traditions. It could have been argued that it would have been better to wait a year until the next "correct" date to organize the Passover with the whole people.

The pragmatic rescheduling of the date for the Passover and all other actions and instructions of Hezekiah, even though they were given and implemented very quickly, were blessed by God and were a complete success all along the line. The rescheduled Passover became a gigantic collective repentance, a conversion to God and cleansing from the evil ways, with all the participants becoming deeply inwardly delighted and their hearts overflowing with gratitude.

> *The whole assembly of Judah rejoiced, also the priests and Levites, all the assembly that came from Israel, the sojourners who came from the land of Israel, and those who dwelt in Judah. So, there was great joy in Jerusalem, for since the time of Solomon the son of David, king of Israel, there had been nothing like this in Jerusalem. Then the priests, the Levites, arose and blessed the people, and their voice was heard; and their prayer came up to His holy dwelling place, to heaven. (2 Chr 30:25–27)*

Nor is it that Hezekiah introduced new, modern or contemporary things, no, he brought the people back to the orders of Moses, which were given to him by God almost eight hundred years earlier. Eight centuries is a long period of time, and one might think that during this time many new currents and events tried to influence the way the worship should be done. And that is how it is today. Many wish or demand that our worship services become more "modern" or "contemporary." Well, it may be that "rocking" music or more modern Bible translations lead to fuller halls, but not always automatically to a more spiritual attitude. And that is what our God and Father wants, after all, that his children be with him with all their hearts.

> *For man looks at the outward appearance, but the Lord looks at the heart. (1 Sam 16:7b)*

If you are an active member in your church, then when deciding on the framework and form of your worship service, you might always think of this verse first, God always looks at the heart, not what is in front of your eyes! Hezekiah reintroduced the centuries-old Mosaic orders, but most of all he tried to give his people a spiritual renewal. This was much more important to him! So important, in fact, that he simply changed the date of the Passover by one month, so that as many as possible of his people had the opportunity to come to Jerusalem to repent, to sacrifice, and to purify themselves. And his plan succeeded! Let us simply read it again:

> *The whole assembly of Judah rejoiced, also the priests and Levites, all the assembly that came from Israel, the sojourners who came from the land of Israel, and those who dwelt in Judah. So, there was great joy in Jerusalem, for since the time of Solomon the son of David, king of Israel, there had been nothing like this in Jerusalem. Then the priests, the Levites, arose and blessed the people, and their voice was heard; and their prayer came up to His holy dwelling place, to heaven.* (2 Chr 30:25–27)

More than 250 years later, the Bible tells us, Nehemiah, then still in Babylon in the Diaspora, was allowed to return to Jerusalem and began to rebuild the city walls. But of course, these too were initially outward appearances, albeit very important ones, as they were necessary for the security of the city. But what happened when the walls of Jerusalem were rebuilt?

> *Now all the people gathered together as one man in the open square that was in front of the Water Gate; and they told Ezra the scribe to bring the Book of the Law of Moses, which the Lord had commanded Israel. So Ezra the priest brought the Law before the assembly of men and women and all who could hear with understanding on the first day of the seventh month. Then he read from it in the open square that was in front of the Water Gate from morning until midday, before the men and women and those who could understand; and the ears of all the people were attentive to the Book of the Law.*
> (Neh 8:1–3)

And further:

> *And Ezra opened the book in the sight of all the people, for he was standing above all the people; and when he opened it, all the people stood up. And Ezra blessed the Lord, the great God. Then all the people answered, "Amen, Amen!" while lifting up their hands. And they bowed their heads and worshiped the Lord with their faces to the ground.* (Neh 8:5–6)

And the reaction?

> *Now on the twenty-fourth day of this month the children of Israel were assembled with fasting, in sackcloth, and with dust on their heads. Then those of Israelite lineage separated themselves from all foreigners; and they stood and confessed their sins and the iniquities of their fathers. And they stood up in their place and read from the Book of the Law of the Lord their God for one-fourth of the day; and for another fourth they confessed and worshiped the Lord their God.* (Neh 9:1–3)

So once again, at least 250 years after Hezekiah, the Jewish people came to repentance, conversion and spiritual renewal by reading the Mosaic orders. These orders were then already over one thousand years old. Please let us never forget, it does not depend on the outer forms, these should of course be good and appealing, but God depends on the heart, only that counts! The author is convinced that the growth of a church can only come from filled hearts, not from filled rooms. Full rooms are naturally great, but full rooms of people whose hearts are filled with God really bear fruit for God, because only the one whose heart is filled will tell others about it and win others for God and his love in his Son.

Don't we all know Luke 6:45b?

> *For out of the abundance of the heart his mouth speaks.*

After the moving and spiritually renewing celebrations around the Passover feast (715 BC) in Jerusalem, which was postponed by one month, many of those present at that time went full of joy and spiritual fulfillment to other cities of the tribes of Judah and Benjamin (= *Southern Kingdom*) and partly even to Ephraim and Manasseh (= *Northern Kingdom*), in order to destroy the idols and places of worship there as well, to tell about the LORD and to call for conversion.

After these certainly unique comprehensive spiritual renewal events Hezekiah immediately set about establishing a regular temple service. He determined the twenty-four departments necessary for this and he even gave animals from his own property for the daily, weekly, monthly, and annual sacrifices. He asked the people to give the tenth part of their income, and the people followed his wish joyfully and in great numbers, so that the collection of the offerings lasted from the third to the seventh month—that is, over four months—and the priests and Levites found so much abundance that Hezekiah had to have pantries built in which everything that the priests and Levites did not consume themselves could be brought in and stored. Hezekiah went even further and hired selected men who were responsible for ensuring that the priests and Levites were regularly and correctly distributed the portions due to them.

It is worth mentioning that Hezekiah <u>asked</u> the people to donate the tenth part, he did not issue a decree, which he could have done without any problems as king. He trusted in the voluntariness of the believing Jews and their joyfulness. It was certainly also clear to him that God only accepts and blesses the donations (sacrifices) that are joyfully given, and not those that are forced or brought in discontent.

The idols were destroyed, the temple was cleansed, its doors and gates were repaired, the whole people had asked God for forgiveness and were cleansed, the priests and Levites were reinstated, and their provision was assured. Thus, the regular temple service could begin and be maintained permanently.

Hezekiah thus made sure that after the conversion to God, the conditions were created to "keep at it" with the faith. He did not leave it with the conversion of the people, but he also wanted to make it possible for his people, to encourage them to be steadfast in their faith, not to let themselves be turned away again through other gods, new idols, but to create the possibility to come to God again and again, to be able to come again and again to the temple for the forgiveness of their sins.

So, it is also in our time tremendously important to give a newly converted child of God the opportunity to "stick with it" in faith. Of course, Christians no longer have to make sacrifices in the temple because of the one, unique, and forever valid sacrifice of Jesus Christ, but they should regularly remember the sacrifice of Christ, live in it, carry it in their hearts, celebrate it once a week, remember it, and meet with other believers, with brothers and sisters. This makes them grow in faith and protects them from doubts and attacks from outside.

Hezekiah already knew this and therefore he provided for an orderly and regular temple service. And he himself was also a frequent guest there. Where did Hezekiah submit to God the impudent and the God slandering letter of the Rabshakeh, and where did he say the decisive prayer that moved God to save Jerusalem from the Assyrian siege and conquest?

In the temple!

Although this temple had no treasures left, because Hezekiah had paid all gold and silver to the Assyrians (which, by the way, had not brought salvation either), God still let himself be heard here by his faithful and humble servant Hezekiah. Another fine example of the fact that appearances count for nothing. The temple was no longer beautiful to look at, everything of value had been torn down. But God always sees the inside, God always looks at the heart. Here, in the naked, half-torn down temple, God heard Hezekiah's prayer and worked the miracle of the salvation of Jerusalem.

The Architect

In the Bible we find some hints about strong building activities at the time of the reign of Hezekiah in Judah. Especially in 2 Chr 32 in verses 5 (fortification of the city of Jerusalem) as well as 29a (construction of many new cities) and 30 (construction of the underground tunnel) we find descriptions of one or the other major project. The truly gigantic extent of the building activities in Judah towards the end of the eighth century BC, however, has only been revealed to us by archaeologists in recent decades.

Population Explosion and Urban Development

The archaeologists state that in the late eighth century BC the number of settlements in the Judean mountainous region increased from 86 to 122 and in the Shephelah (the area between the coastal plain of the Mediterranean Sea and the Judean mountainous region) from 19 to 277! The populated area is said to have increased from 17 acres to 103.5 acres—i.e., almost five times as much. These are explosive developments. The situation is similar with Jerusalem. According to the evidence available to them, archaeologists assume that Jerusalem grew from about 43.2 to 164.3 acres in the second half of the eighth century BC, i.e. it quadrupled.

We find a very beautiful suitable indication in the Bible in 2 Chr 32:5:

> *And he strengthened himself, built up all the wall that was broken, raised it up to the towers, and built another wall outside; also he repaired the Millo in the City of David, and made weapons and shields in abundance.*

Here it is reported how King Hezekiah, in the face of the approaching Assyrian army under Sennacherib around 703/702 BC, begins to fortify the city of Jerusalem, repairing the inner-city wall and erecting watchtowers on top of it. In addition, we learn from the text that he had an outer-city wall built and secured with a rampart.

Fragments of this outer city wall have been uncovered by the archaeologists and they were able to establish that there were indeed houses outside the inner-city wall before the outer wall was added on the orders of Hezekiah. And that is perfectly logical! Because with the growth of Jerusalem described above, it was of course completely impossible to build all the new houses and settlements within the old walls, that is, within the old boundaries of the city. Therefore, the new houses and districts were built in front of the old walls of the city—so that Hezekiah had to have a new outer wall built around them for their protection. He had this wall then protected by a fortification wall. Thus, Jerusalem, under Hezekiah, got a new outer wall appropriate to its new size.

What the "Millo" mentioned in the above-mentioned verse (2 Chr 32:5) was, exactly, can unfortunately no longer be said precisely today. In any case, it was a building that is mentioned for the first time in 2 Sam 5:9 and then again in the books of the Chronicles (1 Chr 1:8) as part of the city of David. Since the mentions, as here with Hezekiah, always have to do with military securing or fortification of the city, and since some linguists suggest the translation "fill" for "Millo" from the word stems, one can cautiously assume that this was one of the first fortifications of the city of Jerusalem. Be that as it may, Hezekiah apparently fortified the "Millo" once again according to 2 Chr 32:5.

Now the question immediately arises where all the additional inhabitants of Jerusalem and the many new cities came from. A healthy natural increase of the existing population may have contributed to this, but it cannot explain these explosive developments by far. There must have been large-scale immigration. Here, historians and archaeologists make the very obvious assumption that this immigration came from the Northern Kingdom of Israel. After a three-year siege in 722 BC, the Assyrians under Shalmaneser V and then his successor Sargon II had taken possession of the capital Samaria (it is not quite clear under which Assyrian king Samaria fell). The Assyrians then immediately began their deportation policy, taking away the inhabitants of the Northern Kingdom and Samaria and settling other ethnic groups. These deportations always took place in waves, the first of which took away the upper classes, followed by the lower classes in subsequent waves. In the case of the Northern Kingdom of Israel, these waves can be traced back to around 669–668 BC under the Assyrian king Assurbanipal—he is even mentioned in the

Bible in this very context (Ezra 4:10). The deportations of the Assyrians in the Northern Kingdom of Israel thus began around 722 BC (outside Samaria probably even earlier) and extended over a period of fifty to fifty-five years (cf. again Isaiah's prophecy to Ahaz in Isa 7:8). In this respect, it is obvious that many Hebrews of the Northern Kingdom, namely all those who had not yet been deported but had to fear being led away, considered whether they should not flee to nearby Judah. It is equally obvious that many did so. This is a very plausible explanation for the population explosion at the end of the eighth century BC in Jerusalem and all of Judah.

Archaeologists have found little difference in the lifestyles of the inhabitants in the many new cities of Judah compared to the older cities. This circumstance also fits well into the picture, for in fact the people from the Northern and Southern Kingdoms were actually one people who lived only in a divided kingdom. In this respect no great differences are to be expected. If other peoples or ethnic groups had immigrated to Judah, this would have been more clearly visible in cultural differences in the archaeological findings.

Judah, Jerusalem, and King Hezekiah were thus apparently confronted with massive streams of refugees from Samaria and the Northern Kingdom of Israel, which led to major construction activities and many new settlements.

According to 2 Chr 32:29b Hezekiah was able to acquire a considerable fortune. This is now well understandable due to the increase in population, the flourishing economy and the associated increase in taxes.

Hezekiah's Tunnel

An extremely exciting construction project of King Hezekiah, which is still perfectly preserved and easy to visit today, is the famous underground tunnel, mentioned several times in the previous chapters, which leads from the Gihon spring to downtown Jerusalem to the Siloam Pond. Today this tunnel is called <u>Hezekiah's Tunnel</u> or Siloam Tunnel.

> *The newer Siloam Tunnel (Hebrew:* נִקְבַּת הַשִּׁלֹחַ, *Nikbat HaShiloaḥ), also known as Hezekiah's Tunnel (Hebrew:* תעלת חזקיהו, *Teʾalát Ḥizkiyáhu), is a water tunnel that was carved within the City of David in ancient times, now located in the Arab neighborhood of Silwan in eastern Jerusalem. Its popular name is*

due to the most common hypothesis that it dates from the reign of Hezekiah of Judah (late 8th and early 7th century BC) and corresponds to the "conduit" mentioned in 2 Kings 20:20 in the Hebrew Bible. According to the Bible, King Hezekiah prepared Jerusalem for an impending siege by the Assyrians, by "blocking the source of the waters of the upper Gihon, and leading them straight down on the west to the City of David" (2 Chronicles 32:30). By diverting the waters of the Gihon, he prevented the enemy forces under Sennacherib from having access to water.

Support for the dating to Hezekiah's period is derived from the Biblical text that describes construction of a tunnel and to radiocarbon dates of organic matter contained in the original plastering. The tunnel leads from the Gihon Spring to the Pool of Siloam. If indeed built under Hezekiah, it dates to a time when Jerusalem was preparing for an impending siege by the Assyrians, led by Sennacherib. Since the Gihon Spring was already protected by a massive tower and was included in the city's defensive wall system, Jerusalem seems to have been supplied with enough water in case of siege even without this tunnel. According to Aharon Horovitz, director of the Megalim Institute, the tunnel can be interpreted as an additional aqueduct designed for keeping the entire outflow of the spring inside the walled area, which included the downstream Pool of Siloam, with the specific purpose of withholding water from any besieging forces. Both the spring itself, and the pool at the end of the tunnel, would have been used by the inhabitants as water sources. Troops positioned outside the walls wouldn't have reached any of it, because even the overflow water released from the Pool of Siloam would have fully disappeared into a karstic system located right outside the southern tip of the city walls. In contrast to that, the previous water system did release all the water not used by the city population into the Kidron Valley to the east, where besieging troops could have taken advantage of it.

The curving tunnel is 583 yards (533 m; about 1/3 mile) long and by using the 12 inch (30 cm) altitude difference between its two ends, which corresponds to a 0.06 percent gradient, the engineers managed to convey the water from the spring to the pool.

According to the Siloam inscription, the tunnel was excavated by two teams, one starting at each end of the tunnel and then meeting in the middle. The inscription is partly unreadable at present, and may originally have conveyed more information than this. It is clear from the tunnel itself that several directional errors were made during its construction. Recent scholarship has discredited the idea that the tunnel may have been formed by substantially widening a pre-existing natural karst. How the Israelite engineers dealt with the difficult feat of making two teams digging from opposite ends meet far underground is still not fully understood, but some suggest that the two teams were directed from above by sound signals generated by hammering on the solid rock through which the tunnelers were digging.[2]

The inscription describing the event in which the two construction teams, approaching from different directions, actually met was discovered in 1880.

This so-called Siloam inscription reports in ancient Hebrew script and language about the work shortly before the tunnel breakthrough and is of archaeological interest. It was found not far from the southern entrance to the tunnel. After an attempt was made to steal it in Ottoman times and the thief was caught, it was taken to Istanbul, where it is still kept today in the Museum of Antiquities.

Here is the text as it can still be read today (ellipses indicate missing text):

> ... the tunnel ... and this is the story [the thing—"dvar"] of the tunnel while ... the axes were against each other and while three cubits [were left] to cut ... the voice of a man ... called to his fellow, for there was a through-passage ["Zedah"] in the rock, from the right ... and on the day of the tunnel [being finished] the stone hewers struck [literally "hit"] each man towards his fellow, ax against [literally: "on"] ax, and the water went from the source to the pool for two hundred and a thousand cubits. And one hundred cubits was the height over the head of the quarrymen.[3]

The entire area of the Gihon Spring and the tunnel, as well as the Siloam Pond, is now a unique archaeological site that can be visited. With a hand lamp, about 1,500 feet of the tunnel can also be walked through. You can wade through the cold spring water, which is up to twenty-seven inches deep. The tunnel is located near the old town below the Temple Mount.

The Hezekiah Tunnel is an impressive and well-preserved legacy of our protagonist King Hezekiah. What this unique construction project from that time can mean for us today is discussed later.

---

2. Wikipedia, "Siloam Tunnel," https://en.wikipedia.org/wiki/Siloam_tunnel.
3. Wikipedia, "Siloam Inscription," https://en.wikipedia.org/wiki/Siloam_inscription.

The Foreign Affairs Expert

After Hezekiah's assumption of sole rule following the death of his father Ahaz, he initially concentrated directly and very consistently on spiritual renewal in the land and among the people of Judah. He also had to take care of other internal affairs, such as the massive influx of refugees from the Northern Kingdom of Israel, where the people were threatened by the waves of Assyrian deportation, which we discussed in detail in the previous chapter.

Only after the internal affairs of the country allowed it to some extent, Hezekiah set about regaining part of the land lost under his father's terrible rule. Perhaps this was urgently needed in view of the rapid growth of the population. In any case, Hezekiah succeeded in pushing the Philistines back to Gaza, that is, to the Mediterranean.

> *And he rebelled against the king of Assyria and did not serve him. He subdued the Philistines, as far as Gaza and its territory, from watchtower to fortified city.* (2 Kgs 18:7b-8)

Only these victories and the extension of his sphere of influence into Philistine can explain why King Hezekiah was able to depose the pro-Assyrian governor of the city of Ekron, located in the land of Philistine north of Gaza. He had Padi taken from Ekron to Jerusalem and placed him under arrest there, and later released Padi along with Hezekiah's tribute payment to Sennacherib. Ekron was an important trading city and the largest oil producer in the world at that time. Thus, certainly also a financially strong metropolis, which could pay the Assyrians quite a bit of tribute.

Hezekiah had probably long since realized that Judah was threatened with destruction, because over the decades the Assyrians had extended their sphere of influence further and further and completed this each time by conquering the respective countries, after which they subsequently resettled the originally resident population. It was only a matter of time before Judah would suffer the same fate. Therefore, he tried to free himself from the Assyrian embrace. He made (according to Sennacherib's records) a covenant with the city-state of Ashkelon, brought the Philistines under his influence as described above, and set them up against the Assyrians. Against the insistent advice of the prophet Isaiah (Isa 30:1–7), he made a covenant with Egypt, which was confirmed by the Rabshakeh of Sennacherib in his speech before the walls of Jerusalem (2 Kgs 18:21).

And he waited for a favorable opportunity to escape the stranglehold of the Assyrians; he lurked for a period of weakness among them. This moment seemed to have come when the dreaded Assyrian king Sargon II was unexpectedly ambushed and killed during a campaign in 705 BC. Sargon's son Sennacherib had to take over the reign and had his hands full with the task of bringing the surrounding peoples, who all believed they could now take advantage of this favorable moment, back under control. This was also the moment for Hezekiah to start the rebellion against the Assyrians, and it can be assumed that the formulation of the Bible "*and he rebelled against the king of Assyria and did not serve him*" in particular means that Hezekiah stopped paying tribute payments.

Hezekiah had thus brought about an anti-Assyrian coalition, consisting of Ashkelon, the Philistines, and above all the Egyptians. Now that the Assyrian Empire was preoccupied with itself and revolts around it after the sudden death of Sargon, Hezekiah saw the right moment to break away from Assyria.

One who also rehearsed the uprising and wanted to take advantage of the situation was Merodach-Baladan, who proclaimed himself king of Babel in 703 BC for the second time after 721–710 BC and began to rule there. Merodach-Baladan, however, came directly into the sights of Sennacherib, so that the latter started a campaign against the self-appointed king of Babel in the same year, which is why Merodach-Baladan had to flee Babylon again after only nine months. This did not, however, prevent him from sending a legation from his retreat in the Persian Gulf to King Hezekiah of Judah to confer with him on joining Hezekiah's anti-Assyrian alliance, which Hezekiah, having just recovered from his fatal illness, obviously liked very much.

Hezekiah's abilities in foreign policy are difficult to assess. It remains to be noted, however, that he partly acted against the advice of the prophet Isaiah and that he did not always fully trust in God the LORD in these matters. It also remains to be noted that the Assyrians then actually moved against the insurgent Judah. Perhaps Hezekiah had not really expected an attack, or he felt strong enough in his coalition. Hezekiah's anti-Assyrian alliance, however, could then offer little resistance to the approaching army of Sennacherib. Ashkelon was overrun, Philistine as well, Ekron was brought back under Assyrian control, and according to Sennacherib's report, the supporters of Hezekiah who had helped depose the previous governor Padi were killed. Later, after his release by Hezekiah, Padi returned to Ekron as governor. The greatest disappointment for Hezekiah was the Egyptians, who, although they started a relief attack against the Assyrians sometime near Libnah (or, according to Sennacherib's report, near the city of Eltheke, north of Libnah), then disappeared from the scene again, presumably because this attack was not successful. As Isaiah had predicted, this covenant with Egypt was very dangerous. He had given Hezekiah in deceptive safety and now he was completely on his own. The Assyrians had defeated all of Hezekiah's allies or had put them to flight. King Hezekiah's quite arbitrary foreign policy must be considered a failure from a human point of view. Now total annihilation threatened.

The Warlord

> *He subdued the Philistines, as far as Gaza and its territory, from watchtower to fortified city.* (2 Kgs 18:8)

As we discussed in the previous chapter, King Hezekiah apparently succeeded in regaining the territories occupied by the Philistines and also in exerting political influence on Philistine territory. Whether this applied to the entire territory of Philistine is difficult to say, but in any case, it seemed to apply to the extremely important trading city of Ekron. So far, so good, Hezekiah had obviously been successful in military and political terms. After regaining the occupied territories, Hezekiah apparently left the conquests behind and limited his power to political influence.

But now the Assyrians were actually threatening to attack, and Hezekiah had to prepare his country, his military and the capital Jerusalem for this war.

> *After these deeds of faithfulness, Sennacherib king of Assyria came and entered Judah; he encamped against the fortified cities, thinking to win them over to himself. And when Hezekiah saw that Sennacherib had come, and that his purpose was to make war against Jerusalem, he consulted with his leaders and commanders to stop the water from the springs which were outside the city; and they helped him. Thus many people gathered together who stopped all the springs and the brook that ran through the land, saying, "Why should the kings of Assyria come and find much water?"*
>
> *And he strengthened himself, built up all the wall that was broken, raised it up to the towers, and built another wall outside;*

also he repaired the Millo in the City of David, and made weapons and shields in abundance. Then he set military captains over the people, gathered them together to him in the open square of the city gate, and gave them encouragement, saying, "Be strong and courageous; do not be afraid nor dismayed before the king of Assyria, nor before all the multitude that is with him; for there are more with us than with him. With him is an arm of flesh; but with us is the Lord our God, to help us and to fight our battles." And the people were strengthened by the words of Hezekiah king of Judah. (2 Chr 32:1–8)

Reading this biblical text, one cannot help the impression that Hezekiah was indeed surprised by the Assyrian attack, for apparently, he did not begin his military preparations until after the Assyrian attack against Judah had already begun. At least this can be said of the fortification of Jerusalem for the imminent siege. This also makes it clear why the tunnel project, which on the one hand was supposed to secure the water supply for the city, but on the other hand was also supposed to affect the water supply for the advancing besiegers, was carried out in such a hurry that one actually had to dig from both directions. Otherwise, it would probably not have been completed in time. The water from the Gihon Spring was piped through the hidden underground tunnel, which had to be built in such a hurry, directly to Jerusalem in the Siloam Pond, the spring itself carefully covered and hidden. Hezekiah had all other water sources around Jerusalem blocked so that the expected besiegers would not find water to supply them. The Gihon spring was so well covered that it could not be found. In this way Hezekiah had provided Jerusalem with a constant supply of fresh water, while leaving as little water as possible for the besiegers who were about to move in.

At the same time the defense of Jerusalem had to be prepared. The city walls were strengthened and renewed, watchtowers and defense towers were built on top of them. An additional outer wall was raised around Jerusalem and a defensive wall was built. Weapons were made in large numbers; an army was formed and "military captains" were deployed. Hezekiah spoke to the inhabitants of Jerusalem in an address about the coming events, appealing to them not to be afraid, *"with him is an arm of flesh; but with us is the Lord our God, to help us and to fight our battles"* (2 Chr 32:8). And the people in Jerusalem trusted him.

King Hezekiah now had to assume that his anti-Assyrian alliance would lose the war and that the Assyrian army would very soon appear before Jerusalem. Thus, Jerusalem was threatened with the same fate as

Samaria a good twenty years earlier, which fell to the Assyrians after a terrible, painful three-year siege. Perhaps Hezekiah had analyzed this and came to the conclusion that he had to prevent the besieging army from becoming self-sufficient for several years before the city was captured. Perhaps this is why he came up with the highly intelligent idea for the tunnel project and its urgent execution, which killed two birds with one stone: on the one hand, it secured a permanent water supply for the besieged city, which was cut off from any external supply and not visible to the Assyrians. On the other hand, all other water sources in the area were blocked, so that the Assyrians, Hezekiah hoped, had difficulties themselves in ensuring a stable supply for their circumvallation around Jerusalem. A clever move.

In an open military conflict, Judah had nothing left to oppose the Assyrians. This would have been hopeless. Here it was only a matter of isolating oneself, of hoping and praying, and of enduring as long as possible.

In one of the prophetic predictions of Isaiah, an invasion route of the Assyrian army in Judah is described, which we want to reproduce here:

> He has come to Aiath, He has passed Migron; At Michmash he has attended to his equipment. They have gone along the ridge, They have taken up lodging at Geba. Ramah is afraid, Gibeah of Saul has fled. Lift up your voice, O daughter of Gallim! Cause it to be heard as far as Laish—O poor Anathoth!
> Madmenah has fled, The inhabitants of Gebim seek refuge. As yet he will remain at Nob that day; He will shake his fist at the mount of the daughter of Zion, The hill of Jerusalem. (Isa 10:28–32)

Some of the cities mentioned here can be identified and located. They describe a rather northeastern route of the Assyrian army to Judah, while Sennacherib's campaign report actual describes a northwestern route, first following the Mediterranean coast. Maybe somewhere it is possible to combine both routes, but that is not the topic of this book.

The fact is that Hezekiah's military alliance had failed, the Assyrians now conquered the cities of Judah and easily advanced to Lachish, which was the last major bulwark before an attack on Jerusalem. When Lachish was about to fall, Hezekiah tried to avert the worst and to change Sennacherib's mind by paying a horrendous tribute, but he failed: The treasures of Judah changed hands, but Sennacherib took Lachish anyway and raised a large part of his army against Jerusalem. According to the personality structures of the Assyrian rulers known to us, this was not really surprising behavior either. According to Sennacherib's report and the pictorial representations on the relief he had made of this siege and conquest of Lachish, which he had hanged in his palace, the capture of the city was by no means an easy task, but rather a quite laborious one that took several months. So Hezekiah had obviously had Lachish well-fortified, but in the end, all this was not enough; Lachish fell and Sennacherib made the city his main camp and military base for the coordination of further operations. At some point, the Egyptians appeared, but were defeated and withdrew again. Thus, King Hezekiah's war strategy could only deal with the fortification and defense of Jerusalem. Although he developed intelligent ideas with the tunnel project, in the end Jerusalem was facing a terrible and very long period of suffering with the upcoming siege. Despite the hopelessness of the situation, he did not give in to Sennacherib's massive calls for surrender, transmitted by the Rabshakeh. King Hezekiah remained firm and steadfast. And he continued to trust in God, who had promised him to save Jerusalem from the Assyrians. In the same way he had also told the inhabitants of Jerusalem. *"And the people were strengthened by the words of Hezekiah king of Judah"* (2 Chr 3:8).

It is also difficult to assess Hezekiah's military achievements. He was obviously successful against the Philistines; his fortification ideas were very intelligent and groundbreaking for the time. His political assessments and the forged alliances, partly against the advice of God and that of the prophet Isaiah, are rather questionable. Of course, Hezekiah had correctly recognized that Judah was in a dangerous situation due to the Assyrian pressure to expand. But his means to free himself from it were rather less suitable from a human point of view. Hezekiah's greatest achievement as a warlord was certainly that he did not capitulate to the Assyrians in a completely hopeless situation, contrary to all human logic, but turned to God the LORD in prayer. This was Hezekiah's greatest military achievement! Trust in God's promises . . .

The Terminally Ill

> *In those days Hezekiah was sick and near death. And Isaiah the prophet, the son of Amoz, went to him and said to him, "Thus says the Lord: 'Set your house in order, for you shall die, and not live.'"*
> (2 Kgs 20:1)

In chapter 2 we have explained that Hezekiah's illness "in those days" is to be placed in chronological order at the beginning of the campaign of the Assyrians under Sennacherib against Judah, i.e., around 702 BC. That the fatal illness was an ulcer, we learn interestingly enough only six verses later, when Isaiah had it externally treated after God's promise of healing and prolongation of Hezekiah's life for another fifteen years.

> Then Isaiah said, "Take a lump of figs. So, they took and laid it on the boil, and he recovered." (2 Kgs 20:7)

Before that we know from verse 1 only that Hezekiah became terminally ill, but at first, we learn nothing about the cause.

Hezekiah was not only facing a major foreign policy and military crisis, but he was also facing a war against an over-powerful enemy, and he was in the process of rearming the army, strengthening the fortification of Jerusalem, and securing the water supply. He now also had a very serious health problem. Since Isaiah later had a fig cake spread on it, it must have been an outwardly recognizable and outwardly expanding boil-like growth. Presumably this ulcer had been recognized and treated according to the methods of the time, but apparently without success.

In the relevant literature we read that it could have been leprosy or the plague. Leprosy was hardly curable at the time, but did not lead directly to death, but rather to a longer, albeit fading life. Hezekiah's great-grandfather Azariah (Uzziah) had such a disease and lived with it for another ten years in a seclusion especially set up for him (see chapter 2). Now, however, Hezekiah was immediately announced of imminent death, since he was at the same time called upon to "order his house," i.e., to settle everything concerning his death: succession in royal rule and military leadership, the care of wives and children, etc. In this respect, leprosy is probably not to be assumed to be his disease, especially since such a disease would not really be called an ulcer. The plague, on the other hand, manifests itself through bulge-like external excrescences, but in the case of a plague disease they appear in a multitude all over the body and one would very probably not only speak of an ulcer here. In addition, the plague is highly contagious, and it would have to be assumed that there would have been many more infections and deaths at the royal palace of Hezekiah, but nothing is reported about this. In this respect, the plague is probably also ruled out as Hezekiah's disease. So we do not know exactly what Hezekiah was suffering from, except that it was a fatal ulcer. The course of the disease must have been very serious, and the fatal diagnosis actually came directly from God, who had the prophet Isaiah go to Hezekiah to bring him the terrible news and make him take all the necessary precautions for his imminent death. This must have been a terrible shock for King Hezekiah. He was nearing the age of forty, so he was still in his prime. He faced himself and the whole land of Judah with gigantic challenges, for the Assyrian army had invaded Judah during Sennacherib's third campaign, taking it city by city and heading inexorably towards Jerusalem, while Hezekiah was in the process of organizing the city's defense. Certainly, he was also in constant contact with his ally Egypt as well as potential allies such as Merodach-Baladan. He obviously knew of Hezekiah's fatal illness, otherwise he would not have sent a delegation with congratulations on his recovery. All in all, this is extremely disturbing news for the very worried Hezekiah, but of course also for the inhabitants of Jerusalem, who of course also wondered what would become of them in the face of the approaching Assyrians, who seemed to be invincible, with their king dying at the same time.

> *Then he turned his face toward the wall, and prayed to the Lord, saying,*
> "Remember now, O Lord, I pray, how I have walked before You in truth and with a loyal heart, and have done what was good in Your sight." And Hezekiah wept bitterly. (2 Kgs 20:2–3)

How did Hezekiah, very ill and full of worries in this extremely difficult situation, react to this terrible news, which—not to forget—was communicated to him directly by God through the prophet Isaiah, that is, it was final?

Hezekiah became very sad; <u>he cried</u>. Later, in his psalm of thanksgiving, he speaks of bitter suffering (Isa 38:17) that he felt. This is an extremely interesting passage in the biblical account. In what other world literature that tells of historical events is a great and successful ruler portrayed in this way? Deadly ill, sad, full of bitter suffering . . . this description is so profound, so moving, so authentic, as people would not, and have never, told about their "glorious" rulers. We read here in the word of God the pure truth about the events of that time, no fake news, no glossed over or censored description, no glorification of King Hezekiah. He was in this situation completely at the end of his rope, full of worries and almost insoluble problems and on top of that he was now terminally ill. And he can't help it, he must cry! And this is exactly what is recorded in the word of God, we may still read and know this today, more than 2,700 years later.

The tears were Hezekiah's immediate unconscious and uncontrollable reaction to the terrible news. But what was his conscious reaction?

> *Then he turned his face toward the wall, and prayed to the Lord . . .* (2 Kgs 20:2a)

Why do you think Hezekiah turned to the wall? That could have had two reasons: either he didn't want the people present to see his emerging tears, which for us is still a very obvious and understandable reason, or Hezekiah, by turning to the wall, wanted to turn completely inwards and concentrate without distraction on the prayer he now wanted to say to God.

So Hezekiah's immediate reaction was to turn to God. He had to start crying and at the same time he turned directly to God. Immediately, he turned to the wall for a moment, then he began to pray to God and ask for salvation.

He did not sink into rigidity or anger. He immediately understood the consequences of what had just been revealed to him. He would die soon, his son Manasseh was with his seven years much too young to take over the king's rule, the Assyrians were approaching, and the fortification of Jerusalem was probably not yet completed. From one moment to the next, everything seemed to be lost forever. But Hezekiah did not sit there in shock and do nothing, he did not start to quarrel with his fate or even shout at Isaiah. It is only reported that he turned to the wall and began to pray. And that he cried a lot.

What Hezekiah prayed, we read in the following chapter.

Let's just try to learn a little from King Hezekiah of Judah. If we ever get into a similarly difficult or sad situation, we might remember this Hezekiah 2,700 years ago. Of course, we may be sad, we may feel bitter suffering. But we may also know that we can turn to God always and everywhere. We do not need to despair or get angry or maybe even blame God. We should turn to God immediately, as Hezekiah did, and ask him to help us. We should search and sweep out our heart, pour it out to the point of purging it to God and ask him from the bottom of our purified heart.

We see from this example that a prayer said in this way with a full and purified heart can be heard by God. He can heal fatal diseases. God is almighty. God is all-powerful. And we can move his holy arm with our prayers. The honor is due to him, also for what he did with his servant King Hezekiah.

The Praying Man

From all that we now know about King Hezekiah, we can assume that he prayed often to his God, the LORD. So, he had an intimate and living relationship with God. In the Bible we are told five of his prayers.

These are

1. the prayer for the purification of the people,
2. the prayer for the rescue of Judah from the Assyrians,
3. the prayer for his healing from the deadly disease,
4. the prayer of thanksgiving for his healing, and
5. the prayer for the rescue of Jerusalem from the siege of the Assyrians

We want to have a look at them now.

1. The Prayer for the Purification of the People

Immediately after taking over the royal rule from his idolatrous father Ahaz, Hezekiah began a comprehensive reformation and reversion of the people to God the LORD. As already described before he began the renewals with the abolition of idolatrous cults and idolatrous altars, the opening and cleansing of the temple and a nationwide call for a common Passover celebration, to which he then even additionally invited all people from the Northern Kingdom of Israel. In addition to the external cleansing and restoration, Hezekiah was especially concerned with the internal cleansing of the people. He wants everyone to go to Jerusalem to come to repentance, to cleanse the heart, to regret and turn away from the ungodly times under Hezekiah's father Ahaz. They all should and wanted to wipe the slate clean and from there start again a new lasting living relationship with God, the LORD. In the Old Covenant, however, it was necessary to bring a sacrifice, which had to die in your stead to cover the guilt, the sins that had been committed. But since obviously so many people had followed Hezekiah's call, even some who did not come directly from Judah ("*Many from Ephraim and Manasseh, Issachar and Zebulun . . ."*), it was obviously no longer possible to perform all the necessary sacrifices for all those who wanted and were supposed to.

> *For there were many in the assembly who had not sanctified themselves; therefore the Levites had charge of the slaughter of the Passover lambs for everyone who was not clean, to sanctify them to the Lord. For a multitude of the people, many from Ephraim, Manasseh, Issachar, and Zebulun, had not cleansed themselves, yet they ate the Passover contrary to what was written. But Hezekiah prayed for them, saying, "May the good Lord provide atonement for everyone who prepares his heart to seek God, the Lord God of his fathers, though he is not cleansed according to the purification of the sanctuary." And the Lord listened to Hezekiah and healed the people.* (2 Chr 30:17–21)

Hezekiah recognized the situation and he also saw that many would have liked to have been purified by sacrifice, but this was simply no longer possible when the Passover celebration then began (already one month late). And so he came before God in prayer and asked him to forgive all those who were pure in heart and could no longer purify themselves through sacrifice according to the divine and Mosaic commandments before the Passover. And God heard Hezekiah! Here we can see that Hezekiah was very caring and really concerned about the salvation of the hearts of his people, even of all people, because those who had come from Ephraim or Manasseh (i.e., from the tribes of the Northern Kingdom) did not formally belong to his people. Many of them in particular could no longer purify themselves in time through sacrifice, and it was precisely for them that Hezekiah prayed to God. How wonderfully caring . . .

2. The Prayer for the Rescue of Judah from the Assyrians

Sennacherib and his Assyrian army had already invaded far into Judah, many of the cities had already been conquered or had to surrender. The important city of Lachish had been besieged and then, despite Hezekiah's tribute payment to Sennacherib, had been taken and had become its current military base. Sennacherib then had some of its officials move against Jerusalem with a large part of the army to call upon King Hezekiah to surrender. The Rabshakeh of the Assyrian king gave a very populist speech outside the city wall, so that all inhabitants of Jerusalem could understand his words. Hezekiah apparently did not attend this event, because he was told about it afterwards.

> *And so it was, when King Hezekiah heard it, that he tore his clothes, covered himself with sackcloth, and went into the house of the Lord. Then he sent Eliakim, who was over the household, Shebna the scribe, and the elders of the priests, covered with sackcloth, to Isaiah the prophet, the son of Amoz.* (2 Kgs 19:1–2)

After he was told what the Rabshakeh had proclaimed, Hezekiah first changed his clothing style in a fierce emotion. He tore his royal garment, at that time always an expression of deepest emotion, for example in great sadness, greatest despair and fierce indignation. And afterwards he wrapped himself in sackcloth. So, he tore his royal clothes to simply put on sackcloth afterwards. This again was a sign of repentance; it documented the strong will to repent. Why was Hezekiah so shaken? There were, of course, many reasons. For one thing, Sennacherib had not cared about the immense tribute payment of Hezekiah, but had conquered Lachish nevertheless, and he now, by his revenge-taking, pretended to want to take Jerusalem as well and to lead its inhabitants away and resettle them later—no matter whether after the conquest or capitulation. So here it was about the fate of Judah, the people of God. Let us not forget that these deportations were very real and very conscious of all the inhabitants of Judah, since they have been happening year after year since the fall of Samaria in 722 BC with the people of the Northern Kingdom of Israel before their very eyes. On the other hand, the polemic speech of the Rabshakeh had a very clear goal: he wanted to unsettle the inhabitants of Jerusalem. To force upon them the thought that it would be better to survive—even if then perhaps in another country—instead of now going through a terrible time of suffering, misery, hunger, and thirst, possibly even dying. For the inhabitants of Jerusalem trusted their king, as the Bible tells us:

> *Then he set military captains over the people, gathered them together to him in the open square of the city gate, and gave them encouragement, saying, "Be strong and courageous; do not be afraid nor dismayed before the king of Assyria, nor before all the multitude that is with him; for there are more with us than with him. With him is an arm of flesh; but with us is the Lord our God, to help us and to fight our battles." And the people were strengthened by the words of Hezekiah king of Judah.* (2 Chr 32:6–8)

The Rabshakeh thus tried very massively to shake the confidence of the people in their king and in their God. But Hezekiah himself continued

THE LIFE OF HEZEKIAH FROM DIFFERENT POINTS OF VIEW   73

to trust in God. What was the very first thing he did after he heard about the Rabshakeh's speech?

> *And so it was, when King Hezekiah heard it, that he tore his clothes, covered himself with sackcloth, and went into the house of the Lord.* (2 Kgs 19:1)

Hezekiah dresses like a repentant sinner in sackcloth and goes to the temple <u>to pray to God!</u> Unfortunately, we do not know what he said to God there, this has not been handed down to us through the word of God, but we do know that immediately after changing clothes he went to the house of the LORD to pray to his God.

Returning from the temple, he sends two of his officials and the elders of the priests to the prophet Isaiah to ask him to pray to God as well. Our eyewitness has recorded in his book very precisely what message Hezekiah had delivered to him:

> *And they said to him, "Thus says Hezekiah: This day is a day of trouble and rebuke and blasphemy; for the children have come to birth, but there is no strength to bring them forth. It may be that the Lord your God will hear the words of the Rabshakeh, whom his master the king of Assyria has sent to reproach the living God, and will rebuke the words which the Lord your God has heard. Therefore lift up your prayer for the remnant that is left." So the servants of King Hezekiah came to Isaiah.* (Isa 37:3–5)

3. <u>The Prayer for His Healing from the Deadly Disease</u>

In the section before we discussed how Hezekiah fared when he had to receive the terrible news of his near death from Isaiah. He turned his face to the wall and had to cry bitterly. And he immediately began to pray to God.

> *"Remember now, O Lord, I pray, how I have walked before You in truth and with a loyal heart, and have done what was good in Your sight." And Hezekiah wept bitterly.* (2 Kgs 20:3)

Hezekiah is deeply moved, he can no longer hold back tears in the face of imminent death and in great concern for the people, who are now defenselessly at the mercy of the Assyrians without a king. And the prayer he is saying now is short and simple. Here we see once again that God is not concerned with elaborate wise words, a certain liturgy or special form. <u>God always looks at the heart.</u> The terminally ill King Hezekiah is deeply moved and can only say a short, simple prayer, but this comes from the bottom of his heart, and it speaks to God's heart! God repented his death announcement to Hezekiah, and he changed his mind! Isn't this a wonderful example that we can reach God with our prayers? That we can move something through our prayers? That we can even change God's mind? Wonderful! And tremendous at the same time! We can change the course of events with our prayers! God had let Hezekiah announce the near death. And now a short, simple prayer from Hezekiah, but coming from his heart, changed God's mind! And this immediately! Hezekiah received his answer to his prayer immediately. For the prophet Isaiah has just left again, he is already on his way home, but has not yet come very far. According to 2 Kgs 20:4, he is still within the inner part of the city when God has already ordered him back and he is allowed to announce the good news of his answer to prayer to Hezekiah.

Unbelievable!

Incredibly beautiful.

4. The Prayer of Thanksgiving for His Healing

Hezekiah was extremely grateful for the God-given healing from the deadly disease. And he expressed this gratitude in a prayer to God, which the prophet Isaiah passed on to us literally and which can be read in Isa 38:9–12. This prayer of thanksgiving is also called the <u>Psalm of Hezekiah</u>. We will read more about this in the next section.

5. The Prayer for the Rescue of Jerusalem from the Siege of the Assyrians

In the Chronicles book of the Bible the prayers of Hezekiah and Isaiah for the salvation of Jerusalem are summarized quite briefly.

> *And Hezekiah the king and Isaiah the prophet, the son of Amoz, prayed for it and cried to heaven for help.* (2 Chr 32:20)

However, the very strong expression "they cried to heaven" is used here, which we do not find otherwise. Interesting!

For this, the prayer is handed down to us in the book of Isaiah and in the book of Kings, which Hezekiah spoke to God in the temple after he had received the letter of Sennacherib through the Rabshakeh with the renewed call to surrender and further insults to God.

> *And Hezekiah received the letter from the hand of the messengers, and read it; and Hezekiah went up to the house of the Lord, and spread it before the Lord. Then Hezekiah prayed before the Lord, and said: "O Lord God of Israel, the One who dwells between the cherubim, You are God, You alone, of all the kingdoms of the earth. You have made heaven and earth. Incline Your ear, O Lord, and hear; open Your eyes, O Lord, and see; and hear the words of Sennacherib, which he has sent to reproach the living God. Truly, Lord, the kings of Assyria have laid waste the nations and their lands, and have cast their gods into the fire; for they were not gods, but the work of men's hands—wood and stone. Therefore they destroyed them. Now therefore, O Lord our God, I pray, save us from his hand, that all the kingdoms of the earth may know that You are the Lord God, You alone." (2 Kgs 19:14–19; Isa 37:15–20)*

In the face of the seemingly certain victory, Sennacherib's and Rabshakeh's words, this time even written in a letter, become increasingly improper and blasphemous. Hezekiah goes with them to the house of the LORD, puts the letter at God's feet, so to speak, and says what is probably his most important prayer ever. Now that the situation is completely hopeless according to human judgement, King Hezekiah of Judah continues to trust in the God of Israel unwaveringly. And Hezekiah, as we will see later in chapter 3.13, once again receives his answer to prayer directly. First, he receives a very extensive verbal answer from God, which the prophet Isaiah is allowed to convey to him (Isa 37:21–35), until then, that very night, an angel of the LORD strikes the Assyrian army in such a way that Sennacherib must leave.

King Hezekiah's trust in God has not been disappointed. Even in the greatest crises Hezekiah could always rely on him. And so, Hezekiah's prayers could change the course of events, his personal affairs, but also the course of world history. Through God's goodness and grace.

In summary, we can say that King Hezekiah of Judah led a very lively prayer life and turned directly to his God in (almost) every situation. In spite of his kingship, he was not too bad to kneel down in humility (or even to dress in sackcloth) and step before God to ask him for something. Yes, rather, he constantly sought the proximity of God and lived in it. And even though he did not always act according to God's pleasure and God had to lead his child through some difficult situations first, so that he could entrust himself completely to him, God the LORD. God did indeed fulfill every prayerful wish of his child Hezekiah, which is handed down to us in the Bible!

Check it! Anyone.

> *He trusted in the Lord God of Israel, so that after him was none like him among all the kings of Judah, nor who were before him. For he held fast to the Lord; he did not depart from following Him.*
> (2 Kgs 18:5–6a)

Hezekiah considered himself not too good for self-correction. After recognizing his arrogance, he bowed down and repented. The same with his doubts: after he realized that he only had to trust God completely and could not add any more of his own works for salvation, he placed himself completely into the arms and hands of God, who then gave him victory. And so it is today! We cannot add anything to the grace-giving gift of the redeeming work of Jesus Christ, no matter how much and how often our old human nature tries to do so. The victory over sin is achieved only by our Lord Jesus Christ, the Son of God. We may accept this in faith and claim it for ourselves. But we are not allowed and not able to add something suitable—no matter how hard we try, visibly or invisibly.

What do our neighbors, our work colleagues, our families actually think about us? How would they write about us? Do they know what our prayer life is like? Do they know how close we are to the LORD? Do they know how great our trust in God and in his Son is? And do they know whether we want to add anything spasmodically? Do we pray with a full heart? Do we pray at all?

This king Hezekiah of Judah had himself corrected by God and he then trusted him completely. He put his fate and that of his entire people into the hands of God. He sought God's nearness, again and again, in prayer. Yes, he was even able to change his mind in his counsel.

Isn't Hezekiah a wonderful example to follow? We have a God and Father to talk to. Yes, who longs very much for us to talk to him! God wants to talk to us! Talk to him!

The Psalmist

When Hezekiah, in his fortieth year of life, recovered from his fatal illness by the grace of God, he writes a praise of God out of gratitude, a psalm of thanksgiving. It is and remains his only psalm. It is not in our book of Psalms, but the prophet Isaiah, who was very close to King Hezekiah in these difficult days, recorded this psalm. We find it in the book of the prophet Isaiah (38:9–20):

This is the writing of Hezekiah king of Judah, when he had been sick and had recovered from his sickness:
I said, "In the prime of my life I shall go to the gates of Sheol;
I am deprived of the remainder of my years."
I said, "I shall not see Yah, The Lord in the land of the living; I shall observe man no more among the inhabitants of the world.
My life span is gone, taken from me like a shepherd's tent; I have cut off my life like a weaver. He cuts me off from the loom;
From day until night You make an end of me.
I have considered until morning—Like a lion,
So He breaks all my bones; From day until night You make an end of me.
Like a crane or a swallow, so I chattered; I mourned like a dove; My eyes fail from looking upward. O Lord, I am oppressed; Undertake for me!
What shall I say? He has both spoken to me, And He Himself has done it. I shall walk carefully all my years in the bitterness of my soul.
O Lord, by these things men live;
And in all these things is the life of my spirit;
So You will restore me and make me live.
Indeed it was for my own peace that I had great bitterness; But You have lovingly delivered my soul from the pit of corruption,
For You have cast all my sins behind Your back.
For Sheol cannot thank You, Death cannot praise You; Those who go down to the pit cannot hope for Your truth.
The living, the living man, he shall praise You, as I do this day; The father shall make known Your truth to the children.
The Lord was ready to save me;
Therefore we will sing my songs with stringed instruments All the days of our life,
in the house of the Lord."

The Proverbs Collector

Please do us the favor of reading Prov 26:27.

Did you know until just now that this wisdom, which is still very well known in our times, comes from the Bible and can be traced back to Solomon, but that we owe it to Hezekiah that we can still read it today?

Also, little known and also a little surprising is that we owe the entire chapters 25 to 29 in the book of Proverbs to our protagonist King Hezekiah. Please read Prov 25:1:

> *These also are proverbs of Solomon which the men of Hezekiah king of Judah copied.*

As this verse tells us, at the time of his reign, King Hezekiah assembled a group of men and instructed them to gather and write down Proverbs of Solomon. Why did he do this? We know from his known life and work that he was faithful to God and thus also to God's word. We also know that he placed his royal rule under God's grace and that he wanted to lead the whole people of Judah back to God in faithful ways. We also know that he very often sought God's advice in prayer, we know of his closeness to the prophet Isaiah. In other words, Hezekiah was not a complacent, single-minded, and decisive king, but he always sought instruction and advice from God, his Lord, and also from wise and experienced men of God. In this light, it is no longer so surprising that he put together a team to collect previously unrecorded sayings of the wise King Solomon and write them down for him and for posterity.

We know from 1 Kgs 5:12 that Solomon wrote or composed 3000 sayings and 1005 songs (an astonishingly precise statement). In the Bible only a fraction of this is recorded. This was certainly not different during the lifetime of Hezekiah, more than two hundred years after Solomon. In fact, we owe five of the thirty-one chapters of the book of Proverbs to the collecting efforts of Hezekiah, in total <u>137 individual proverbs</u>.

From the contents and themes of these 137 sayings, we can see that Hezekiah was not only interested in collecting and recording them for posterity, but that his intention was to learn something for himself and for his reign as king of Judah. Many of these sayings deal with how a king should behave.

Here are some nice examples:

> *It is the glory of God to conceal a matter,*
> *But the glory of kings is to search out a matter.* (Prov 25:2)

> *As the heavens for height and the earth for depth,*
> *So the heart of kings is unsearchable.* (Prov 25:3)

> *Take away the dross from silver,*
> *And it will go to the silversmith for jewelry.*
> *Take away the wicked from before the king,*
> *And his throne will be established in righteousness.* (Prov 25:4–5)

A ruler who lacks understanding is a great oppressor,
But he who hates covetousness will prolong his days. (Prov 28:16)

The king establishes the land by justice,
But he who receives bribes overthrows it. (Prov 29:4).

If a ruler pays attention to lies,
All his servants become wicked. (Prov 29:12)

Many seek the ruler's favor,
But justice for man comes from the Lord. (Prov 29:26)

Also the sayings from Hezekiah's collection, which do not directly allude to a king or ruler, almost always have something to do with good, godly, and also humble behavior.

Here is a small selection of further beautiful sayings of Solomon from Hezekiahs's collection:

Whoever has no rule over his own spirit
Is like a city broken down, without walls. (Prov 25:28)

As a door turns on its hinges,
So does the lazy man on his bed. (Prov 26:14)

Whoever digs a pit will fall into it,
And he who rolls a stone will have it roll back on him. (Prov 26:27)

The wicked flee when no one pursues,
But the righteous are bold as a lion. (Prov 28:1)

Evil men do not understand justice,
But those who seek the Lord understand all. (Prov 28:5)

A man's pride will bring him low,
But the humble in spirit will retain honor. (Prov 29:23)

And at the very end of Hezekiah's collection of Solomon's Proverbs, we find the proverb that helped King Hezekiah most in his most difficult times and which he actually really took to heart and acted upon, despite all the burden of responsibility he had to bear for his country and his people, even after a few detours and teachings from God:

> *The fear of man brings a snare, But whoever trusts in the Lord shall be safe.* (Prov 29:25)

King Hezekiah of Judah did not always do everything right in his fifty-four years of life, like all people, like all of us often do things wrong. But he was really serious about God. He tried the best he could to be faithful to God in humility and to serve his people well as a ruler. The order to some of his men to find and collect wise sayings of Solomon, which help him to be a good, faithful, and God-fearing king, is another interesting, impressive, and little-known indication of this, which we should not underestimate.

The Doubter

We find God's overall judgement of King Hezekiah several times in the Bible, and it is absolutely and unreservedly very good.

> *He trusted in the Lord God of Israel, so that after him was none like him among all the kings of Judah, nor who were before him. For he held fast to the Lord; he did not depart from following Him, but kept His commandments, which the Lord had commanded Moses. The Lord was with him; he prospered wherever he went.* (2 Kgs 18:5–7a)

> *And he did what was good and right and true before the Lord his God. And in every work that he began in the service of the house of God, in the law and in the commandment, to seek his God, he did it with all his heart. So he prospered.* (2 Chr 31:20b–21)

Already beginning with Hezekiah's name "My strength is the LORD," we see the main theme of his life: to rely on the LORD God completely and without restriction. Hezekiah was absolutely faithful to God, he believed and trusted and relied on God, his LORD. And in his responsibility as king over Judah he also led his people back to this path. But as is the case with us human beings, we are not always perfect, we are human, and in addition, as with all of us, there are also weaknesses, mistakes, and sins in Hezekiah. Whether in thoughts or in deeds, as long as we are human, we will make mistakes, but we may then sincerely repent and lay them at the feet of Jesus Christ, who forgives us and erases them forever, since he has paid for our misdeeds, whether already done or future ones, with his flawless divine life. Out of weakness, doubts also quickly arise. If we cannot fully trust God, then we are weak, we begin to fear and doubt.

So, Hezekiah did not always live up to his name, there were situations in which he did not want to rely on God completely, there were situations in which he doubted and tried to take fate into his own hands. What were these situations and how did they end?

Hezekiah's Covenant with Egypt

Hezekiah had rightly recognized that Judah had to free itself from the Assyrian grip that his father Ahaz had brought about in order to retain a chance of survival as an independent country. Therefore, he forged a long-term plan to free himself from the Assyrian yoke. An essential part of this plan was of course the necessary drastic spiritual reforms with the unconditional turning to God, but also many other measures, such as very extensive building activities. New cities were built, and new fortifications were constructed (the city of Lachish was not so easy to capture by Sennacherib, as the relief from the entrance hall of his palace in Nineveh shows very impressively and in detail). The army was strengthened, and through military successes against the surrounding countries, such as the Philistines, the national borders were again extended to their original size, and the overall position of Judah in the region as a whole was significantly strengthened and stabilized. Then Hezekiah was waiting for a favorable moment. This came with the death of the dreaded Assyrian king Sargon II (who probably had destroyed Samaria in 722/721 BC), who was unexpectedly killed in a campaign in 705 BC, so that his son Sennacherib succeeded him on the throne. In this situation the oppressed countries sensed a period of weakness of the Assyrians and launched a rebellion, as did the Babylonians with Merodach-Baladan as ringleader. Hezekiah now also saw the chance to shake off the Assyrian embrace and commenced the uprising by stopping tribute payments and having the Assyrian-controlled city prince Padi deposed from Ekron, an important trading city in Philistine, and arrested in Jerusalem. He also sought an additional alliance with Egypt as a safeguard. But here he obviously acted completely against the advice of the prophet Isaiah, who, on behalf of God, expressly advised against an alliance with and a call for help to Egypt. Isaiah dedicates two full chapters (30 and 31) to this topic in his book. Let us read, for example, Isa 30:3:

> *Therefore the strength of Pharaoh Shall be your shame, and trust in the shadow of Egypt Shall be your humiliation.*

But the key verse here is Isa 30:15:

> *For thus says the Lord God, the Holy One of Israel: "In returning and rest you shall be saved; In quietness and confidence shall be your strength." But you would not.*

And then still a little later in Isa 30:18–19:

> *Therefore the Lord will wait, that He may be gracious to you; And therefore He will be exalted, that He may have mercy on you. For the Lord is a God of justice; Blessed are all those who wait for Him. For the people shall dwell in Zion at Jerusalem; You shall weep no more. He will be very gracious to you at the sound of your cry; When He hears it, He will answer you.*

God also clearly promises in Isa 30:31 to strike the Assyrians:

> *For through the voice of the Lord Assyria will be beaten down, As He strikes with the rod.*

He also promises to protect Jerusalem in Isa 31:5:

> *Like birds flying about, so will the Lord of hosts defend Jerusalem. Defending, He will also deliver it; Passing over, He will preserve it.*

All these passages are connected with the warning against a covenant with Egypt instead of trusting in God.

As we know from the Assyrian and Egyptian sources and from 2 Kgs 19:9, Egypt under its leader Tirhakah (the word "Kush" = Southern Egypt) tried to help Judah, but apparently rather half-heartedly and above all unsuccessfully.

Interesting that also the Rabshakeh, sent by Sennacherib to ask Hezekiah and Jerusalem to surrender, judges Egypt similarly as God judges through Isaiah. What does the Rabshakeh say in Isa 36:6 outside the city walls of Jerusalem to the three officials of Hezekiah: "*Look! You are trusting in the staff of this broken reed, Egypt, on which if a man leans, it will go into his hand and pierce it. So is Pharaoh King of Egypt to all who trust in him.*" In the Bible, Egypt is always an image for the world, the temptations of the worldly life, the opposite pole to a spiritual life pleasing to God. And now his faithful king Hezekiah allies himself with this very Egypt, the symbol of the worldly, which in the end always takes its toll, even if it brings you joy or help for a short time, because it slowly and imperceptibly removes man from God and a spiritual life. In this respect, the Rabshakeh of Sennacherib has indeed spoken the truth in one point, by drawing the picture that anyone who allies himself with Egypt and relies on it ultimately cut off his nose to spite his face and harm himself.

And so it happened to Hezekiah, who rebelled against Assyria, demonstrated strength and relied on his ally Egypt, which made a timid attempt to help, but then ceased to appear. After the first defeat against Sennacherib, the Egyptians withdrew and abandoned Judah and Jerusalem. But that was obviously God's plan, too, he wanted to see Hezekiah king of Judah all alone, to make him rely only on his God. Hezekiah obviously had slight doubts about his actions against the Assyrians and God's promises that he would help his people, so he preferred to organize an alliance with the mighty Egyptians as a precaution, but this quickly evaporated when it mattered. How very human was this Hezekiah, actually so loyal to God, so full of faith and confidence. And then he had to help a little bit in his confidence himself. But God brought his faithful king exactly where he wanted him to be. Without the Egyptians he is now completely on his own. Judah was lost, Jerusalem was facing a catastrophe, the situation was hopeless.

Hezekiah's Tribute Payment to Sennacherib

Fully aware of the hopelessness of his situation, Hezekiah undertook a last, desperate, and again very human attempt to avert the impending doom. He let Sennacherib, who was on the verge of taking the storm-ridden city of Lachish, know that he had done wrong in trying to break away from the Assyrians. He now offered to fulfill any condition if Sennacherib would only stop his cruel attack. Here Hezekiah now completely threw his trust in God overboard. Likewise, he threw overboard his (completely correct) convictions that Assyrian bondage meant slow, creeping spiritual and physical death for Judah. And now he offered all possible worldly means to change the Assyrian king's mind. This was the moment of greatest doubt in Hezekiah's life. Here in this situation, he did not trust in God. The terrible worries about his people, about the city of

Jerusalem, had overwhelmed him. It is all too human, very human—but still not right towards God.

Sennacherib made a gigantic demand, which Hezekiah could only fulfill by plundering his treasuries and even had the gold removed from the temple doorposts (which he had had installed). Hezekiah was so completely desperate, so thoroughly controlled by fear, that he did not ask God what to do at that moment. He did not let Isaiah come and did not ask him for a prayer, for advice or for support. No, he acted quite humanly, as <u>he</u> now felt it was right and necessary. And what did God do? God let him grant. What happened afterwards?

Sennacherib received all the silver and gold with thanks—and then he took Lachish anyway and had part of his mighty army march against Jerusalem and lay siege to it. And he sent his officials with the Rabshakeh as spokesman to announce to Hezekiah the downfall of Jerusalem unless he would capitulate unconditionally. Hezekiah's all too human action to avert disaster had failed magnificently. All silver and gold was with Sennacherib, but the situation was still at least as hopeless as before. Hezekiah had to realize that he could do nothing more against the Assyrians now. He was completely at the end of all human judgement and advice. But this was exactly the state where God wanted Hezekiah to be—with all his human wits at his end. Hezekiah had to realize that he was lost without God. Now Hezekiah can, no, <u>must</u> finally trust God completely and exclusively! And so it happens, now Hezekiah begins to pray, to seek out Isaiah, the prophet of God, to ask him and God for advice, to plead urgently. And now he can only trust in God and his promises. And this is exactly what Hezekiah will bring about the victory over the Assyrians. From this moment on, we will find no more doubting king Hezekiah. We know the rest of the story: the Assyrians were defeated by God, Jerusalem was saved. But God had achieved an equally great victory with his faithful child Hezekiah. God had also reached the goal with him, a spiritual goal. And that is exactly why the word of God can judge this good King of Judah without restriction:

> *He trusted in the Lord God of Israel, so that after him was none like him among all the kings of Judah, nor who were before him. For he held fast to the Lord; he did not depart from following Him.*
> (2 Kgs 18:5–6a).

And Hezekiah now also knows for certain why the following saying of Solomon at the very end of his collection is so valuable:

The fear of man brings a snare, But whoever trusts in the Lord shall be safe. (Prov 29:25)

The Fallen

An even less beautiful chapter in Hezekiah's life is his reaction to the visit by the legation from Babel. Let us recall once again where this episode fits into the sequence of events.

Sennacherib had driven the rebellious self-proclaimed king Merodach-Baladan out of the capital Babylon and had begun his campaign to Judah, which also progressed quickly. Hezekiah had fortified Jerusalem and made great efforts to secure the water supply for the city through a hidden underground tunnel and to hide all other sources of water from the approaching besiegers. Then Hezekiah became seriously ill, so that Isaiah had to announce his imminent death. Because of his very earnest prayer, God gave Hezekiah a cure from the disease with the promise to add another fifteen years to his life. God sealed the whole thing with a miracle by making the sundial of Ahaz, which was probably placed directly in the royal palace, go back ten steps. As announced by God, Hezekiah became healthy after three days.

The news of these two miracles, the quick healing of the king of Judah from the deadly disease and the miraculous backward movement of the sundial will have spread like wildfire. Especially the latter is so unusual that this event will have been on everyone's lips for weeks. It is not known how this could have happened, whether the sun really ran backwards here and thus also the time, or whether God "solved" this differently. Neither is it known whether this was a locally limited or a worldwide event. In any case, it was an important sensation, and it was certainly not local, because these sensational news must have reached Merodach-Baladan in a very short time and caused the latter to send a legation to Jerusalem to Hezekiah.

According to 2 Kgs 20:12 and Isa 39:1, the main reason for the legation from Babel were probably the congratulations to Hezekiah for his recovery. But was that really all? Of course not. There were at least <u>two other</u>, more profound reasons for Merodach-Baladan to send its messengers to Hezekiah.

1. The Babylonians Worshiped the Sun

Among the Babylonians, sun worship was the highest religion. They had personified the sun as the supreme deity, given it a name, and set aside a day for its worship, in order to commemorate their highest god with a sun festival. Incidentally, we still find remnants of this Babylonian tradition today, quite surprisingly, in the name of our seventh day of the week, the "Sunday." Beyond that, or perhaps because of it, the Babylonians were also the inventors of the sundial. The sundial of Ahaz, possibly located in the royal palace in Jerusalem, was indeed a Babylonian invention. And now there is here a divine intervention in Jerusalem, in which a terminally ill Judean king is healed after a prayer to his God, and in addition, through divine intervention, the sun moves backwards! Obviously, someone here has power over the sun, the highest deity of the Babylonians. If this is not a reason to send someone there and to have the events reported and checked on the spot!

2. Allies against Assyria

Merodach-Baladan is still called the king of Babel here. In fact, shortly before, Sennacherib had deposed him by force, so that Merodach-Baladan had to flee to Chaldea in 703/702 BC, the easternmost region of Babel, farthest away from Assyria, directly on the Persian Gulf. The Assyrian records call this the "sea areas." So, he was in fact still in Babel, though no longer in the capital Babylon, and still called himself the king of Babel. This, however, became his undoing in 701/700 BC, when Sennacherib, on his retreat from Judah to Assyria, again passed over Babel ("back on the way he had come" 2 Kgs 19:33), since the rebellion still flared up here and perhaps also out of frustration over his previous defeat, in order to at least finally bring the matter with Merodach-Baladan in Babel to an end. Therefore, Merodach-Baladan had to leave Babel in 700 BC for good and go into exile in the land of Elam (today's Persia/Iran), with which he had allied himself against Assyria three years before, where he died six years later in 694 BC.

In the year 702 BC at the time of Hezekiah's recovery, Merodach-Baladan was still in Chaldea in the south of Babylon and continued to call himself King of Babylon. Since he himself could not visit Hezekiah, which would have been far too dangerous in view of the advancing Assyrians in Judah, Merodach-Baladan obviously sent a delegation to Hezekiah to explore a possible alliance. Apparently, he was dealing with a powerful ruler who had influence over the sun, the supreme god of Babylon. This might have been the actual reason for the visit from Babel: they wanted to reach an agreement about a possible military alliance against Assur. Merodach-Baladan must also have known that Judah had formed an alliance with Egypt. So perhaps he wanted to join this coalition.

Hezekiah's reaction to the visit from Babel was again very human. The author of these lines would like to distance himself explicitly from many comments that describe Hezekiah's behavior at this point as "his foolish sin," "Hezekiah's inglorious pride," "shameful fall," or similar disrespectful constructions of terms. Neither the authors of these commentaries nor the author of this book are entitled to write in this way about a believing man to whom God issues this judgment in his word:

> He trusted in the Lord God of Israel, so that after him was none like him among all the kings of Judah, nor who were before him. For he held fast to the Lord; he did not depart from following Him. (2 Kgs 18:5–6a).

Besides the doubts discussed in the previous section, this is the only sin of Hezekiah that is recorded and discussed in the word of God. Presumably there will have been more of them, but God did not have them written down. Now let each of the authors of the Bible commentaries, who describe Hezekiah's sin as stupid, shameful or inglorious, examine where he himself stands on his way with God, and whether Hezekiah, for all his mistakes, would give him such a good testimony as he did with King Hezekiah. To commit a sin is certainly not good, and we must then live with the consequences, as Hezekiah did. But we are all sinners without exception, with the unfathomable privilege of being saved by the work of redemption of Jesus Christ, the Son of God. The one who is clearly aware of this does not label another believer who has spent his whole life trying to be faithful to God, even under the enormous burden of a kingdom, because of one known sin, as stupid, shameful or inglorious. And certainly not over 2,700 years after all these events. Let each one first examines himself before he judges and condemns others.

Hezekiah, perhaps still under a euphoric and exuberant impression of his recovery from the deadly illness, full of energy and zest for action, was very happy about this visit from Babel, the gift, and letter that Merodach-Baladan had delivered. Likewise, we must not forget that God promised him not only healing and an additional fifteen years of life, but also salvation from the hands of the Assyrians (2 Kgs 20:6b). Perhaps Hezekiah again thought very humanly and concluded for himself that with the Babylonians rescue was now approaching.

In any case, he did everything to impress and win over the Babylonian guests. In this respect, the accusation of arrogance is perhaps justified, but we can also see here again that Hezekiah did not fully trust in God, but still hoped for alliances, just as he had already entered into one with Egypt against the advice of Isaiah. Presumably both were true. According to 2 Chr 32:31 God probably wanted to show Hezekiah once again what was not quite right in his heart. Hezekiah was proud of his riches, of his kingdom and his rule, and he showed this too. There is indeed a little pride. But perhaps even worse, he still didn't trust God unconditionally, he hoped to make another alliance, like with Egypt, which expressly did not approve of God, which still existed at that time and was one of Hezekiah's hopes. And this, after God had promised him shortly before, besides the miraculous healing, the rescue from the Assyrians. Hezekiah did not ask God in prayer here either, he did not ask the prophet Isaiah for advice. He did what <u>he</u> thought was right. He did not fully trust God.

Sins that we commit always have consequences. Even if God takes the guilt from us through his Son Jesus Christ and does not take it into account, we must still deal with the consequences in our further worldly life. This was the case with Hezekiah: Isaiah had to announce to him that all the treasures and achievements that Hezekiah had joyfully presented to his visitors from Babylon would one day be taken away to Babylon. And so it came to pass. It should not be forgotten that at the time of this announcement Babylon was a rather insignificant country in the immediate vicinity of the all-dominant Assyrians. So this announcement of judgment must have been very astonishing at that time.

In fact, it took place in several stages. Only a short time later, in his desperation, Hezekiah already gave a large part of the treasures from his treasuries to Sennacherib, namely, almost all gold and silver as tribute payment in the hope that Sennacherib would break off his campaign against Judah, which he did not do. But now Sennacherib was Assyrian and not Babylonian. Later he actually brought all his spoils to Nineveh in Assyria. However, ninety years later, in 612/611 BC, Nineveh fell into the hands of the Babylonians under Nabopolassar in a massive attack and long, hard siege battles. All gold and silver that Sennacherib had brought from Jerusalem to Nineveh would then be fallen into the hands of the

Babylonians and carried off to Babylon. Thus, all the gold and silver that Hezekiah's visit from Babylon in 702 BC had seen in Jerusalem has arrived in Babylon, as predicted—with a stopover in Nineveh. Everything else besides the gold and silver that Hezekiah presented to his guests from Babylon fell into the hands of the Babylonians, first a few years later in 597 BC at the first defeat of Jerusalem against the Babylonian king Nebuchadnezzar and then in 587 BC at the final destruction of Jerusalem by Nebuchadnezzar. Thus, the prophecy of Isaiah on Hezekiah in 587 BC was completely fulfilled, exactly one hundred years after Hezekiah's death in 687 BC. Some chronologies put Hezekiah's death on the year 686 BC and also the fall of Jerusalem on 586 BC which is only a postponement of one year and means again the fulfillment of this prophecy exactly one hundred years after Hezekiah's death. God loves numbers, they always have a meaning with him. God loves order. Anyone who knows anything about the biblical symbolism of numbers, which we really only want to go into a little bit here, knows that the number ten in the Bible always symbolizes the responsibility of man. Giving the Ten Commandments, the ten virgins, the ten plagues of Egypt, the ten pounds entrusted to us, the tithe—these are only a few excellent examples of this. With 10 x 10 = 100, the author does not wish to engage in cabalistic number acrobatics here, but somehow one cannot get rid of the feeling that the fulfillment of the prophecy to Hezekiah exactly one hundred years after his death is not a coincidence, but part of the divine orders and arrangements.

Besides the treasures and possessions that would be taken to Babylon, Isaiah announced Hezekiah as a further punishment: "*And they shall take away some of your sons who will descend from you, whom you will beget; and they shall be eunuchs in the palace of the king of Babylon*" (2 Kgs 20:18). Has this now been fulfilled? Well, already Hezekiah's son Manasseh is imprisoned in Babylon, but is released again after he urgently asks God for forgiveness. The word of God is really great, it forgets nothing and even every little detail, which we might otherwise just read over, has a meaning. The prophet Nehemiah, who later saw to it that the walls of Jerusalem were rebuilt after the Jews were allowed to return to their land from the Babylonian captivity, lists in chapter 7 of his book in detail how many people from which family return from Babel to Judah and Jerusalem. In exactly one of these listed families, and exactly only there, one finds a small addition in verse 21:

> *These are the inhabitants of the province of Judah who went up from captivity, the captives whom Nebuchadnezzar king of Babylon had led away, and who returned to Jerusalem and Judah, each to his own city, all who came with Zerubbabel and with Yeshua, Nehemiah, Azariah, Raamah, Nahamani, Mordecai, Bilshan, Mispereth, Bigwai, Nehum, and Baana. This is the number of the men of the people of Israel: The sons of Parosh 2172; the sons of Shephatiah 372; the sons of Arach 652; the sons of Pahat-moab, of the sons of Jeshua and Joab 2818; the sons of Elam 1254; the sons of Sattu 845; the sons of Sakkai 760; the sons of Binnui 648; the sons of Bebai 628; the sons of Asgad 2322; the sons of Adonikam 667; the sons of Bigwai 2067; the sons of Adin 655; the sons of Ater, of* **Hezekiah:** *98.* (Neh 7:6–21; Ezra 2:1–16)

So, the "sons of Ater" of Hezekiah were in Babylonian captivity and have now returned to Jerusalem. Any more questions?

Some exegetes criticize Hezekiah in that he asked to be cured of the deadly disease, which enabled him to prolong his life by fifteen years. They argue that Hezekiah did not want to accept God's death sentence in obedience to the faith and then fell into great sin during his visit from Babylon, which would not have happened if he had not prayed to God for his healing. Then he would not have been healed and the Babylonians would not have had such a great interest in a visit. These exegetes argue that Hezekiah would not have fallen into that sin and therefore judge that his prayer was not good.

Such a view by a believing Bible interpreter is already very questionable and must be rejected outright! Why?

God Makes No Mistakes!

The view presented above implies that God made a mistake by answering Hezekiah's prayer, since after his healing he fell into sin, as it were, in recklessness. This is not possible. God does not make mistakes. God is omniscient and not bound by time and space. He knows the future, but he is just as capable of shaping and changing it. If he decides that Hezekiah must die, then it is good and fulfills his plans for future developments, and if he gives Hezekiah healing and another fifteen years of life after his very intimate prayer, then it is also good and fulfills his plans and thoughts about future developments as well. It is not possible for us humans with our limited minds to fully understand this, but we may know that God never makes a mistake.

God Answers Prayers!

There are many examples in the Bible of believing men and women asking God the LORD for something, even after God has already announced his counsel. Just think of Moses, how often he struggles with God in prayer for the people of Israel. If this were not so, what kind of life would it be? We really could no longer influence anything; everything would be preordained. Exaggeratedly depicted, we could sit in an armchair and wait for years and years to see what happens. Everything would be preordained anyway. But it is not so! God rejoices in a personal relationship of people with him. That is the real meaning of our life, God created us humans to have community with us. Unfortunately, we humans have severely impaired this through sin, but God has created solutions for this in the old and especially in the New Covenant. He wishes that we communicate with him, he wishes that we pray to him. In the New Covenant we even have an extremely powerful intercessor in God's Son, Jesus Christ, who intercedes for us before God (Rom 8:26; Heb 7:25). And what we will ask in his name, the Father will give us (John 14:13)! God rejoices in our prayers, even if he does not always fulfill them. But sometimes they are fulfilled, and then it is also good. It is even very good.

The Son of God as an Example

Who would dare to criticize our Lord Jesus Christ for his prayer in the Garden of Gethsemane? Does he not ask his Father there with the famous words "*O My Father, if it is possible, let this cup pass from Me; nevertheless, not as I will, but as You will*" (Matt 26:39) precisely because he did not carry out something that God the Father had decided in his eternal counsel? What Jesus was about to do here was so frightening that the incarnate Son of God—although divine in nature—was so afraid of it that he asked his Father whether there was not a way to avoid what was about to happen. In this case, however, there was apparently no other way. Our Lord Jesus Christ accepted that his prayer was not answered, bowed to the counsel of his Father and carried the sins of the whole world to the cross.

So, if even the Son of God can ask his Father to deviate from his counsel, if it were possible, then this is obviously nothing wrong or reprehensible.

So, it is not for us to criticize Hezekiah for his prayer for healing. It is not for us to suggest that it was not good that God prolonged his life. God does not make mistakes. On the contrary, it is only through the events that follow that God can reach his goal with his faithful child King Hezekiah. Only then after his bad reaction to the visitors from Babylon can Hezekiah realize what is in his heart and that he must repent and change. And isn't that also written in the same way in 2 Chr 32:31? *"God withdrew from him, in order to test him that He might know all that was in his heart."*

God took Hezekiah into a teaching, he showed him step-by-step what was important to him and what was still working against it in Hezekiah's heart. God brought Hezekiah step-by-step to the point where he could only rely on him completely and exclusively. To trust him completely and entirely. No longer in his own strength, intelligence, or wealth. Hezekiah had not asked God for advice when the legation from Babel arrived; he had not consulted Isaiah, the prophet of God. He was again striking out on his own, wanted to control the fate of Jerusalem through his own destiny. But God had announced several times long ago that he would save Jerusalem and that Hezekiah and the inhabitants of the city should only trust in it calmly. Hezekiah had made an alliance with Egypt, which did not please God. He had made great efforts to fortify Jerusalem, had secured the underground water supply in an unprecedented construction project, and was now in the process of making an additional alliance with the Babylonians. But with what result?

The alliance with Egypt was no help, the Egyptians withdrew after the first defeat against Sennacherib and did not continue to fight for Judah. The alliance with the Babylonians did not come about anymore. The immense tribute paid to Sennacherib had no effect. The fortification of Jerusalem was not needed at all, because the Assyrians did not have the time to attack Jerusalem. In the end, all the human considerations and efforts of Hezekiah <u>did nothing to save</u> Jerusalem from the Assyrians. It was only God's intervention. And that was the goal that God achieved with Hezekiah. In the end, Hezekiah had no choice but to trust God completely. He recognized what was in his heart, namely still a little bit of human vanity and human arrogance and the will to contribute something to the salvation wrought by God despite God's announcements. After all human efforts and considerations, God led Hezekiah into a final total dependence on him and his promises. And Hezekiah understood all this. He did not agree to surrender, as Sennacherib's Rabshakeh demanded of him and Jerusalem. Although all his human efforts had been destroyed, although Hezekiah, from a human point of view, now had nothing more to oppose the Assyrian attack, he did not capitulate. A capitulation might have saved a large portion of the lives in Jerusalem, but the people would have been led away from their land, somewhere else, according to Assyrian practices. Judah would have ceased to exist, as it had happened to Samaria and the Northern Kingdom of Israel twenty years earlier. No, Hezekiah had understood his teachings. What did he do? He went into prayer! After the Rabshakeh's call to surrender, he consulted the prophet of God, and he went into prayer earnestly. And what happened beyond that? After the Rabshakeh had left for Sennacherib, he immediately sent a letter to Hezekiah with another ultimate call to surrender. And what did Hezekiah do with this letter? What did Hezekiah do with the letter of Merodach-Baladan, which the Babylonian messengers had brought with them? He probably read it; we do not know the content of this letter. But he had <u>not presented</u> this letter to <u>God</u>, he did not disclose the contents of this letter—presumably it was about a covenant against the Assyrians—and he did not consult with the wise men of God. But Hezekiah had now learned his lessons. He now knew that he could trust in God completely, took the letter of the Rabshakeh, went with it to the temple, <u>spread this letter before God</u>, and began another haunting prayer.

God had come to his goal with his faithful child, King Hezekiah. Hezekiah put aside all his doubts, fear, and human vanities. He placed his fate and that of the city of Jerusalem with all its people completely in the hands of God, who had promised his protection on several occasions. Hezekiah now trusted in God. He could have agreed to the surrender. That would have been the only reasonable decision according to human judgment. That would have saved the lives of many people, even if they had been deported to another country. Now a very long, terrible siege was about to begin, in which many people would suffer or die. Afterwards the city would have been taken and plundered by the Assyrians. Many people would have died in this process as well. But Hezekiah was now at peace with God. He had gone into repentance, had changed his attitude of heart. Now, as God had long wished him to do, he put the whole further course of events into the hands of God. What a trust. What confidence Hezekiah now gained from the power of his prayers. And all this would not have been possible if he had died before and not asked for his healing. Nor would it have been possible if he had not been able to search his heart and repent of his misconduct during the visit from Babel.

Now the strength of this king of Judah is the recognition of his weakness. And the knowledge of the faithfulness of his God. The God of Israel. And now Hezekiah can finally live up to his name: My strength is God! Just as God had announced to Hezekiah through Isaiah long before:

> "In returning and rest you shall be saved; In quietness and confidence shall be your strength." (Isa 30:15).

And now God can finally glorify himself in his child Hezekiah, who trusts in him completely, and save Jerusalem from destruction by the Assyrians.

Just as the Lord Jesus Christ told Paul,

> *My grace is sufficient for you, for My strength is made perfect in weakness.* (2 Cor 12:9b)

The Father

After Hezekiah's death, his son Manasseh becomes (*sole*) ruler over Judah. Manasseh immediately regresses, like his grandfather Ahaz, into terrible, idolatrous, murderous times.

How could this happen?

According to our chronology, Manasseh was born in 709 BC through his mother Hephzibah ("my joy is in her" [2 Kgs 21:1]). The father of Hephzibah is not mentioned by name. In the Jewish tradition it is handed down that the prophet Isaiah is said to have been her father. So, Isaiah would have been the father-in-law of Hezekiah. However, there is no real proof of this. Since Hezekiah was born in 741 BC, he was already thirty-two years old when his heir to the throne, Manasseh, saw the light of day—relatively late for those times. According to Sennacherib's campaign report, some of Hezekiah's daughters were also part of the immense tribute Hezekiah paid to Sennacherib to persuade him to cancel his campaign, which he did not do after all. The tribute was paid in 701 BC, so Manasseh must have been about eight years old. It can be assumed that Sennacherib rather brought daughters of Hezekiah to Nineveh, who were older than Manasseh. From this we can conclude that Hezekiah probably produced children even before Manasseh, but they were daughters. So, Manasseh had older sisters, but was the first-born male heir to the throne, unless there had already been male descendants of Hezekiah who died early. This was not unusual at that time; the infant mortality rate was much higher than today. Maybe Manasseh was not the firstborn heir to the throne, but the one who survived. This would be a possible explanation, in addition to the apparently prior born daughters, why the age difference between Hezekiah and his heir Manasseh is relatively large by the standards of the time.

Manasseh grew up in what we would call a well-protected home. At the age of approximately seven years (702 BC) he had to watch his father fall fatally ill, but he also had to see how his father was healed by God. When he was eight years old, he experienced the crisis surrounding the siege of Jerusalem by Sennacherib's army, but also saw how God protected the city and the people in it and how the Assyrians had to leave defeated.

After that he grew up in a peaceful environment, there were no more wars. At the age of twelve years (697 BC), after which, according to Hebrew tradition, a boy becomes responsible for his own actions (*gadol*), his father Hezekiah appointed him coregent. Hezekiah knew that he only had ten years to live, because five of the additional fifteen years of life given by God had already passed. He now began to prepare his son for the succession to the throne in ten years at the earliest possible time, when Manasseh would be twelve years old. Hezekiah, by the way, knew how it felt for a son, since he himself was proclaimed coregent by his father Ahaz at the age of twelve or thirteen.

Ahaz, however, had tried to hold his son Hezekiah responsible for his evil, rebellious actions against God. Hezekiah, on the other hand, took Manasseh into his reign in order to introduce him to his future task as king in loyalty to God. Although Manasseh, like Hezekiah, was led into codomination at the age of about twelve, this obviously happened under completely contradictory conditions.

So Manasseh had all the best prerequisites to become a good king. He grew up protected in peaceful times, he saw his faithful father and how he was devoted to God, regularly consulted the prophet Isaiah and was extremely successful. He experienced how the people of Judah rejected idolatry and, under his father's guidance, entrusted themselves entirely to the LORD God and served him. He will have visited the temple regularly and experienced how the temple services went, which his father had reinstated. In everything his father was a good example to him.

Then his father took him into responsibility early on and Manasseh was allowed to rule together with him. So Manasseh had all the prerequisites to become a good king. But he did not become one.

What could have gone wrong? Was Hezekiah responsible for it? Had Hezekiah failed as a father?

Manasseh's turnaround after his father's death and after taking over sole rule was both truly incomprehensible and inexplicable. The descriptions in 2 Kgs 21:1–9 are terrifying:

> *Manasseh was twelve years old when he became king, and he reigned fifty-five years in Jerusalem. His mother's name was Hephzibah. And he did evil in the sight of the Lord, according to the abominations of the nations whom the Lord had cast out before the children of Israel. For he rebuilt the high places which Hezekiah his father had destroyed; he raised up altars for Baal, and made a wooden image, as Ahab king of Israel had done; and he worshiped all the host of heaven and served them. He also built altars in the house of the Lord, of which the Lord had said, "In Jerusalem I will put My name." And he built altars for all the host of heaven in the two courts of the house of the Lord. Also he made his son pass through the fire, practiced soothsaying, used witchcraft, and consulted spiritists and mediums. He did much evil in the sight of the Lord, to provoke Him to anger. He even set a carved image of Asherah that he had made, in the house of which the Lord had said to David and to Solomon his son, "In this house and in Jerusalem, which I have chosen out of all the tribes of Israel, I will put My name forever; and I will not make the feet of Israel wander anymore from the land which I gave their fathers—only if they are careful to do according to all that I have commanded them, and according to all the law that My servant Moses commanded them." But they paid no attention, and Manasseh seduced them to do more evil than the nations whom the Lord had destroyed before the children of Israel.*

And then additionally 2 Kgs 21:16:

> *Moreover, Manasseh shed very much innocent blood, till he had filled Jerusalem from one end to another, besides his sin by which he made Judah sin, in doing evil in the sight of the Lord.*

The Roman-Greek historian Flavius Josephus (AD 37–100) reports of daily executions in Jerusalem under Manasseh's rule. And according to the Jewish tradition in the Talmud and other sources, Manasseh had the prophet Isaiah, who at some point hid from him in a hollowed-out trunk of a cedar tree, cut up together with the tree after discovery on the spot. It should be mentioned in addition that Manasseh was <u>twenty-two years old</u> when his father Hezekiah died in 687 BC, he took over the <u>sole reign</u> in Judah and thus began his terrible work.

What had gone wrong? Had Hezekiah's education been so bad? Was he not a good father? Had he not given Manasseh a good education? Was Hezekiah not a good example for his son after all? Manasseh had not met his grandfather Ahaz, who had similar terrible inclinations, who died in 716 BC, seven years before his birth. So, the evil grandfather could not have been to blame. What had happened?

These questions are difficult to answer. Actually, they cannot be answered at all.

Isn't it still the same today? Don't some people who grew up in terrible childhood conditions, overwhelmed by the grace of God and the work of the Lord Jesus Christ, suddenly come to faith and stay there for the rest of their lives? But don't some of the children who grew up in a good Christian home, who had loving parents loyal to God, fellowship with Christian brothers and sisters, regular children's and teenagers' hours, don't some of these children also stray from the path at some point and one day find themselves completely far from God? Yes, we know all these cases. And they show us that the decision to live a life with God not depends solely on the person who has to make that decision for him or herself. The natural man is always in rebellion against God at first. This is also the case with our children, when they then grow up and take responsibility for themselves. A loving Christian home, a Christian upbringing in humility, much knowledge from the Holy Scriptures, fellowship with brothers and sisters of all ages in faith—all these are wonderful conditions for a good childhood and to wish for many more children than are given such a childhood today. But all these are <u>no guarantees</u> that our children will become faithful Christians, faithful to God. In all that we give or do not give to our children, at the very end, there is both the personal recognition demanded of each person by God and his Son Jesus Christ of his own sinfulness and the impossibility of reaching God through his own actions, as well as the very personal decision to believe in the redeeming work of the Son of God and to claim it for themselves. Our children are completely responsible for their own affairs with God.

Of course, as parents we try to give them good basics. But in the end they are all alone before God. The decision which way they take is made entirely by them. There is nothing more we parents can do for them here—except bring them before God in our prayers.

We would like to pass this on as a consolation to all parents whose children no longer walk the path with God, who at present want to know nothing more about the Lord Jesus, although they may have been given a good Christian foundation in their childhood. <u>Dear parents, you are not responsible for this!</u> Your upbringing was certainly the best you could have given your children. Your children are absolutely responsible before God. It is not your fault, not your responsibility, if your child has currently turned away from God. We know that this hurts. Please do not blame yourself! Please do only one thing: <u>pray for your child . . .</u>

And parents, who (could not) let their children grow up in a non-Christian way, in whatever circumstances, and who now regret this—let the following be said: your children are also responsible before God! If your child does not convert to the Lord Jesus Christ, then it is not because you did not bring him up in a Christian way in the past. It is not your fault, not your responsibility, if your child has not yet turned to God. Please do not blame yourself! Please do only one thing: pray for your child . . . God is a just God. If your child has not heard the gospel from you, he or she will receive it from someone else. And then he or she will be alone before God, and you cannot help him or her.

<u>Pray for your child!</u>

Hezekiah was certainly not a bad father. Of course, nothing is handed down about his upbringing and how he dealt with Manasseh. We don't know whether he took a lot of time for him, whether he treated him lovingly or rather rough and very demanding. We do not know. We would probably judge his personality to be rather gentle and loving after all we know about Hezekiah by now—but we do not know.

But we know that Manasseh had a sheltered childhood and that his father must have been a God-fearing role model for Manasseh.

> *And he did what was good and right and true before the Lord his God.*
> *And in every work that he began in the service of the house of God, in the law and in the commandment, to seek his God, he did it with all his heart. So he prospered.* (2 Chr 31:20b-21)

But Manasseh obviously wants to go different ways than his father under all circumstances. After his father died and he was thus the sole ruler and got free rein, he completely and unbelievably radically reversed all the good that made up his father's government. This is his very personal rebellion against God—and probably also a rebellion against his (dead) father.

We do not know what it was like in Manasseh's heart that brought him on this terrible path. We only know, unfortunately, that after ten years of co-regency under his faithful and God-loyal father, he initiated a conversion just as radical as his father did when he took over the sole reign, unfortunately in a completely different direction. Unbelievable...

We do not want to repeat here what Manasseh did all that was terrible. We do not want to repeat his inglorious deeds again. In summary, however, it can probably be said that he most likely did not omit any sin, no infamous deed. It is hard to imagine much worse.

And then an event occurs in Manasseh's life that heralds another radical change: he is captured by Assyrian army commanders and taken in bronze fetters to Babylon (not to Nineveh!):

> *And the Lord spoke to Manasseh and his people, but they would not listen.*
> *Therefore the Lord brought upon them the captains of the army of the king of Assyria, who took Manasseh with hooks, bound him with bronze fetters, and carried him off to Babylon.*
> (2 Chr 33:10–11)

We do not know why Manasseh was captured and taken away. Nor do we know why he was taken in captivity to Babylon and not to Nineveh. But we can reasonably deduce when this must have taken place. The historians are largely agreed that this no longer happened under the Assyrian king Esarhaddon (681–669 BC), but under his son Assurbanipal (669–627 BC). Let us recall that Manasseh's reign lasted from 697 to 642 BC, the first ten years of which were spent as a coruler under his father Hezekiah. Babylon as the place of his captivity was under Assyrian rule at this time and Assurbanipal had appointed his brother Shamash-shumu-ukin as king over the city around 667 BC. In the Assyrian records Manasseh and the kingdom of Judah are explicitly mentioned as supporters of the campaign of Assurbanipal against Egypt, which began in 667 BC and ended victoriously with the conquest of Thebes in 664 BC. At that time Manasseh had not yet fallen into disgrace with the Assyrians. As already described in chapter 2, however, a fratricidal war broke out in 652 BC between the two Assyrian king's sons, which ended in 648 BC with the death of Shamash-shumu-ukin. It can be assumed that Manasseh was captured in Babylon shortly before the outbreak of the fratricidal war but was released relatively quickly as a result of the trials and tribulations. In any case, there is no record of another king being appointed over Judah during the time of his captivity, which would certainly have been the case if the captivity had lasted several years.

So, Manasseh came to Babylon in Assyrian captivity, and this according to the passage in 2 Chr 33:10b at the instigation of God, who simply could no longer bear the atrocities of Manasseh. What happened then?

> Now when he was in affliction, he implored the Lord his God, and humbled himself greatly before the God of his fathers, and prayed to Him; and He received his entreaty, heard his supplication, and brought him back to Jerusalem into his kingdom. Then Manasseh knew that the Lord was God. (2 Chr 33:12–13)

Manasseh repents!

Manasseh realized in captivity what a terrible godless life he had led. If we once assume, as explained in chapter 2, that his captivity and his conversion took place at the beginning of the war between the Assyrian king's sons—that is, 652 BC—Manasseh was already fifty-seven years old at that time and had made about thirty-five years of his reign as horrible as the word of God in 2 Kgs 21 tells us. Manasseh was converted at the age of fifty-seven! Who could have expected this after three and a half decades of his reign of terror? We humans would have given up all hope. We would have thought that such an evil man was lost forever. And yet Manasseh is obviously repenting. The Bible tells us about it, and his actions and deeds after his return from captivity, which was given to him by God, prove the authenticity of his repentance. Obviously, Manasseh had a lot of time for reflection during his imprisonment, a lot of time to reflect on his life and realize how terribly he had fallen into sin and wickedness all these years. And at the latest there he will have remembered his father and his life according to God. He will have remembered how often and how intensively his father had gone into prayer with God, how often and how intimately his father Hezekiah had placed himself completely in the hands of God, and how often God gave answers to prayer. He will have remembered the prayer that Hezekiah spoke when he asked for the salvation of Jerusalem from the siege of Sennacherib, which is recorded and handed down through Isaiah (Isa 37:15–20). He will have remembered a great deal from his childhood. And now we can see that probably not everything was in vain, what Hezekiah the father exemplified to his son, what he gave him in education and training and experiences. Even if Hezekiah was not allowed to experience this during his lifetime, towards the end of the life of his son Manasseh it still bore fruit. Manasseh turns back! After all these terrible years, after three and a half decades of open enmity against God. Manasseh goes into repentance! He confesses his guilt and repents deeply. And in the last ten or so years of his life, he still tried, as best he could, to correct much of what he had done wrong.

My dear parents whose children are not going through life with God at the moment: there is always hope! You do not know whether your child will one day turn to God again. You don't know whether your child will remember everything that you have given him/her on the path of life. You do not know whether your child will remember his or her believing parents and what you have shown him or her. Perhaps you are then already long since no longer on this earth when this happens. There is always hope, there is always the possibility that you could sow a seed in the heart of your child, which will finally come up in due time and lead your child into the arms of God. Maybe you will not experience it yourself anymore, maybe at least not in this world. Everything has its time. And my dear parents, if you feel that you have not done enough for your child, if you feel that you have not prepared him enough for a Christian life or that you have not set a good example—bring all this before the Lord Jesus Christ. Bring all your worries and needs to him in prayer, ask for forgiveness if you think that your education was not good enough for your child. He will forgive you! And he will again give you a joyful heart in this regard. You will then realize that it is always your child's personal responsibility if he or she is not living with God at the moment. God the Father and the Lord Jesus are ultimately <u>not</u> dependent on your good and Christian upbringing when it comes to the spiritual battle for a human soul.

There is always hope! Even a seemingly completely hopeless case like Hezekiah's son Manasseh, who for decades wallowed in sin in open enmity with God like pigs in mud, even this Manasseh still manages to repent, to repent and to find God.

Pray for your children . . .

There is always hope. Pray for your children and trust in God and the Lord Jesus Christ.

> *My sheep hear My voice, and I know them, and they follow Me. And I give them eternal life, and they shall never perish; neither shall anyone snatch them out of My hand. My Father, who has given them to Me, is greater than all; and no one is able to snatch them out of My Father's hand. I and My Father are one.* (John 10:27–30)

Excursus: Metals in the Bible

> *Therefore the Lord brought upon them the captains of the army of the king of Assyria, who took Manasseh with hooks, bound him with bronze fetters, and carried him off to Babylon.* (2 Chr 33:11b)

Why does the word of God explicitly mention here that Manasseh will be led away to Babylon in fetters of <u>bronze</u>? Why, for example, is the Nehushtan, the brazen serpent, also made of bronze?

The metals gold, silver, and bronze are often found in the Bible. Even though they are mentioned in different contexts, a basic tendency can clearly be seen in which context and with which meaning these metals occur. Gold is very often a symbol of the holiness of God. Let us think of the new Jerusalem in the books of Revelations, which is made entirely of gold, or of the Blessed Sacrament in the temple and tabernacle, whose walls and all the utensils inside are made entirely of gold.

Silver is often a symbol of the redeeming work of Jesus Christ—let us think of the thirty pieces of silver to which he was "sold."

Bronze is clearly a symbol of sin and atonement. The brazen serpent was to be made by Moses from bronze. All the devices in <u>front of the</u> innermost part of the temple were made of bronze, as they were used for sacrifices and thus for cleansing from sin. There are many other similar examples. And Manasseh's shackles are also made of bronze. The Bible mentions such a detail not without reason! The fact that his fetters, in which he is led away to Babylon, are made of bronze, is a very clear sign that he is bound in his sins and now must atone for them.

Excursus: Manasseh's Prayer of Repentance

In the AD first century, a scripture appears which is called "Manasseh's Prayer." It is supposed to reflect the contents of his prayer of repentance during his Assyrian captivity in Babylon and is subsequently appended in some editions of the Bible as an addition to the books of Chronicles. Although it is a beautiful prayer, it cannot be said whether it was really Manasseh who formulated it in this way or whether another author wrote it afterwards and only attributed it to him. That a first proof is probably possible at the earliest in the second century BC, i.e., at least two-hundred years after the writing or completion of the Chronicles, weakens the credibility regarding Manasseh as the original author. Nevertheless, this cannot be completely ruled out. For we find in the Bible (2 Chr 33:18–19) the clear indication that Manasseh's Prayer of Repentance at that time was actually already recorded and reproduced (even several times). But we do not know whether what we know today as "Manasseh's Prayer of Repentance" was really his prayer in captivity in Babylon. The text we have as Manasseh's Prayer is considered apocryphal by nearly all Jews, Catholics, as well as Protestants, but nevertheless by some Orthodox Christians as a canonical book. Luther inserted it behind the Apocrypha. However, we want to reproduce this prayer here. When reading it, the reader should keep in mind that it is very uncertain whether it really comes from Manasseh and corresponds to his prayer of repentance in the prison in Babylon:

> *O Lord, Almighty God of our fathers, Abraham, Isaac, and Jacob, and of their righteous seed; who hast made heaven and earth, with all the ornament thereof; who hast bound the sea by the word of thy commandment; who hast shut up the deep, and sealed it by thy terrible and glorious name; whom all men fear, and tremble before thy power; for the majesty of thy glory cannot be borne, and thine angry threatening toward sinners is importable: but thy merciful promise is unmeasurable and unsearchable; for thou art the most high Lord, of great compassion, longsuffering, very merciful, and repentest of the evils of men.*
>
> *Thou, O Lord, according to thy great goodness hast promised repentance and forgiveness to them that have sinned against thee: and of thine infinite mercies hast appointed repentance unto sinners, that they may be saved. Thou therefore, O Lord, that art the God of the just, hast not appointed repentance to the just, as to Abraham, and Isaac, and Jacob, which have not sinned against*

thee; but thou hast appointed repentance unto me that am a sinner: for I have sinned above the number of the sands of the sea. My transgressions, O Lord, are multiplied: my transgressions are multiplied, and I am not worthy to behold and see the height of heaven for the multitude of mine iniquities.

I am bowed down with many iron bands, that I cannot life up mine head, neither have any release: for I have provoked thy wrath, and done evil before thee: I did not thy will, neither kept I thy commandments: I have set up abominations, and have multiplied offences. Now therefore I bow the knee of mine heart, beseeching thee of grace. I have sinned, O Lord, I have sinned, and I acknowledge mine iniquities: wherefore, I humbly beseech thee, forgive me, O Lord, forgive me, and destroy me not with mine iniquities.

Be not angry with me forever, by reserving evil for me; neither condemn me to the lower parts of the earth. For thou art the God, even the God of them that repent; and in me thou wilt shew all thy goodness: for thou wilt save me that am unworthy according to thy great mercy.

Therefore I will praise thee forever all the days of my life: for all the powers of the heavens do praise thee, and thine is the glory for ever and ever. Amen.

Excursus: Hezekiah Had (At Least) One More Son

King Hezekiah apparently had at least one more son and thus Manasseh at least one brother. His name was Amariah, from whom the prophet Zephaniah descended in a later line. Zephaniah is therefore Hezekiah's great-great-grandson.

The word of the Lord which came to Zephaniah the son of Cushi, the son of Gedaliah, the son of Amariah, the son of Hezekiah, in the days of Josiah the son of Amon, king of Judah. (Zeph 1:1)

Hezekiah's son Amariah does not appear otherwise.

The Miracles—God Intervenes

In the Bible we are told of <u>three miracles</u> that Hezekiah is allowed to experience through God's intervention. These three miracles were the backward movement of the sundial, his healing from the deadly disease and the destruction of the Assyrian army at the gates of Jerusalem overnight. The first miracle is meant as a confirmation of God's decision to give Hezekiah healing from the deadly disease (the second miracle). Thus, the first miracle takes place to confirm that God will indeed let the second miracle happen.

The Shadow of the Sun Moves Ten Steps Backwards

It is quite astonishing that Hezekiah specifically asks the prophet Isaiah for a sign of God as a quasi "confirmation miracle." Isaiah had just brought him the unbelievably joyful news that Hezekiah's prayer, his plea for salvation from the deadly disease was answered by God—and Hezekiah has nothing better to do instead to rejoice and fall on his knees before God in gratitude, he has nothing better to do than to ask for a sign of confirmation? How is that possible?

In order to be able to explain this, we must once again deal with a childhood experience of Hezekiah's. After the entry of his father Ahaz into the coregency in 735 BC together with his father Jotham, Judah was attacked by the alliance of Rezin, the king of Aram (Syria), and Pekah, the king of the Northern Kingdom of Israel—with the goal of making the son of Tabeel (this name seems to be Syrian) king of Judah. This attack was unsuccessful, but it was the reason for the hate-filled Ahaz to persuade the Assyrians under their then leader Tiglath-Pileser III to attack Aram and its capital Damascus in 732 BC and raze it to the ground. As already described in previous chapters, the Assyrians did not stop in Syria but continued their conquests in the Northern Kingdom of Israel until its capital Samaria fell in 722 BC after a three-year siege. So, when the newly crowned king Ahaz faced this hostile alliance of Aram and Israel around 735/734 BC, God sent his prophet Isaiah to Ahaz to tell him to keep calm and not to be afraid (Isa 7:1–6). The LORD then went on to tell Ahaz to ask for a sign to confirm (and certainly to reassure), "in the deep or in the high places" (Isa 7:11). But Ahaz refused to demand this sign, which led Isaiah to comment that Ahaz was tiring God with it. At this point at the latest, Ahaz's aversion to his God began, and at this point at the latest, his desire to always take over control of all action begins. The whole thing then developed with Ahaz into an abysmal hatred against the God of Israel and the beginning of a frenetic idolatry.

Hezekiah will have been about six or seven years old at that time, so he got all this quite well. And of course, he also witnessed the terrible further development of his father. Now thirty-three years later, the LORD God announced to him through Isaiah a supernatural intervention, namely his recovery within three days and his salvation from the approaching Assyrians. This time Hezekiah wanted to get it right, not like his father, who even rejected God's request for a sign to confirm. This time Hezekiah, the son of Ahaz, himself demanded a sign from God! And God granted it to him: Hezekiah may choose whether the hands of the sundial should go ten steps forwards or backwards. Here the term "the sundial of Ahaz" (2 Kgs 20:11) is mentioned in the translations of the Holy Scriptures known to us today. The sundial was an invention of the Babylonians (more on this later, see the excursus at the end of this section), who worshiped the sun as the supreme deity. So, it is quite possible that Hezekiah's father Ahaz, who took part in just about every idolatry just to document his hatred of the God of Israel, had this sundial made by Babylonians in his palace in Jerusalem.

Hezekiah was allowed to choose between forward or backward, just as his father was allowed to choose between up and down ("in depth or up in height" [Isa 7:11]). In contrast to Ahaz, God determined for Hezekiah where and on which object the sign would be visible. The miraculous sign that God did for Hezekiah was performed on the sun, the supreme deity of a pagan nation (Babel = unbelieving seductive world)—more precisely, on an object that Hezekiah's deeply ungodly father Ahaz, who rejected such a sign of confirmation from God, erected himself! God thus understood very clearly why Hezekiah demanded this sign for confirmation and the choice of the object on which it was to be seen could be considered ironic by human standards. By God's standards, however, this was quite simply just.

The reaction of God to Ahaz's refusal to demand a sign was, by the way, very astonishing. For his part, he nevertheless determined a sign, but then one that no longer had anything to do with Ahaz and his current situation, but had an eternal character and was known to all believing Christians:

> *Therefore the Lord Himself will give you a sign: Behold, the virgin shall conceive and bear a Son, and shall call His name Immanuel.* (Isa 7:14)

Most amazing how God's infinite goodness and grace, even in the face of the greatest disbelief and disobedience, can still proclaim something so good in the end!

So, Hezekiah wants to do it better than his father, who refused to demand a sign from God, even when the latter asked him to do so. Hezekiah demanded for himself his announced recovery and the salvation from the Assyrians this sign; Isaiah asked God for it. And he granted it and let it happen. Hezekiah's sign was very noticeable, and it spread quickly to all the surrounding countries, which was one of the reasons for the visitors from Babylon sent by Merodach-Baladan to Jerusalem. Today we do not know how this miracle was performed by God, whether the sun really ran backwards or only its shadow. We do not know whether this event was locally limited to Jerusalem or whether it could be perceived worldwide. But that is not really relevant either; what is important is that it took place and that it was obviously not doubted, otherwise the messengers from Babel would not have taken the long and dangerous road to get to the bottom of it all.

A miracle had taken place. Completely unnatural and visible to all, the shadow of the sun went backwards by a certain way (ten steps). What might this have triggered in Hezekiah, in Isaiah and the people in Jerusalem?

Today we are granted to know what the people of that time were also allowed to experience: with God nothing is impossible. He wants to be there for us and he always keeps his promises!

Even today God still works miracles, often in silence and often not as dramatically as happened here. Sometimes it is also the very personal miracles that take place in a human life. It is important to know that God is omnipotent, he can always and at any time work a miracle, also for us.

Also, for you. You only have to ask him . . .

Excursus: Was the Sundial of Ahaz Perhaps not a Sundial at All?

The Hebrew original text in 2 Kgs 20:11 is difficult to translate and it is by no means certain whether a sundial is really meant here. If you take it quite literally, you would have to translate it like this:

> *And he made the shadow go back by ten steps around the steps he had gone down on the stairs of Ahaz.*

In the famous complete Isaiah scroll found at Qumran, there is even (in one of the very few deviations from our present texts, which we know from the Isaiah scriptures) still talked about an "upper room of Ahaz," to which the stairs are said to have led up once.

Stairs or sundial?

The principle of the sundial and the use of a pinhole or a shadow stick (gnomon) to determine the time of day has been known in China since about 1100 BC. The first forerunners can already be found in the thirteenth century BC among the Egyptians, even if only very rudimentary versions.

Herodotus (approx. 484 to 425 BC), an ancient Greek historian, geographer, and ethnologist, wrote about 450 BC that the Greeks took over the sundials from the Babylonians. Aha! So, the Western world received the sundials from the Babylonians. Whether the Babylonians once had contact with the Chinese or invented the sundial themselves or simply improved the Egyptian pre-versions is hard to say. Scientists today assume that "real" sundials (not the rudimentary predecessors from the eleventh or thirteenth century) were actually invented by the Babylonian Chaldeans, which fits very well with their sun worship cult. Our historians believe, however, that this invention did not occur until about 600 BC. Our story here, however, is about 700 BC and thus one hundred years earlier. Did the sundials of the Chaldeans already exist then? Our scientists might be a little off in their time estimates. The general context in terms of time and content (Hezekiah apparently received a visit from the people who invented the sundial in Western culture) is at least somewhat appropriate, and perhaps Hezekiah's father Ahaz, in his inexhaustible idolatry, simply had the latest in the Babylonian sun cult purchased and built in his palace in Jerusalem.

On the other hand, the text speaks quite clearly of "steps." Ten steps the shadow went backwards. Were the steps actually divisions on the sundial? Or were they simply steps of a staircase on which the shadow of the sun fell?

We can no longer make a final decision on this today, but it is not really important. What is really important is that God has let the shadow of the sun run backwards, something that cannot really exist in reality. God actually caused this miracle, because it spread to all neighboring countries. Whether the shadow running backwards fell on the steps of a staircase or on the steps of a sundial of the Babylonians, which was very modern by the standards of the time, is irrelevant to the event as such and especially its significance. We just do not want to leave you in the dark about the fact that there are different opinions here, which probably cannot be resolved. The author of this book is more inclined to the opinion that it was about steps of a staircase, but would find the story with a "modern sundial of the Ahaz" even a bit more "exciting."

Most of today's Bible translations speak of the sundial, which is why we have left this term unchanged in our book in the mentions of these Bible passages.

Hezekiah Is Cured of the Deadly Ulcer

So, after God had confirmed his promise to heal Hezekiah through the sign on the sundial of Ahaz discussed above, Hezekiah had to wait and see if he actually healed. Isaiah had a fig cake spread on Hezekiah's ulcer. So, it was obviously not enough to sit back and wait for God to act. As so often, God expected a bit of initiative (sometimes he expects to wait for his intervention in peace and quiet, but then he explicitly asks us to do so).

Such fig cakes were often made at that time, simply to be able to store the figs better. By the way, this is actually coming back into fashion in our time. Either the figs were placed on top of each other until they stuck together and looked like a cake, or the fresh figs were squeezed into a mass and then baked into a real cake (1 Sam 25:18; 1 Sam 30:12; 2 Sam 16:2).

However, such fig cakes were of course intended for consumption rather than for the treatment of ulcers.

Figs, or the fig tree, occur surprisingly often in both the Old and New Testaments. The Lord Jesus often uses the fig tree in his parables either for the people of the Jews or for man in general, who may or may not bear fruit. In fact, we find the fig tree or fig leaves right at the beginning of human history. In Gen 3:7, Adam and Eve, after recognizing their nakedness, make aprons (coverings) from fig leaves.

Nowadays, archaeologists can also prove through corresponding finds that figs were harvested, dried, stored, and naturally consumed by man right from the very beginning of human civilization.

Here now Isaiah has the fig cake spread on Hezekiah's ulcer for treatment. How long did Hezekiah's recovery take? How long did it take him to recover from his fatal illness?

> *Return and tell Hezekiah the leader of My people, "Thus says the Lord, the God of David your father: I have heard your prayer, I have seen your tears; surely I will heal you. On the third day you shall go up to the house of the Lord."* (2 Kgs 20:5)

Of course, God did not miss the opportunity to give an image of the healing of Hezekiah for the healing of all people, which he planned through his son, who completed it a good 730 years later through his unique sacrifice for the salvation of all.

Just as the Lord Jesus Christ rose from the dead after his cruel death on the cross through the intervention of God on the third day and brought about the healing of all mankind from the deadly "sickness," the ugly and eternally gluttonous ulcer of sin, so Hezekiah also receives his healing with the third day. As in so many other events of the Old Testament, God lets the coming work of his Son shine through and thereby glorifies it in a foresight.

> *I will heal you. On the third day you shall go up to the house of the Lord.* (2 Kgs 20:5b)

But did Hezekiah really go to the temple after his recovery on the third day? In fact, this is not really written down. It is simply assumed. It was clear! Of course, on the third day, the day of his recovery, Hezekiah went to the house of the LORD, to the temple to worship and thank God, just as God had foretold in his promise to Hezekiah.

We even know what he said to God in his gratitude! We find this in Isa 38:9–20 in the beautiful psalm that Hezekiah speaks here in his gratitude for his God the LORD.

Hezekiah was miraculously healed. By human standards he could not be saved, his illness must have progressed so far that God, through the prophet Isaiah, asks him to prepare himself for death and also to arrange his succession (*"Thus says the LORD: Order your house!"* [2 Kgs 20:1]). And now he had been saved by divine intervention. Here we see—and why should it be different in our times?—that God, our LORD, can be moved by prayers, by our petitions. The author is convinced that this is as valid today as it was then. Why should it be different? Unfortunately, we do not know if and when our requests will be fulfilled, sometimes he does not give us what we ask for.

But we may know that to those who love God all things serve for the best (Rom 8:28)! So in the end it is always about trusting him. If we trust him, we may know with certainty that it will be good for us. In the

Garden of Gethsemane, the Lord Jesus asked his Father to let this cup, this terrible approaching death, pass by him. But he placed all his trust in the hands of his Father, "not as I will, but as You will" (Mat 26:39). And so it is just the same for us today: we may, indeed we should ask God, and we may expect answers to prayers and also miracles. But if he does not give them, we can still feel completely safe in his hands and trust him that it is good. Even if we cannot or do not always want to understand this. But: it is good. Always.

> And we know that all things work together for good to those who love God, to those who are the called according to His purpose. (Rom 8:28)

God Strikes the Assyrians and Saves Jerusalem from Destruction

Already in his promise to heal Hezekiah from the deadly ulcer, God promised without being asked to save Hezekiah and the whole city of Jerusalem "from the hand of the king of Assyria" (2 Kgs 20:6). In chapter 2 of our book, we have worked out that this must have happened at a time when the Assyrian campaign against Judah had already begun, when the first cities of Judah had probably already fallen into the hands of the Assyrians, and when Hezekiah was preparing Jerusalem for the imminent siege by Sennacherib's army. In doing so, he certainly always had in mind the terrible events surrounding the three-year siege of Samaria, the capital of the Northern Kingdom. The fall of Samaria was about twenty-one years ago at that time and Judah had taken in a large number of refugees from the Northern Kingdom.

In the meantime, Hezekiah had recovered, but the Assyrians had now reached Lachish. An immense tribute paid by Hezekiah did not stop Sennacherib from taking the city and sending his Rabshakeh to Jerusalem with very brazen and polemical calls for surrender. Hezekiah, in his greatest need, turned to God in an urgent pleading prayer, and Hezekiah confirmed once again what he had actually already promised him, that the king of Assyria would not enter Jerusalem. Yes, he even strengthened and concretized his promise and added that Sennacherib would not shoot an arrow into the city and would not raise a wall against it (2 Kgs 19:32–34). This, incidentally, indicates that the siege of Jerusalem cannot have lasted very long.

Even among scholars who do not believe in the Bible, there is little doubt that the Assyrians under Sennacherib did not actually take Jerusalem. There is sufficient extrabiblical evidence for this, and even Sennacherib, who is all too happy to glorify himself in his campaign reports, reported a difficult siege of the strategically important city of Lachish for several months and its successful capture, but he definitely did not report the capture of Jerusalem. Instead, Sennacherib told only that he locked Hezekiah in Jerusalem "like a caged bird."[4] There is no mention of the capture or conquest of the city. Nor does he mention the duration of the siege, so it can be assumed that it must have been relatively short indeed. So nonbelieving scientists cannot deny this, but they are equally surprised, because Jerusalem would certainly not have been able to withstand an Assyrian siege for long. So why did Sennacherib leave after a seemingly short siege without taking Jerusalem? If one does not want to believe in the supernatural intervention of God, then of course other explanations must be used. Various approaches have been suggested.

Explanation Attempt: Sennacherib Did Conquer Jerusalem After All, but the Bible Conceals This

This is an unsuitable attempt to exclude a divine miracle. There is practically no evidence for this explanation. For there is neither archaeological evidence of the capture of Jerusalem in the time of Hezekiah nor are there any such records. One could try to argue that the Bible shamefully conceals this, which in itself is very implausible, since all other defeats and misfortunes of the people of Israel and the Jews are mentioned and reported very precisely. Why should one conceal exactly this event? Even more important is the written report of an extremely renowned eyewitness, namely Sennacherib himself, who in his campaign report speaks of a very long and difficult, but then successful and victorious siege of Lachish (a very well-preserved huge wall relief was discovered in Sennacherib's royal palace). He definitely does not speak about the capture of Jerusalem in his self-glorifying campaign report.

> The account of the blockade erected around Jerusalem is different from the sieges described in Sennacherib's annals and the massive reliefs in Sennacherib's palace at Nineveh, which depict the

---

4. Wikipedia, "Sennacherib's Annals," https://en.wikipedia.org/wiki/Sennacherib%27s_Annals.

successful siege of Lachish rather than events at Jerusalem. Though the blockade of Jerusalem was not a proper siege, it is clear from all available sources that a massive Assyrian army was encamped in the city's vicinity, probably on its northern side. Though it is clear that the blockade of Jerusalem ended without significant fighting, how it was resolved and what stopped Sennacherib's massive army from overwhelming the city is uncertain.[5]

The inscription on the Taylor Prism gives a detailed account of the events in the Jerusalem region by Sennacherib himself. There he tells the story in his own words:

> As for the king of Judah, Hezekiah, who had not submitted to my authority, I besieged and captured forty-six of his fortified cities, along with many smaller towns, taken in battle with my battering rams. . . . I took as plunder 200,150 people, both small and great, male and female, along with a great number of animals including horses, mules, donkeys, camels, oxen, and sheep. As for Hezekiah, I shut him up like a caged bird in his royal city of Jerusalem. I then constructed a series of fortresses around him, and I did not allow anyone to come out of the city gates. His towns which I captured I gave to Mitinti, king of Ashdod; Padi, ruler of Ekron; and Silli-bel, king of Gaza.[6]

Sennacherib may have conquered large parts of Judah, the Bible confirms this, but not Jerusalem: then he would have told the story differently and not glorified the siege of Lachish so much. And then the archaeologists would also have found evidence of such a conquest of Jerusalem. No, Sennacherib was not in Jerusalem.

Explanation Attempt: Hezekiah Has Capitulated

A further attempt to explain the situation is that Hezekiah had capitulated after all and Sennacherib had left satisfied. Sennacherib had already received the extraordinary tribute payments and certainly Hezekiah's assurance to be a loyal Assyrian vassal again, who continued to pay punctually and regularly. There are several arguments against this theory. Such a behavior of the Assyrians would have been completely unusual: they would certainly have besieged and conquered Jerusalem with great joy or, after a surrender, would certainly have tried to get some of this satisfaction. To

---

5. Wikipedia, "Sennacherib," https://en.wikipedia.org/wiki/Sennacherib.
6. Wikipedia, "Sennacherib's Annals."

make matters worse, the Rabshakeh himself had already said something about the conditions of surrender before the walls of Jerusalem in his speech to the inhabitants of the city. He said that it would surely be better to stop the resistance and give up now. He cited the terrible example of how Samaria, the capital of the former Northern Kingdom of Israel, had fared. He added that instead of dying now or suffering terribly, it would be better to <u>continue</u> life without hardship <u>in another country</u>:

> *Do not listen to Hezekiah; for thus says the king of Assyria: "Make peace with me by a present and come out to me; and every one of you eat from his own vine and every one from his own fig tree, and every one of you drink the waters of his own cistern; until I come and take you away to a land like your own land, a land of grain and new wine, a land of bread and vineyards."* (Isa 36:16–17)

So, Sennacherib lets Jerusalem be told by his Rabshakeh that they should capitulate in order to save their lives, and he promises a life that is definitely worth living (including vine and fig tree!), but—this is clearly announced here—in another country! This would correspond exactly to the Assyrian procedures of deporting, leading away and resettle peoples from the countries they had conquered. They had done the same with the Northern Kingdom of Israel. The resettlement of the Hebrews of the Northern Kingdom was still in full swing at that time, and the Assyrians wanted to proceed in the same way with the Jewish people. The ten tribes of the Northern Realm are considered lost to this day according to the Assyrian expulsions, so the Assyrians were quite thorough in this. And they wanted to proceed in the same way with Judah and Benjamin. But then this never happened! According to all we know today, the Assyrians withdrew and nothing else happened. All we know is that afterwards Hezekiah was highly regarded and respected by all other peoples. There were no displacements or resettlements. There were no further major confrontations with the Assyrians after that. Only Hezekiah's son Manasseh was once captured by the Assyrians, but this was probably not the result of a war or military conflict, but presumably had reasons in personal sensitivities or differences. It was as the Bible writes:

> *The Lord was with him; he prospered wherever he went. And he rebelled against the king of Assyria and did not serve him.* (2 Kgs 18:7)

Explanation Attempt: Sennacherib is Satisfied after the Tribute Payments and Turns Back

This attempt at explanation is very similar to the previous one. The only difference is that Hezekiah did not have to capitulate here, but the Assyrian king Sennacherib, after the immense tribute payments, which he also listed in his campaign report, returned to Nineveh satisfied and spared Jerusalem. This, too, does not really seem plausible, for the Assyrian army was already standing before Jerusalem, and the siege had begun with at least a part of the Assyrian army. It would have been very obvious to take the city now, especially since the tribute payments of Hezekiah obviously went to Sennacherib before the fall of Lachish, in order to prevent the downfall of Lachish and subsequently of Jerusalem as well. Why then should Sennacherib still have besieged Jerusalem or sent the Rabshakeh with his calls for surrender? Besides, in this age it was still a question of honor to experience military victories or defeats. Now the victory over Jerusalem and Judah was so close at hand, why should the Assyrians have proceeded here completely differently than they had done a few years earlier with Samaria? Let us note that at that time the deportations from the Northern Realm were still taking place and at least for several decades. So why should they have proceeded quite differently here? This attempt at an explanation is just as implausible as the previous one.

The obvious and, by human standards, unexpected non-capture of Jerusalem by the Assyrians must therefore have had a superior reason. Since obviously undeniable extraordinary circumstances prevented Jerusalem from being conquered by the Assyrians, further attempts at explanation were made so that one did not have to believe in a miracle of God.

Explanation attempt: An Epidemic or Plague Has Decimated the Assyrian Army

Both the ancient Greek historian Herodotus (approx. 484 to 425 BC) and the Roman-Jewish historian Flavius Josephus (approx. AD 37 to 100) try to explain the Assyrian retreat by the outbreak of a plague of mice and the pestilence. These would have weakened the Assyrian attackers to such an extent that they had to return home. Josephus describes it like this:

> Now when Sennacherib returned to Jerusalem from the campaign against Egypt, he found that the troops left behind under Rapsakes

[= Rabshakeh] *were suffering severely from the plague. On the first night, as he continued the siege together with these troops, the plague killed one hundred and eighty-five thousand men in his army, along with their leaders and captains.*[7]

Are pestilence or plague of mice plausible? A plague of mice is certainly very unpleasant, but can it really have been the reason for the large, famous, and terrifying Assyrian army to break off the siege? Hard to believe. In any case, it can hardly produce 185,000 dead Assyrian warriors overnight. Pestilence, on the other hand, can easily claim that many lives. In the Bible we even find a comparable story in 2 Sam 24, where it threatened to strike Jerusalem. But it is very unlikely that as many as 185,000 healthy men would all die in one night from pestilence!

Nowadays we know how epidemics spread, in waves of infection and not all at once. One can only understand the account of Herodotus as an attempt to mix the apparently quite accepted biblical account with natural explanations for the supernatural. The main thing is that one now does not have to believe in a divine miracle.

Explanation Attempt: A Samum Has Burned the Assyrians

Samum is the local term for a sandstorm in the North African-Arabic region. The word comes from the Arabic and means "poison wind." This indicates the danger that is attributed to this type of sandstorm. The Samum is partly loaded with dust and can develop into a desert wind with temperatures of up to 130 degrees Fahrenheit (54 degrees Celsius). In fact, such sandstorms may occasionally occur in the Jerusalem area, but it is extremely unlikely that they occur at night and remain unnoticed until the morning. Moreover, they should not cause such high death rates among Assyrian soldiers sleeping in tents.

Explanation Attempt: The Egyptian Army Attacked the Assyrians at Night

None other than the famous devout British scientist Sir Isaac Newton, in his book on the past kingdoms, tried to find an explanation for the death of the 185,000 Assyrian soldiers, assuming that they were attacked

---

7. Flavius Josephus, *The Antiquities of the Jews*, Book 10, Section 4 (Hollywood, FL: Simon and Brown, 2013), 602.

and killed by the approaching Egyptians under their leader Tirhakah at night. He believed that an army hostile to the Assyrians could be interpreted as angels of the LORD, who executed the judgment of God. But this is extremely implausible, there are some arguments against such a presumption. First of all, there is no other similar case in the Bible: there at no point is an angel equated with an army. Furthermore, it is not very plausible if the author of the book of Kings a few lines before (verse 9) calls the Egyptians under Tirhakah exactly by name and then some verses later speaks of an angel of the LORD. Moreover, the Egyptian army would have to operate extremely quietly if it killed 185,000 men in one night, which nobody noticed until the morning awakening! And would the Egyptians then have simply disappeared again unnoticed and without a sound after this terrific victory? In such a way that no one noticed anything more of them in the morning? No, even this attempt at explanation leads nowhere.

In our opinion it makes little sense to believe a part of the biblical account, namely the 185,000 dead Assyrians, but then not in the reported cause of death, namely the divine intervention by an angel. What natural cause could kill 185,000 strong Assyrian soldiers unnoticed within one night? Hard to imagine. Logical and consistent is to trust the biblical account completely or reject it entirely.

No, all "normal" attempts at explanation are not sufficient or they are simply not plausible. Something extraordinary must have happened. God had indeed intervened in a very drastic supernatural way.

The Assyrians simply withdrew—no further siege, no conquest, no abductions. Sennacherib mentioned the successful siege and conquest of Lachish and had it colorfully depicted on a relief in his palace. But there is no evidence that Jerusalem was conquered, not even that it suffered. No, Sennacherib could not harm Jerusalem. It seems then that a phase of many peaceful years has also occurred. The Assyrians gave way and the people of the Jews could breathe a sigh of relief and rebuild the land and the conquered cities.

The LORD God had protected Hezekiah and Jerusalem from the Assyrians, as he had promised Hezekiah king twice.

> *For I will defend this city, to save it For My own sake and for My servant David's sake. And it came to pass on that certain night that the angel of the Lord went out, and killed in the camp of the Assyrians one hundred and eighty-five thousand; and when people arose early in the morning, there were the corpses—all dead.*

> *So Sennacherib king of Assyria departed and went away, returned home, and remained at Nineveh.* (2 Kgs 19:34–36)

We even know quite well when God had the Assyrians beaten by his angel. If we read our text again very carefully, we find that the judgment on the Assyrians was carried out "on that certain night." What does "that certain night" refer to? The events before <u>that day</u> were the letter of Sennacherib, delivered to Hezekiah by the Rabshakeh, who then presented it to God, urging him to be saved, and God's promise to save Jerusalem from the Assyrians and to execute judgment on them. This had happened that <u>day</u>, and now <u>on that night</u> the angel of the LORD comes and carries out the punishment on the Assyrians. The judgment of God apparently followed exactly that night of the day, on which Hezekiah prayed to God and who promised him salvation. So immediately afterwards.

The Bible does not tell us exactly how the Assyrian soldiers died. As we have explained above, speculations about this do not lead to anything, but it is not really relevant. Nor do we know exactly when it happened at night, at what hour, and how long it lasted. We may only know that the surviving Assyrians apparently only noticed the terrible event in the morning after getting up (2 Kgs 19:35b). So, the angel of the LORD must have acted very quietly and very bloodlessly, so that one could obviously assume until the morning that everyone was still sleeping. This dramatic event caused Sennacherib to abandon the siege and return to Nineveh (we know by now that he was passing through Chaldea to finally set Merodach-Baladan down in his exile in the Persian Gulf). What was the reason for his abandonment of the siege? Was his army now so weakened that he no longer considered the siege promising? Or was he aware that a divine judgment was indeed being carried out on him? Or possibly both?

The death of 185,000 of his men in a single night, and this immediately after Sennacherib had his letter in which he reviled the God of Israel delivered to Hezekiah, already speaks a lot for the fact that the king of the Assyrians understood that he was dealing with a supernatural intervention of a power he could not oppose. The Assyrians also believed in gods (even very many) and the power they could give or exercise. In this respect, the main reason for Sennacherib's retreat may have been that, in addition to the considerable military weakening, he recognized this divine power and did not want to run the risk of being completely wiped out in a further confrontation. The Bible also does not leave us in the dark about the fact that this victory of God over the Assyrians was final.

They did not return to Nineveh to replenish the army with fresh men and to try the attack against Jerusalem once again. Nor did they stay outside Jerusalem with the rest of the troops and request reinforcements from Assyria. Nothing of the sort happened. The Assyrians will never again attack Judah and Jerusalem. The Holy Scripture tells us quite plainly:

> So Sennacherib king of Assyria departed and went away, returned home, and remained at Nineveh. (2 Kgs 19:36)

And he remained in Nineveh. He never came back. Sennacherib had seen enough. He was defeated and he feared the power of the God of Israel. The battle was won. For good.

The LORD God had won them for Hezekiah, the people of Jerusalem, and all the people of Judah. The remaining two tribes of Judah and Benjamin were not taken away and no other peoples were settled.

God had kept his promises to Hezekiah.

Excursus: The Army Camp of the Assyrians

> And it came to pass on that certain night that the angel of the Lord went out, and killed in the camp of the Assyrians one hundred and eighty-five thousand. (2 Kgs 19, 35a)

The already mentioned Roman-Jewish historian Flavius Josephus (approx. AD 37 to 100) is an eyewitness of the later siege and conquest of Jerusalem by the Romans in AD 70. In his report, which is part of his work "De Bello Judaico" (= Of the Jewish War), he mentions twice an area near Jerusalem, which at that time was probably called "The Army Camp of the Assyrians." Apparently, Emperor Vespasian's son Titus also set up his headquarters there in AD 70. Further passages in Josephus's work suggest that this area was located in the northwest of Jerusalem. Perhaps the name "The Army Camp of the Assyrians" had been used for the almost 770 years between the Assyrian siege (701 BC) and the Roman siege (AD 70). It was a place where God worked a mighty miracle and where the people of the Jews were saved from the Assyrians. It is obvious that this special area was given a name—"The Army Camp of the Assyrians." Since the Assyrians actually stood only this one time before Jerusalem, it could perhaps really be the very area where the angel of the LORD struck the 185,000 Assyrian men. So, we apparently have a reasonably well-founded assumption as to where the camp of the Assyrians was located when the angel of the LORD came in the night.

Excursus: God's Sign for the Coming Harvest

> *This shall be a sign to you: You shall eat this year such as grows of itself, and in the second year what springs from the same; Also in the third year sow and reap, Plant vineyards and eat the fruit of them. And the remnant who have escaped of the house of Judah shall again take root downward, and bear fruit upward. For out of Jerusalem shall go a remnant, and those who escape from Mount Zion. The zeal of the Lord of hosts will do this.* (2 Kgs 19:29–31)

This is what God says exactly before he lets Hezekiah know to his joy that he will not let the Assyrians enter Jerusalem (2 Kgs 32–34). What is it about these harvests? What does God say? <u>In this year</u>, the year of the siege of Jerusalem, the people are to eat from the offspring of the harvest. <u>In the second year</u> of its wild growth, then <u>in the third year they shall</u> sow and reap and plant vineyards. It seems obvious that in the year of the Assyrian attack, with the capture of countless Jewish cities, the siege and conquest of Lachish, and the siege of Jerusalem, the Jewish people could hardly have cared for the cultivation of the fields. Therefore, God tells Hezekiah that the people can eat from the naturally regrowing. The actual harvest could probably still be brought in in a hurry, but a further cultivation of the fields, including a new sowing, was apparently no longer possible. So now, after the Assyrians had left, the people should feed themselves on what would grow again from the current harvest. Israel was then (and is again today) a very fertile country, so that a "reharvest" must have been possible. But since a timely sowing for the coming harvest was obviously no longer possible, God promised that in the second year the people would even be fed by the "wild growth." So, although no controlled cultivation was possible due to the Assyrian attack, the people would be satisfied by what then grows wild. Only in the following year can and should the Jews sow and harvest extensively again. God thus reassures Hezekiah of an impending famine as well as of a possible renewed Assyrian attack in the coming years. As a result, more time and resources were indeed available for the reconstruction of Judah and the cities conquered by the Assyrians. After all, God's promises meant that at first, no attention had to be paid to the cultivation of crops. God would provide for sufficient offspring and wild growth of the harvests.

Some exegetes interpret that the second year must have been a sabbatical year, because otherwise the harvest would have been cultivated. According to Exod 23:10–11, after six years of cultivation, the people of Israel had to leave the land fallow in the seventh year. This was the Sabbatical year and served to recover the soil. We now know with great certainty from Flavius Josephus and his records that the years 164/163 BC and 38/37 BC were Sabbatical years. This makes it very easy to determine, by backward calculation, that the next Sabbatical year after the year 701 BC, in which we are now here, must have been 696 BC. In this respect this interpretation is to be rejected. In fact, God tells Hezekiah here that he need not worry, because when the Assyrians have left, there will be enough crops left to prevent famine. And even in the following year, the Jews are supposed to take care of the reconstruction of the country, God even lets enough grow from the wildly grown grain so that there is enough for everyone. In the third year, the normal cultivation of the harvest could be started again, and it would be very profitable.

God simply lets Hezekiah know, "Don't worry, the Assyrians will not return for years to come. Take care of the reconstruction of the country, I will take care of your supplies." Only then, in the verses that follow, does he let Hezekiah know that he will save Jerusalem from the Assyrian attackers and their king Sennacherib. So, the LORD God is not only taking care of the current threat to the people, but also of the time after that, of the necessary supply of the people in the post-war and reconstruction period.

What a caring God we have!

Excursus: The Apocryphal Book Tobit (Tobias)

Tobit chapter 1 (KJV):

> *The book of the words of Tobit, son of Tobiel, the son of Ananiel, the son of Aduel, the son of Gabael, of the seed of Asael, of the tribe of Nephthali;*
>
> *Who in the time of Enemessar king of the Assyrians was led captive out of Thisbe, which is at the right hand of that city, which is called properly Nephthali in Galilee above Aser.*
>
> *I Tobit have walked all the days of my life in the ways of truth and justice, and I did many almsdeeds to my brethren, and my nation, who came with me to Nineve, into the land of the Assyrians.*
>
> *And when I was in mine own country, in the land of Israel being but young, all the tribe of Nephthali my father fell from the*

house of Jerusalem, which was chosen out of all the tribes of Israel, that all the tribes should sacrifice there, where the temple of the habitation of the most High was consecrated and built for all ages.

Now all the tribes which together revolted, and the house of my father Nephthali, sacrificed unto the heifer Baal.

But I alone went often to Jerusalem at the feasts, as it was ordained unto all the people of Israel by an everlasting decree, having the firstfruits and tenths of increase, with that which was first shorn; and them gave I at the altar to the priests the children of Aaron.

The first tenth part of all increase I gave to the sons of Aaron, who ministered at Jerusalem: another tenth part I sold away, and went, and spent it every year at Jerusalem:

And the third I gave unto them to whom it was meet, as Debora my father's mother had commanded me, because I was left an orphan by my father.

Furthermore, when I was come to the age of a man, I married Anna of mine own kindred, and of her I begat Tobias.

And when we were carried away captives to Nineve, all my brethren and those that were of my kindred did eat of the bread of the Gentiles.

But I kept myself from eating;

Because I remembered God with all my heart.

And the most High gave me grace and favour before Enemessar, so that I was his purveyor.

And I went into Media, and left in trust with Gabael, the brother of Gabrias, at Rages a city of Media ten talents of silver.

Now when Enemessar was dead, Sennacherib his son reigned in his stead; whose estate was troubled, that I could not go into Media.

And in the time of Enemessar I gave many alms to my brethren, and gave my bread to the hungry,

And my clothes to the naked: and if I saw any of my nation dead, or cast about the walls of Nineve, I buried him.

And if the king Sennacherib had slain any, when he was come, and fled from Judea, I buried them privily; for in his wrath he killed many; but the bodies were not found, when they were sought for of the king.

And when one of the Ninevites went and complained of me to the king, that I buried them, and hid myself; understanding that I was sought for to be put to death, I withdrew myself for fear.

Then all my goods were forcibly taken away, neither was there any thing left me, beside my wife Anna and my son Tobias.

THE LIFE OF HEZEKIAH FROM DIFFERENT POINTS OF VIEW 123

> *And there passed not five and fifty days, before two of his sons killed him, and they fled into the mountains of Ararath; and Sarchedonus his son reigned in his stead; who appointed over his father's accounts, and over all his affairs, Achiacharus my brother Anael's son.*
>
> *And Achiacharus intreating for me, I returned to Nineve. Now Achiacharus was cupbearer, and keeper of the signet, and steward, and overseer of the accounts: and Sarchedonus appointed him next unto him: and he was my brother's son.*

The book of Tobit (Tobias was called Tobit's son, but Martin Luther somehow calls both father and son Tobias) does not belong to the biblical canon. It is assigned by Luther to the Apocrypha and thus attached to the Old Testament. It was also not included in the Jewish canon but is found in the Septuagint as well as in Hebrew and Aramaic fragments from the famous Qumran Caves. However, the Roman Catholic and Orthodox churches assign the book directly to the Old Testament. Its origin is dated to about 200 BC, which would then be more than five centuries, or half a millennium, away from the allegedly described events.

This book tells the story of a Hebrew named Tobit, who evidently led a good and righteous life with his family in the Northern Kingdom of Israel, until he was taken away by the Assyrians under the then king Shalmaneser when the Northern Kingdom was conquered by the Assyrians, and from then on had to live in captivity in Nineveh. There Tobit boasted together with his son Tobias to do good for all the other Israelites in captivity. The situation worsened dramatically when Sennacherib became king, went against Judah, and returned defeated. He must not have coped well with his defeat, and from then on, he let out his anger on the Hebrews still in captivity in Assyria, which Tobit and his family also felt directly. This became so bad that Tobit and his family and friends had to hide from Sennacherib until, after forty-five days, Sennacherib was killed by his sons and Tobit could breathe again.

This stretches Tobit's alleged history relatively far, because the conquest of the Northern Kingdom of Israel began with Shalmaneser V (here called *Enemessar*), but he probably died about 722 BC during the siege of Samaria. He was followed by his brother Sargon II (of whom Tobit reports nothing). So, Tobit's story must have begun before 722 BC and, since there are other chapters in his book after this first chapter, it continued beyond 681 BC, when, as we know for certain, Sennacherib was slain by his sons. Likewise, the difficult period of oppression and persecution by Sennacherib described by Tobit after his defeat and return from Judea must have lasted from about 700 BC (the year of the return from the Judaic campaign) to 681 BC (the year of the death of Sennacherib). This does not quite fit in with Tobit's description that Tobit and his family only had to hide from Sennacherib for forty-five days until he was slain by his sons. Besides the rather late writing of this book, there are also some question marks regarding the correct chronological classification of the events mentioned. Moreover, Tobit refers to Sennacherib as the son of Shalmaneser, which is definitely wrong, because Sennacherib was the son of Sargon, who had taken over the royal throne from his brother Shalmaneser.

This makes the book of Tobit already a bit questionable, and thus it was probably rightly not assigned to the biblical canon, but to the Apocrypha. It is interesting to note that after his return to Nineveh, Sennacherib was apparently not very good at talking to people of Hebrew descent, who were then subjected to reprisals. So Sennacherib was perhaps rather angry about his defeat at Jerusalem and took it out on the Hebrews who were still in his country and under his control.

The Letters

The Bible tells us about two letters Hezekiah received, which he dealt with in very different ways. Certainly, King Hezekiah received many more letters in his life, but the word of God apparently only cared about exactly these two, since it only lets us know about them. We want to take a closer look at them now.

The Letter of Merodach-Baladan (2 Kgs 20:12-19; Isa 39)

The self-proclaimed still-king of Babel Merodach-Baladan, who was probably already driven out of the city of Babylon by Sennacherib and who was likely already in exile on the Persian Gulf at that time, sent a legation to Hezekiah around 702 BC.

He did this superficially to congratulate him on his recent recovery from the actually deadly disease—but behind the scenes, political reasons and a large portion of curiosity certainly played a role. Curiosity, as already mentioned, because the Babylonians worshiped the sun as their supreme god and in Jerusalem a miracle had obviously just happened that influenced the course of the sun (2 Chr 32:31). Hezekiah's father, Ahaz, who was devoted to every pagan cult, may have had such a sundial made by their Babylonian inventors in Jerusalem. So, this sundial had now, as a visible divine sign, gone ten steps backwards. Another reason for the visit of the legation of Merodach-Baladan was certainly that they wanted to sound out how strong the Jewish army was with the apparently very resistant and divinely supported leader Hezekiah. It certainly seemed to be clarified whether an alliance could perhaps be formed so that both sides, the Babylonians and the Jews, together with the Egyptians (this alliance still existed at that moment) could do something against the Assyrians.

So Merodach-Baladan sent some men (2 Kgs 20:14) with a letter and gifts (2 Kgs 20:12) to Hezekiah. This visit, the greetings, and the gifts obviously brought great joy to the king, who had just recovered. Let us not forget that Hezekiah still had great worries, since the Assyrian army was approaching, had probably already invaded Judah, and conquered city after city (Sennacherib later speaks in his campaign report of a total of forty-six Jewish cities that he had taken).

Merodach-Baladan also had Hezekiah deliver a letter through his messengers, so he obviously had something to tell him. Did Hezekiah open and read the letter? That is not written down, but we can assume with some certainty. What do we know about the content of this letter? Nothing. Nothing at all. We can only make speculations. It is relatively certain that Merodach-Baladan had greeted Hezekiah and congratulated him on his recovery. This is already a conjecture, although it is provided with a certain probability. More we cannot say.

What we can say, however, is that this visit from Babel (in the Holy Scriptures always also a picture of the temptations and enticements of this world), the greetings and wishes, the gifts and the message of Merodach-Baladan Hezekiah, conveyed by letter, put Hezekiah into a high-spirited state. In this way, to the displeasure of God and the prophet Isaiah, he opened up to his visitors quite a bit and presented what he and Jerusalem had to offer.

King Hezekiah of Judah thus stumbled over the visit, gift, and letter from Babel into an unattractive vanity that would later be punished by God. How could this happen, how could he have prevented it?

The Letter of Sennacherib (2 Kgs 19:9, 14; 2 Chr 32:17; Isa 37:9, 14)

After the Rabshakeh had delivered his demagogic war speech outside the walls of Jerusalem, he went back to the main army (presumably to report to him of Hezekiah's non-capitulation). However, he had to realize that the army was no longer encamped in Lachish but was apparently fighting an Egyptian army (Kush = Nubia = Southern Egyptian Empire) near the village of Libnah. The exact location of the city of Libnah at that time can no longer be fully understood today, but according to the contemplable locations it will have been relatively close to Lachish. The city of Libnah seems to have survived the skirmish relatively well, because later Hezekiah's daughter-in-law Hamutal, the wife of his son Manasseh, comes from there (2 Kgs 23:31). So, the Egyptians kept their word, even if apparently somewhat half-heartedly, and tried to help Judah and his king Hezekiah. So distracted and currently not able to return immediately to Jerusalem, the Rabshakeh wrote a letter to Hezekiah, which in sharpness and polemic once again clearly surpassed his speech outside the city wall. In particular, Rabshakeh now tried to shake Hezekiah's trust in God to the core and did not shy away from accusing God himself of deception. We read again 2 Kgs 19:10:

> Thus you shall speak to Hezekiah king of Judah, saying: "Do not let your God in whom you trust deceive you, saying, 'Jerusalem shall not be given into the hand of the king of Assyria.'"

Mind you, the Rabshakeh here did not doubt the existence of the God of Israel, yes, he was even informed that God had apparently given Hezekiah a promise to save Jerusalem! No, he did not doubt God's existence, but rather accused him of deception! And he emphasized that nobody could resist the Assyrians, not even the God of Israel.

God would punish the terrible arrogance and self-importance of the Assyrians a few hours later by letting 185,000 men of the Assyrian army die at the gates of Jerusalem. To challenge God with the mouth or to blaspheme him was already very bad, sometimes the tongue is faster than the brain. But if you then do this with full intention in writing in an official document, it is terrible.

But how do we know all this?

Here we see the big difference to Hezekiah's actions in the first letter, which he had received only a few months earlier. The first letter, the one from Babel of Merodach-Baladan, which he had not presented to God, which he had not made public, with this letter he did not go into prayer with God. But so now with the letter from Sennacherib's Rabshakeh. He presented it to God at the gates of the temple and asked God for advice and salvation. And that is what Hezekiah had learned, that was the big difference.

He had learned that our own actions and doings are not always good and successful. Especially in decisive life situations we should seek the closeness of God, tell him our situation, our fears, hardships, worries, or simply our thoughts! God will answer us in one way or another. He wants to participate in the life of his children, and he wants them to be well and that we don't get ourselves into trouble. Of course, if we have once again been obstinate, we must bear the consequences, which can sometimes be punishments. But like every loving father, God also wants that this does not happen and that we let him participate in our lives, ask him for advice and help. We know that without him we are not very successful! So now Hezekiah, too, presented this letter to God and went to him in prayer—and God responded immediately with the comprehensive promise of perfect salvation. Yes, even more, he even announced what was to happen twenty years later (also handed down from Assyrian sources): that Sennacherib would be murdered in Nineveh by the sword of his sons.

FIGURE 4

Illustration from 1866

Hezekiah did not conceal this second letter mentioned in the Bible, he brought the content of this letter before God and asked him for advice and help. Do we not see here again a sign of how Hezekiah's relationship with his God became ever closer and more intimate and trusting?

Hezekiah and the Prophets

Isaiah

The Bible tells us in detail about the very intensive and trusting relationship between King Hezekiah and the prophet Isaiah, about which we have already learned a lot in this book. Nevertheless, there must have been a clear difference in age between the two of them, since Isaiah, according to Isa 1:1, was already appointed and active as a prophet under Hezekiah's great-grandfather Azariah (Uzziah).

> The vision that Isaiah, the son of Amoz, had of Judah and Jerusalem in the days of Uzziah, Jotham, Ahaz, Hezekiah, the kings of Judah. (Isa 1:1)

According to Isa 6:1–13, however, Isaiah's calling begins in the year Azariah (Uzziah) dies, which according to our chronology is 740 BC. Since we place Hezekiah's birth year at 741 BC, there must have been an age difference of about twenty-five years between the two men, assuming that Isaiah was in his mid-twenties when he was called by God to be a prophet. As we have already reported, Isaiah probably outlived Hezekiah anyway and then died under or by Hezekiah's son Manasseh around 680 BC. Isaiah will therefore have been just over eighty years old.

Hosea and Micah

In fact, during the reign of Hezekiah, the well-known prophets Hosea and Micah were also active in Israel and Judah, but we learn nothing more about them through the Holy Scriptures during the narration of the life of King Hezekiah.

> The word of the Lord that came to Hosea the son of Beeri, in the days of Uzziah, Jotham, Ahaz, and Hezekiah, kings of Judah, and in the days of Jeroboam the son of Joash, king of Israel . . . (Hos 1:1)

> The word of the Lord that came to Micah of Moresheth in the days of Jotham, Ahaz, and Hezekiah, kings of Judah, which he saw concerning Samaria and Jerusalem. (Mic 1:1)

Micah of Moresheth prophesied in the days of Hezekiah king of Judah, and spoke to all the people of Judah . . . (Jer 26:18a)

Zephaniah

And then there is the prophet Zephaniah, who is in a completely different connection to Hezekiah:

The word of the Lord which came to Zephaniah the son of Cushi, the son of Gedaliah, the son of Amariah, the son of Hezekiah, in the days of Josiah the son of Amon, king of Judah. (Zeph 1:1)

As we have already seen in chapter 3, Hezekiah apparently had another son named Amariah, from whom the prophet Zephaniah obviously descends in the third generation. Can this be fitting in time?

Zephaniah himself claims to have worked under the king Josiah. He reigned for thirty-one years from 640–609 BC in Judah. Assyria's capital Nineveh was not yet destroyed in Zephaniah's writings—this happened in 611 BC by the Babylonians. The time frame with three generations after Hezekiah thus fits well into the classification of Zephaniah's work and his descent from him.

So, the prophet Zephaniah was Hezekiah's great-great-great-grandson.

Did you know that?

The Bronze Serpent . . . Then as Now . . .

Then they journeyed from Mount Hor by the Way of the Red Sea, to go around the land of Edom; and the soul of the people became very discouraged on the way. And the people spoke against God and against Moses: "Why have you brought us up out of Egypt to die in the wilderness? For there is no food and no water, and our soul loathes this worthless bread." So the Lord sent fiery serpents among the people, and they bit the people; and many of the people of Israel died. Therefore the people came to Moses, and said, "We have sinned, for we have spoken against the Lord and against you; pray to the Lord that He take away the serpents from us." So Moses prayed for the people. Then the Lord said to Moses, "Make a fiery serpent, and set it on a pole; and it shall be that everyone who is bitten, when he looks at it, shall live." So Moses made a bronze serpent, and put it on a pole; and so it was, if a serpent had bitten anyone, when he looked at the bronze serpent, he lived. (Num 21:4–9)

This event will have taken place approximately between 1450 and 1400 BC during the desert migration of the people of Israel. Since then, the Israelites and the Jews had obviously kept this "bronze snake on the staff" until the lifetime of King Hezekiah. In the course of history, it must have become a cult object that people worshiped—presumably they prayed to the "Nehushtan" (Hebrew for "bronze") for his physical healing from an illness or infirmity. This worship must have gone so far that people no longer worshiped God the LORD—who had instructed Moses to make the snake and who gave the healing from snakebites when the Israelites trusted him and looked up in faith to the snake—but the bronze snake itself. In 716/715 BC, in the course of the profound spiritual cleansing he initiated in Judah, King Hezekiah caused the pagan, idolatrous worship of Nehushtan to destroy the bronze snake and thus put an end to the cult around it.

> *He removed the high places and broke the sacred pillars, cut down the wooden image and broke in pieces the bronze serpent that Moses had made; for until those days the children of Israel burned incense to it, and called it Nehushtan.* (2 Kgs 18:4)

Interestingly, we find the snake on the staff afterwards again and again throughout the following history of mankind:

Rod of Asclepius (Or Also: Asclepius Staff)

FIGURE 5 Asclepius, a son of Apollo, is called the god of healing in Greek mythology from about the seventh century BC onwards. In the pictorial representations Asclepius always holds a staff with a snake wrapped around it in his hand. The worship of Asclepius can be traced in particular in Athens, Pergamon and on the island of Kos, where Hippocrates studied. Around 300 BC the cult of Asclepius reached as far as Rome—for example, in 298 BC a temple of Asclepius was consecrated in Rome on the Tiber Island.

Even then, the symbol was used in slightly modified form for the guild of pharmacists under the name Caduceus:

FIGURE 6

The Caduceus was a staff wrapped by snakes with wings representing Hermes (in Greek pharmacies) or Mercury (in Roman pharmacies).

After Hezekiah had tried to put an end to the godless pagan cult in Judah at the end of the eighth century BC, the snake on the staff reappeared in Greek mythology in the seventh century BC as the staff of the god Asclepius and continued its triumphal procession in the third century BC over the Roman Empire to this day throughout the world. How persistent are the gods made by humans, if humans cannot let go of them? It is better to worship a piece of metal that God has ordered to be made and attribute healing powers to the metal, instead of wholeheartedly professing one's faith in God, who is actually the one who gives healing—as was the case with the Israelites in the desert at that time. And so today we actually find this symbol worldwide among doctors, pharmacists and health organizations.

Symbol of the Doctors

FIGURE 7

FIGURE 8

FIGURE 9

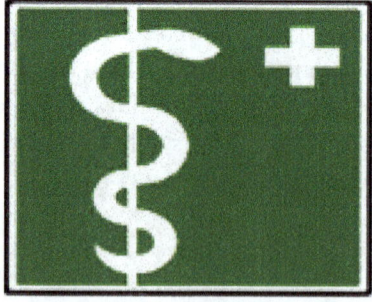

The bronze snake or the staff of Aesculapius can be found practically everywhere in the world as an international symbol for doctors. It is amazing, no matter in which region or city of the world you are, you will always find the winding snake somewhere in connection with the healing professions.

FIGURE 10

The flag of the World Health Organization (WHO)

FIGURE 11

The Star of Life is the international symbol for emergency rescue service facilities

FIGURE 12

The coat of arms of the Medical Office of the German Armed Forces

Symbol of the Pharmacists

Bowl of the Hygeia

You often see the snake wrapped around a bowl. This symbol shows how the snake drinks from the bowl, which means health. It can also be found on the German pharmacy sign "A" ("Apotheke").

FIGURE 13   **FIGURE 14**

FIGURE 15

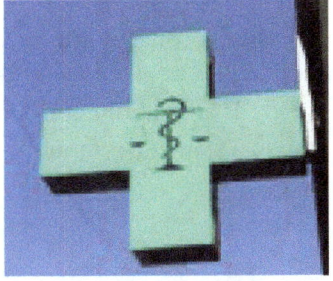

A pharmacy in Bern (Switzerland)

In summary, it can be said that all healing professions and related organizations use this symbol. The physical destruction of the bronze snake by King Hezekiah obviously could not prevent the mythological unfolding of this cult object.

By the way, the bronze snake can sometimes be found somewhere else:

FIGURE 16

Coat of Arms of the Municipality Arnsdorf

Arnsdorf is a community in the district of Bautzen near Dresden (Germany). The symbol in the coat of arms can apparently be explained by the opening of the Royal Saxon Sanatorium and Nursing Home Arnsdorf on April 1, 1912, which was one of the largest and most famous German medical, spa, and healing institutions at that time.

Worldwide!

In fact, we find the bronze snake countless times around the globe—always in a medical context. So always in a broader sense when something has to do with healing. Here is an amazing selection of institutions that use the snake wound around a staff as a symbol:[8]

Asia

- Beijing University of Chinese Medicine
- Academy of Medicine of Malaysia
- International Medical University, Malaysia
- Malaysian Medical Council
- Medical Council of India
- Pakistan Army Medical Corps
- Sultan Qaboos University Hospital
- Indonesia Society for Health Promotors and Educators

Australia and New Zealand

- Australian Medical Association
- Australian Medical Students' Association
- Australian Veterinary Association
- Royal Australian Army Medical Corps
- Medical Council of New Zealand

Canada

- Ambulance Paramedics of British Columbia
- Canadian Association of Physician Assistants
- Canadian Medical Association
- Royal Canadian Medical Service
- Canadian Dental Association

---

8. Wikipedia, "Rod of Asclepius," https://en.wikipedia.org/wiki/Rod_of_Asclepius.

Europe

- Association of Anesthetists of Great Britain and Ireland
- British Medical Association
- British Royal Army Medical Corps
- British Small Animal Veterinary Association
- Emergency medical services in France (SAMU, SMUR, et al.)
- Emergency medical services in Italy
- Emergency medical services in the Netherlands
- Finnish Medical Association
- The London Clinic
- Royal College of Psychiatrists (UK)
- Spanish National Council of Medical Student's Association (CEEM)
- University of Copenhagen Faculty of Health and Medical Sciences
- State Medical Rescue—Polish emergency rescue service

Africa

- Nigerian Medical Association

South Africa

- South African Medical Research Council (former coat of arms)
- South African Military Health Service
- Tygerberg Academic Hospital, Cape Town, South Africa

USA

- American Academy of Physician Assistants
- American Osteopathic Association
- American Medical Association
- American Medical Response
- American Academy of Family Physicians
- American College of Occupational and Environmental Medicine
- American College of Osteopathic Internists
- American Academy of Psychiatry and the Law

- American Hippocratic Registry
- American Medical Student Association
- American Veterinary Medical Association
- Army Medical Department of the US Army (AMEDD)
- Blue Cross Blue Shield Association (US)
- Heritage College of Osteopathic Medicine
- International Medical Corps
- MedicAlert (US)
- Michigan State Medical Society
- National Athletic Trainers Association
- Stanford University School of Medicine
- Kansas City University of Medicine and Biosciences
- Pennsylvania Department of Health
- Student Osteopathic Medical Association (US)
- United States Navy Hospital Corps
- United States Air Force Medical Corps
- Yale University School of Medicine

Worldwide Organizations

- Medical Protection Society (MPS)
- Star of Life
- World Health Organization (WHO)

Hezekiah was able to physically destroy the Nehushtan, which was already over seven hundred years old, over 2,700 years ago. However, he could no longer erase the myth of healing powers created by humans, which emanates from this symbol. Most people of all generations worldwide saw and still see in it a symbol for healing—and so it appears over many centuries, sometimes mixed with pagan deities, in many logos of doctors, pharmacists, and health organizations. That behind this healing effect stands the God of Israel and that this points to the work of redemption of his Son on the cross—and it is actually this event that really brings healing, namely the healing of the soul—unfortunately so many people today do not see this. Yet the Lord Jesus Christ expresses it so simply in a few sentences in his conversation with Nicodemus, one of the leading Pharisaic scholars of his time, and brings it to the crucial point:

> *And as Moses lifted up the serpent in the wilderness, so must the Son of Man be lifted up, that whosoever believes in him may have eternal life. For God so loved the world that he gave his only begotten Son, that whosoever believes in him should not perish but have eternal life.* (John 3:14–16)

May people do not look at the bronze snake on the stick and expect healing from it, but at the exalted Son of God on the cross, who wants to and will heal their souls!

The bronze serpent is mentioned exactly three times in the word of God:

- **Num 21:5–9**
- **2 Kgs 18:4**
- **John 3:14**

At their first mention, God commands their making and promises every Israelite bitten by a snake his healing when he looks up at the raised-up snake.

At the second mention, King Hezekiah of Judah had the bronze snake destroyed, as it had become a cultic, pagan object of worship over the centuries, so that God himself, who had given the healing from the snake bites in the desert, was no longer the focus of worship.

At its third mention, the Lord Jesus, in his conversation with Nicodemus, one of the leading Pharisaic scholars, speaks about the bronze serpent and refers this sign directly to himself and to his forthcoming work of redemption on the cross. And it is only through this that this symbol is fully explained, and only through this does it become clear to us what God intended at the time when he instructed Moses to make the bronze serpent. Let us read again exactly what the Lord Jesus Christ says about it:

> *And as Moses lifted up the serpent in the wilderness, even so must the Son of Man be lifted up, that whoever believes in Him should not perish but have eternal life. For God so loved the world that He gave His only begotten Son, that whoever believes in Him should not perish but have everlasting life.* (John 3:14–16)

And so, it only becomes clear in its entirety what the symbol of the elevated snake is all about. In his work of redemption, through his death, the Lord Jesus carried the sin of the world to the cross and thus for men. And everyone who believes in him and his redemption, for him his sins are blotted out and he will be saved. The serpent has always been a symbol of evil, of sin—ever since Adam and Eve.

Many theologians find it difficult to deal with the events surrounding the bronze serpent, since it does not fit at all into the rest of Israel's history with God, who actually never has any symbols made. But through the words of Christ, it becomes clear! The bronze serpent was an image—a foresight—of Jesus Christ! <u>The serpent raised on the pole symbolizes the sin carried to the cross by the Christ</u>. The serpent on the pole is the sin of the whole world, which Jesus Christ carries to the cross, where it is also lifted, then paid for by his death and once and for all erased. The death of the Son of God on the cross brings healing to the souls of men, who will no longer be lost, but will receive eternal life with God, if . . . <u>IF YOU BELIEVE IN IT</u>! And that is then the only, but tremendously important prerequisite for the salvation and healing of our souls: we must believe in it, we must believe in the Lord Jesus! Let us read the decisive verses again very carefully, word for word:

> *And as Moses lifted up the serpent in the wilderness, even so must the Son of Man be lifted up, that whoever believes in Him should not perish but have eternal life. For God so loved the world that He gave His only begotten Son, that whoever believes in Him should not perish but have everlasting life.* (John 3:14–16)

In these few but very well-known verses, we find twice the condition <u>"so that everyone who believes in him."</u> The work of redemption of Jesus Christ has been accomplished, the Son of God has accomplished it for all of us by the mandate of his Father. It is to be received completely free, the healing of the oppressed souls enslaved by sin and their eternal salvation are a fact! We only have to take it; we only have to believe in it!

Just as the Israelites who were bitten by the serpents in the desert had to believe that they would be (physically) saved if they looked up at the bronze snake that Moses had had made at the behest of God. In fact, this bronze symbol had no healing powers at all, it was God who gave the healing, but only . . . IF LOOKING UP TO THE SNAKE!

Here too, an act of faith was necessary. Anyone who was bitten but did not look up to the snake and did not believe that it could save him, died.

Only those who believed and looked up to the serpent were saved. As it is today, only when we believe in him and look up to his work of redemption on the cross and accept it, then we will be saved.

The storage and the later worship of the iron serpent were thus basically completely meaningless. It was simply a bronze snake on a staff. Only God could give the healing. In this respect, King Hezekiah acted quite rightly by smashing the bronze snake, the Nehushtan, to pieces. The people had worshiped something man-made to ask for healing. Yet it is God who gives the healing—something that Hezekiah would later experience in his own body when the prophet Isaiah had to explain to him that he, Hezekiah, the king of Judah, was terminally ill. Only God could give him the healing.

Despite Hezekiah's deed, the mystification of the snake on the pole in connection with the healing effect could not be stopped. The people who cannot or do not want to believe in God and Jesus Christ as their Savior and Redeemer prefer to look at the snake on the pole. And so it is that this symbol now stands for doctors, pharmacies, and health organizations worldwide.

If only all the people who look at this symbol, which is now over 3,400 years old, every day, whether consciously or unconsciously, would know that this <u>is an image of sin carried to the cross by our Lord Jesus Christ</u>.

Perhaps some of them would be saved by this?

When they look at him and believe . . .

Excursus: Another Dating Attempt

The events in Num 21 took place during the forty-year desert migration of the people of Israel. The date of the exodus from Egypt is hotly disputed among scholars. If one adds up all the year dates in the Bible without interpretation, the entry into Egypt would have been around 1876 BC and thus (according to Exod 12:40) the exodus under Moses 430 years later in 1446 BC (1876 − 430 = 1446). The conclusion of the forty-year desert migration and the subsequent land grab in Canaan would then have taken place in 1406 BC. In the sequence of events in the fourth book of Moses (= Numbers), the events with the poisonous snakes are told <u>after the death of Aaron on Mount Hor</u> (Num 20,22-29). From Mount Hor, the people set out for the Red Sea, bypassing the land of Edom (Num 21:4), and this is how the event of the bronze serpent took place. In the Bible we do indeed find a full chapter with a kind of travelogue (Num 33) about the different stations of the desert migration of the people of Israel. But there is only one single date in the whole chapter, namely in Num 33:38: *"And Aaron the priest went up to Mount Hor by the commandment of the LORD; and he died there in the fortieth year after the sons of Israel came out of the land of Egypt, in the fifth month, on the first day of the month."* So here the exact date of Aaron's death is given. Since the people of Israel set out from Mount Hor one chapter after the death of Aaron, the event around the bronze serpent must have taken place <u>after it</u>, that is to say also in the fortieth year after the exodus from Egypt—thus <u>right at the end of the migration in the desert</u> and some months before the taking of Canaan. And so we can likewise date the story about the bronze serpent and its manufacture by Moses to <u>the year 1406 BC</u>, on the assumption that the derivation of the Exodus of the Israelites from Egypt and the associated beginning of the desert migration, as explained above, is correct.

In our chronology Hezekiah destroyed the bronze snake in 716 or 715 BC in the course of his extensive spiritual cleansing in Judah. At that time the bronze snake was already almost <u>seven hundred years old</u>.

So, more than <u>seven hundred years</u> after the migration into the desert, the Israelites had still kept this object of miracle-working healing by God and had apparently even slowly elevated it to the status of a cult object, to which they then, according to 2 Kgs 18:4b, offered worship in the form of smoke offerings (a kind of incense). The bronze snake had become an idol! King Hezekiah therefore cut the bronze snake into pieces to put an end to the idolatrous cult.

A good <u>seven hundred years</u> later, the Son of God would then come into this world to actually fulfill this image, this foresight of his work of redemption on the cross.

It is quite astonishing that the three mentions of the bronze serpent from its creation through its destruction to the fulfillment of its pictorial meaning by the Lord Jesus Christ take place in approximately seven-hundred-year steps.

1. Creation (Num 21) → around 1406 BC
2. Destruction by Hezekiah (2 Kgs 18:4) → around 716 BC

3. Parable through the Lord Jesus (John 3:14) ➔ around AD 26

(Assuming that Jesus Christ was born in the year 4 BC and not in the year 1 because of the well-known miscalculation of the monk Dionysius. This is also confirmed by the date of death of Herod, who according to extrabiblical sources probably died in the year 4 BC.)

The symbol of the snake on the staff, which we see today in the healing professions and health organizations worldwide, is thus over 3,400 years old and represents nothing more than a forward-looking image of the Lord Jesus Christ, who carries the sin of the world to the cross and thus brings about healing for all people—if they only believe in him . . .

What does Paul say in Athens on the Areopagus to the Greeks present?

> *Therefore, since we are the offspring of God, we ought not to think that the Divine Nature is like gold or silver or stone, something shaped by art and man's devising. Truly, these times of ignorance God overlooked, but now commands all men everywhere to repent . . .* (Acts 17:29-30)

And after having had to put up with a lot of idols before:

> *Now while Paul waited for them at Athens, his spirit was provoked within him when he saw that the city was given over to idols.* (Acts 17:16)

As we have learned above, the Greeks knew the snake on the staff already since the seventh century BC for the healing professions and also in the symbols for the pharmacies. So, it is very possible that Paul in Greece, when he walked through Athens in about AD 50 and stood in front of pharmacies or doctor's offices saw some of these symbols of the iron snake and was naturally reminded of the word of God with the given fact in Num 21.

Perhaps he even had the bronze snake at the back of his mind during his famous speech on the Areopagus.

Excursus: The Snake in the Bible

In the Bible, the snake stands for evil, for sin, for the deceiver, the devil. Right at the beginning of the history of mankind, already in the third chapter of the word of God, it appears suddenly and begins its evil, lying, and seductive work.

> Now the serpent was more cunning than any beast of the field which the Lord God had made. And he said to the woman, "Has God indeed said, 'You shall not eat of every tree of the garden'?" And the woman said to the serpent, "We may eat the fruit of the trees of the garden; but of the fruit of the tree which is in the midst of the garden, God has said, 'You shall not eat it, nor shall you touch it, lest you die.'" Then the serpent said to the woman, "You will not surely die. For God knows that in the day you eat of it your eyes will be opened, and you will be like God, knowing good and evil." (Gen 3:1–5)

The first people fall for the snake and commit their first sin. And thus, the suffering of all mankind begins with the expulsion from paradise and the separation from God. The serpent deceived Eve and Adam, and they willingly let themselves be deceived.

Interesting and, by the way, very sad for the male readers of these lines is Adam's reaction when he is subsequently confronted by God: *"Then the man said, 'The woman whom You gave to be with me, she gave me of the tree, and I ate'"* (Gen 3:12).

Here we see the first case in the history of mankind of stealing from responsibility and shifting the blame on others. Adam has to answer to God and says that the woman is to blame, the woman "whom you gave me." Adam is only a victim? Actually, it was the woman, and strictly speaking it is God's own fault that it has come to this, because it was *the* woman that God had given him! If he had created another woman for him, then perhaps none of this would have happened. No backbone, my dear Adam! Very sad, my dear sex comrade! Sad picture …

There were quite a lot of snakes in the areas of the desert migration of the people of Israel then as now. Interestingly enough, in the report of the forty-year stay in the desert, they only appear in large numbers and in a deadly manner when the people once again begin to grumble and complain about why they were led from the quite bearable life in Egypt to this barren desert landscape. And as we know from the previous excursus, this happened in the fortieth, the last year of the desert migration. Only after this event with the snakes the survivors of the people are allowed to leave the desert for good and move on towards Canaan, where they will move just in a few months.

Here God has once again taken very clear care that only those of the people of Israel may enter Canaan who believe in him and who trust in him. For all those who did not do this died from the bites of the serpents.

Only the faithful Israelites were allowed to move on and enter the Promised Land.

Even though this may be a very strong warning, it must be pronounced: **this is still the case today!** Only those who believe in God and trust in him can enter the promised land, that is, heaven, the presence of God, the new Jerusalem! Only he who looks up to the Son of God on the cross and believes him that his work of redemption will save him will be saved, he will be able to move into his dwelling in heaven when his earthly life comes to an end.

The snake on the pole was then only a picture, a foresight of the Lord Jesus, who defeated the devil, the seducer, the old snake on the cross on Golgotha once and for all!

Since the serpent appears at the very beginning of the Bible and begins its destructive work, we meet it again at the very end of the Word of God. Here we can read how it is dealt with at the end of all times.

> *So the great dragon was cast out, that serpent of old, called the Devil and Satan, who deceives the whole world; he was cast to the earth, and his angels were cast out with him.* (Rev 12:9)

> *He laid hold of the dragon, that serpent of old, who is the Devil and Satan, and bound him for a thousand years . . .* (Rev 20:2)

> *Now when the thousand years have expired, Satan will be released from his prison and will go out to deceive the nations which are in the four corners of the earth, Gog and Magog, to gather them together to battle, whose number is as the sand of the sea. They went up on the breadth of the earth and surrounded the camp of the saints and the beloved city. And fire came down from God out of heaven and devoured them. The devil, who deceived them, was cast into the lake of fire and brimstone where the beast and the false prophet are. And they will be tormented day and night forever and ever. And when the thousand years are ended, Satan shall be loosed out of his prison, and shall go forth to deceive the nations which are in the four corners of the earth, Gog and Magog, to gather them together for war; the number of them is as the sand of the sea. And they went up to the breadth of the earth and surrounded the camp of the saints and the beloved city; and fire came down from heaven and devoured them. And the devil that deceived them was thrown into the lake of fire and brimstone, where the beast and the false prophet are both; and they shall be tormented day and night forever and ever.* (Rev 20:7–10)

God will judge and destroy the serpent, the devil, at the end of all days. Just as Hezekiah cut the bronze snake into pieces, God will judge and destroy the evil one forever. The symbol of the snake on the staff will finally lose its meaning. It will simply cease to exist. It will no longer be found in the new world ruled by the Lord Jesus Christ. It is gone. For God has judged the serpent, it is destroyed once and for all.

The evil will be gone. And healing professions as well as their idolatrous symbols will no longer be needed, because all sickness, all sadness, and even death itself have been defeated. Our Lord Jesus Christ will take care of us, he will be there for us. Let us read it ourselves:

> *"And God will wipe away every tear from their eyes; there shall be no more death, nor sorrow, nor crying. There shall be no more pain, for the former things have passed away." Then He who sat on the throne said, "Behold, I make all things new." And He said to me, "Write, for these words are true and faithful." (Rev 21:4–5)*

Wouldn't you like to be there too?

The Hezekiah Tunnel

The Hezekiah Tunnel is a beautiful picture of the spiritual life of a believing Christian. If you are a believing Christian, then you know how difficult it is to live a life pleasing to God, how difficult it is to resist the constant attacks of evil, the seductions and scattered doubts. This is why the Lord Jesus has placed his Spirit at our disposal, whose outpouring we celebrate year after year at Pentecost fifty days after Easter. It is this Spirit of God who can lead and guide us. He can admonish, encourage, help us through difficult times, tribulations and temptations, he is always there for us. He is our connection to God and to our Lord Jesus Christ, he fills our hearts and our minds with his love and his goodness. He opens the Holy Scriptures for us and leads us to deep insights.

Now imagine the city of Jerusalem surrounded by Assyrian soldiers—that would be you! Jerusalem is the image for a believing Christian who is surrounded day and night in this world by seductions, lewd things, temptations, words, deeds, thoughts of bad people who want to bring you down, just as the Assyrians wanted to bring down Jerusalem. How can one resist such a siege? But only by sticking completely to the Lord Jesus, by letting yourself fall completely into his arms, and by letting yourself be helped and guided by his Holy Spirit through all these challenges that a believing Christian faces every day. This is exactly what the Lord Jesus left us his Spirit for: to take care of us until the Lord returns. The Spirit of God lets you withstand this constant siege. Now, in the Bible, water very often appears as an image for the outpouring of the Spirit of God—so I think we can apply it here as well. So let us imagine that the city of Jerusalem besieged by the Assyrians is an image for the believing Christian who is constantly besieged by this world. Let us imagine that the Gihon spring, which springs from Mount Orphel, would be the Holy Spirit poured out by God and his Son for the believers on earth. The Gihon Spring supplies Jerusalem with fresh water, which it urgently needs to survive. The Spirit of God provides the believing Christian with God's thoughts, his love, he cleanses us, he guides us, he is our counselor. Only through him can we survive in this world. Through him we feel our Lord Jesus living in us. He fills our hearts. He wants to flow from above to us, in us.

But what else does this picture want to tell us? What did the inhabitants of Jerusalem have to do to ensure a permanent water supply? They had to move from both directions, because otherwise it might have been too late, and the enemy could have cut the line! Not only would the water take its natural direction downhill towards the city and a pipe was laid for this purpose, but the inhabitants of Jerusalem also had to move towards the source. It had to be dug from both directions! The tunnel, the pipe for the fresh water, had to be made <u>from both directions</u> at the same time!

And this is what God expects from us as believing Christians. He wants us not only to wait for the fresh water to come to us, no, he also wants us to do something for it, not only to wait for the Spirit to come to us, to come down from the mountain and let us fill ourselves with it. He wants to see that we also build with zeal and joy a way <u>in his direction</u>— and for this he has created something wonderful—<u>prayer!</u>

In prayer we may approach him through his Son Jesus Christ, quasi our connecting tunnel to God, and turn to his Father like a child, with everything that oppresses us and is on our hearts. Regular prayer cleanses the lines to God, it takes away what weighs on our hearts, what oppresses us, what disturbs our connection to God. We may throw all our worries on him! We may even try to move his mighty arm through prayer.

And so, this city of Jerusalem, which is besieged by the Assyrians, is perhaps a beautiful picture for the faithful Christian, who is surrounded and harassed by the temptations of this world and can only withstand them if he lets himself be supplied by the fresh water of God, but in return also has to lay pipes in both directions and keep them regularly clean and pure.

Can you find yourself in this picture?

Excursus: Who Can Remember the Names of the Four Rivers That Flow Through the Garden of Eden?

> *The name of the first is Pishon; it is the one which skirts the whole land of Havilah, where there is gold. And the gold of that land is good. Bdellium and the onyx stone are there. The name of the second river is Gihon; it is the one which goes around the whole land of Cush. The name of the third river is Hiddekel; it is the one which goes toward the east of Assyria. The fourth river is the Euphrates.* (Gen 2:11–14)

Pishon, **Gihon**, Euphrates, and Tigris . . .

The Pregnant Woman Who Cannot Give Birth . . .

> *And they said to him, "Thus says Hezekiah: 'This day is a day of trouble and rebuke and blasphemy; for the children have come to birth, but there is no strength to bring them forth. It may be that the Lord your God will hear the words of the Rabshakeh, whom his master the king of Assyria has sent to reproach the living God, and will rebuke the words which the Lord your God has heard. Therefore lift up your prayer for the remnant that is left.'" So the servants of King Hezekiah came to Isaiah.* (Isa 37:3–5)

Hezekiah has these words spoken by his officials and the elders of the priests of Isaiah, after he himself had first gone to the temple to speak to God. The occasion was, of course, the polemic speech of the Rabshakeh Sennacherib and his unconditional surrender demand, combined with the offer to be allowed to continue living "in another country" (2 Kgs 18:32), i.e., the deportation of the people. Hezekiah first goes alone into the house of the LORD to pray to his God, then he sends a delegation of two eye and earwitnesses of the Rabshakeh's speech outside the city wall with the elders of the priests to the prophet Isaiah with the message quoted above from the word of God. Isaiah apparently memorized these words well, for he wrote them down with remarkable accuracy.

Apart from asking Isaiah to pray to God for salvation for Jerusalem and punishment for the mocking words of the Assyrians, Hezekiah mentions that this is a day of tribulation, chastisement, and abuse. He then uses the astonishing image of children who have obviously not yet been born, but whose birth seems to be imminent, for they have "come to the mouth of their mother" (2 Kgs 19:3; Isa 37:4). But there is no power to complete the birth and give life to the children.

What did Hezekiah mean by that?

The image of children about to be born can only be understood spiritually. He thus describes the people in Judah and Jerusalem who, since Hezekiah's assumption of sole rule in 716 BC and the comprehensive reformations in 715 BC, have developed spiritually, become children of God, and have now matured in faith. Hezekiah still speaks of spiritual embryos, but they have now matured in such a way that they would be able to live on their own, so they could soon see the light of day and leave the protection of the mother's body.

But now the mother has no strength to bear her children, because the mother, in this case Jerusalem, is violently harassed from outside. Hezekiah thus compares his people to small children who have now grown spiritually in such a way that they could leave the mother's womb in order to be able to lead their own independent and autonomous spiritual life. But there the Assyrians come and have something against it. The extremely expansionist empires of that time, especially the Assyrians, not only forced allegiance and tribute payments on the subjugated peoples, but in many cases also a part of their religion.

In their conquests, the Assyrians always exercised perfect control in all areas of life. Be it economic, military, educational, settlement, or religious matters. It is not without reason that the Assyrians always began their waves of expulsion in the conquered territories with the higher strata of the population. They did this in order to be able to exercise control and guidance more easily among the remaining population strata. This would now of course have threatened the people in Jerusalem and all of Judah. In the first fourteen to fifteen years of Hezekiah's reign, after decades of remoteness from God and idolatry, the people had been spiritually begotten and then slowly matured—so that they were now ready to lead an independent spiritual life.

But now the Assyrians are standing here and want to prevent "the delivery" of the people of Judah. Thus, King Hezekiah brings the spiritually newly begotten and matured children of God before God in prayer.

He lets the prophet Isaiah ask God and plead for the salvation of his children, to see to it that the mother may give birth to the mature babies and that the forthcoming birth is not prevented or suppressed by the enemies. As we all know, babies who have already reached the cervix in the birth process should be born very soon, otherwise they are in danger of suffocation.

We now know how this turned out. After the Rabshakeh sent a letter, even more derisive and blasphemous than his speeches outside the city wall, Hezekiah went with this letter once more into the house of the LORD and prayed to his God. That very night the besieging Jerusalem was crushed and withdrew to Nineveh. Jerusalem was free! The affliction was gone, the abuses ended. The children of God, who were still stuck at their mother's mouths a moment ago, were now free, could breathe freely, and were allowed to cut the umbilical cord, to begin their own spiritual life. God had not abandoned his children, as he had promised from the beginning. And it is still the same today.

The Lord Jesus Christ later confirmed this impressively once again:

> *And I give them eternal life, and they shall never perish; neither shall anyone snatch them out of My hand. My Father, who has given them to Me, is greater than all; and no one is able to snatch them out of My Father's hand. I and My Father are one.* (John 10:28–30)

The Post-War period

The Years after the Departure of the Assyrians

> *Thus the Lord saved Hezekiah and the inhabitants of Jerusalem from the hand of Sennacherib the king of Assyria, and from the hand of all others, and guided them on every side. And many brought gifts to the Lord at Jerusalem, and presents to Hezekiah king of Judah, so that he was exalted in the sight of all nations thereafter.* (2 Chr 32:22–23)

The God-wrought defeat of the Assyrians before Jerusalem had of course not remained hidden from the other nations around Judah. Sennacherib had simply gone away and did not come back either.

> *So Sennacherib king of Assyria departed and went away, returned home, and remained at Nineveh.* (2 Kgs 19:36)

THE LIFE OF HEZEKIAH FROM DIFFERENT POINTS OF VIEW

From that time on Judah was at rest from the Assyrians for many years, and the neighboring countries of Judah rubbed their eyes in wonder how this could happen. Of course, King Hezekiah of Judah was highly respected by all nations because no one had ever been able to resist the Assyrians, and certainly not such a small country. It is also very much to be hoped that word got around everywhere that the God of Israel had performed this miracle, how he decided this war for Judah, the people in Jerusalem, and for his child Hezekiah, as he had promised long before.

But what do we also read in these verses? The people of Jerusalem and all of Judah were grateful to God and "many brought gifts for the LORD to Jerusalem." Isn't it beautiful to read that people recognized and did not forget to whom they owed this victory?

In fact, fourteen years of peace and tranquility had now arrived until Hezekiah's death. The people of Judah were able to take a deep breath, rebuild the land and the cities, sow and bring in the harvests again, and move on to a normal, regulated, and undisturbed life. Even in the extra-biblical records we find no extraordinary events or reports concerning the land of Judah during this time. There was simply peace and quiet. Even when the protagonists on both sides changed with the death of Hezekiah and six years later the death of Sennacherib, his successors Manasseh and Esarhaddon and later Assurbanipal would not start a war anymore. The Assyrians would never attack Jerusalem again and would never conquer it. Nor do we learn of any other military conflicts at that time. There simply were none. The people of Judah now had fourteen years of peace under their king Hezekiah.

Hezekiah's Death

> *Now the rest of the acts of Hezekiah, and his goodness, indeed they are written in the vision of Isaiah the prophet, the son of Amoz, and in the book of the kings of Judah and Israel. So Hezekiah rested with his fathers, and they buried him in the upper tombs of the sons of David; and all Judah and the inhabitants of Jerusalem honored him at his death. Then Manasseh his son reigned in his place.* (2 Chr 32:32–33)

Our protagonist King Hezekiah of Judah died in 687 BC at the age of fifty-four years, exactly fifteen years after God healed him from the fatal ulcer in 702 BC and promised him fifteen additional years of life. And so it had come to this.

Hezekiah of Judah is buried with honor directly at the entrance to the tombs of the sons of David, and the people of Judah and Jerusalem paid their last respects to him. It must have been very moving and honorable funeral ceremonies at that time. For Hezekiah's reign was a very good one, for the people of Judah and Jerusalem and also for Hezekiah himself.

The obituary of the king of Judah was written by God himself in his word:

> *And he did what was right in the sight of the Lord, according to all that his father David had done.* (2 Kgs 18:3)

> *Thus Hezekiah did throughout all Judah, and he did what was good and right and true before the Lord his God. And in every work that he began in the service of the house of God, in the law and in the commandment, to seek his God, he did it with all his heart. So he prospered.* (2 Chr 31:20–21)

> *He trusted in the Lord God of Israel, so that after him was none like him among all the kings of Judah, nor who were before him. For he held fast to the Lord; he did not depart from following Him, but kept His commandments, which the Lord had commanded Moses. The Lord was with him; he prospered wherever he went. And he rebelled against the king of Assyria and did not serve him.* (2 Kgs 18:5–7)

If only we could take a little example from this trust in and this intense relationship with God. It would change our life completely. We could see and experience the miracles of God, just as Hezekiah was allowed to do.

4

The Life of Hezekiah in a Historical Context

We have now concluded our reflections on the life of our protagonist, King Hezekiah, and in this chapter, we would like to devote ourselves to extrabiblical testimonies and place the story of Hezekiah in an even broader historical context, while also attempting to satisfactorily explain the last unsolved problems in the harmonization of the biblical times of rule.

The Problem of the Transition from Jotham to Ahaz

In the chronology of the kings of Judah presented in this book, and especially in the historical processes during the lifetime of our protagonist Hezekiah, we have drawn heavily on the chronology of the Hebrew kings created by Edwin R. Thiele and have even modified and expanded it a little in the following. In the process, we have created what we consider to be a harmonious and contradiction-free chronological sequence, which combines the extrabiblical evidence, and their verified dates, with the sequences and chronological indications of the Bible. However, Thiele was not able to completely close a last gap of about three years in the dating of the assumption of the kingships at Jotham and Ahaz. He was well aware of this, and he developed an attempt to explain it, which we will discuss later on. This time we will approach the problem from behind.

With the relatively certain date of death of Hezekiah's son Manasseh in 642 BC, all subsequent royal rule in Judah up to the last king Zedekiah, under whom Jerusalem was then conquered by Nebuchadnezzar in 587 BC, can be easily listed and derived. The reigns of the kings of Judah following Manasseh are:

Amon:	two years
Josiah:	thirty-one years
Jehoahaz:	three months
Jehoiakim:	eleven years
Jehoiachin:	three months
Zedekiah:	eleven years

That makes a total of fifty-five years and six months and thus correctly leads to the year 587 BC (642 − 55 = 587), the year of the destruction of Jerusalem and the beginning of the Babylonian captivity.

After Hezekiah's son Manasseh there are no more problems with the chronologies, the biblical data and the extrabiblical dates. In our chronology, Hezekiah leads his son Manasseh into the coregency in 697 BC, exactly when he became old enough for it at the age of twelve in the Hebrew tradition, and exactly ten years before Hezekiah's death, whom he knew in advance through God's promise to prolong his life.

With the death of Hezekiah in 687 BC Manasseh then became the sole ruler of Judah and began his evil deeds. According to 2 Kgs 21, Manasseh was twelve years old when he became ruler, and his kingship lasted fifty-five years. So it is also clear (697 − 642 = 55) that Manasseh was born 709 BC, 697 + 12 = 709. So far so good, until then everything fits.

Since Hezekiah was twenty-five years old when he became the sole ruler of Judah after 2 Kgs 18 and this reign lasted twenty-nine years, we can close back from his year of death 687 BC to the assumption of sole rule (687 + 29 = 716 BC) and since he was twenty-five years old in that year, we can also calculate his year of birth as 716 + 25 = 741 BC.

His father Ahaz probably led him into the coregency at the age of twelve or thirteen years after 2 Kgs 18, when Hezekiah was old enough according to the Hebrew tradition, and in the third year of the parallel reigning king of the Northern Kingdom Hoshea (who ruled from 731 until the downfall of Samaria in 722 BC).

That will have been 731 − 3 = 728 and of course also 741 − 13 = 728 BC. Hezekiah thus became coregent in 728 BC.

The Bible also gives interesting information about the siege and fall of Samaria. The siege began after 2 Kgs 18:9–10 in the fourth year of the coregency of Hezekiah (728 − 4 = 724 BC) and ended in its sixth year (728 − 6 = 722 BC). Thus we can also deduce the beginning, end, and duration of the siege of Samaria (724–722 BC), which is in complete agreement with the Assyrian records and their relatively reliable year dates.

What the Bible tells us about the last king of the Northern Kingdom Hoshea also fits quite well:

> *In the twelfth year of Ahaz king of Judah, Hoshea the son of Elah became king of Israel in Samaria, and he reigned nine years. And he did evil in the sight of the Lord, but not as the kings of Israel who were before him. Shalmaneser king of Assyria came up against him; and Hoshea became his vassal, and paid him tribute money. And the king of Assyria uncovered a conspiracy by Hoshea; for he had sent messengers to So, king of Egypt, and brought no tribute to the king of Assyria, as he had done year by year. Therefore the king of Assyria shut him up, and bound him in prison. Now the king of Assyria went throughout all the land, and went up to Samaria and besieged it for three years. In the ninth year of Hoshea, the king of Assyria took Samaria and carried Israel away to Assyria, and placed them in Halah and by the Habor, the River of Gozan, and in the cities of the Medes.* (2 Kgs 17:1–6)

Hoshea ruled for nine years (731–722 BC) and the siege of Samaria lasted three years. After that the deportations began. Everything fits. Very interesting is also the mention of a "conspiracy," which Hoshea planned by stopping his tribute payments to Assur and apparently wanted to ally with Egypt under the then Pharaoh "So." Historians are relatively certain that the pharaoh "So" mentioned in the Bible refers to the Egyptian pharaoh Osorkon IV, who ruled from about 732 to 722 BC, and that the request for help to Egypt was made in 725 BC. That also fits.

The history of the kings of the Northern Kingdom of Israel during this period is very turbulent and confused, including conspiracies, murder and manslaughter, depositions, parallel dominations, and attacks by various other powers, including the Egyptians. To list them here would go beyond the scope of this book. We will try to include them only when the year dates are reasonably certain. Let's concentrate again on the kings of the Southern Kingdom.

From our previous considerations followed the assumption of the sole rule of Hezekiah's in 716 BC which must have been the year of the death of his father Ahaz. Since Ahaz took over the sole reign after 2 Kgs

16 at the age of twenty years and held it sixteen years, his sole reign must have begun 716 + 16 = 732 BC.

Thus, we have derived backwards:

587 BC	Destruction of Jerusalem, Babylonian captivity
...	
642 BC	Manasseh dies
687 BC	Manasseh takes over the sole reign
687 BC	Hezekiah dies
697 BC	Manasseh comes into the coregency
709 BC	Manasseh is born
716 BC	Hezekiah takes over the sole reign
716 BC	Ahaz dies
728 BC	Hezekiah comes into the coregency
732 BC	**Ahaz takes over the sole reign**

Let us now try to approach this period from the other direction.

If one sets the division of Israel into Northern Kingdom and Southern Kingdom of Judah after Solomon's death at 931 BC, which is generally assumed, Thiele's royal chronology can then explain the course of the royal dynasties in the Southern as well as in the Northern Kingdom to some extent satisfactorily (as already described with slight difficulties in the Northern Kingdom before Hoshea and the fall of Samaria).

Thus, in the Southern Kingdom of Judah, in the forward view, one comes without major problems to King Amaziah, who must have been born in 821 BC, took over sole rule in 796 BC at the age of twenty-five and died after twenty-nine years at the age of fifty-four in 767 BC. However, in 789 BC Amaziah was captured in a war with the Northern Kingdom of Israel and his son Azariah (Uzziah) had to take over the official duties at the age of sixteen. Although his father returned to Judah from captivity, he obviously could not return to the royal court and then fell victim to an ambush in Lachish in 767 BC (in the twenty-seventh year of King Jeroboam II of Israel: 2 Kgs 14 and 15), after which his son Azariah (Uzziah) officially became sole ruler.

We know from Azariah (Uzziah) that he was very successful, but that this went to his head and he wanted to take the smoke offerings from the priests and perform them himself, so God punished him with leprosy. After that he had to go into seclusion (a kind of lifelong quarantine) and his son Jotham had to take over the government business. This must have happened in about 750 BC, the second year of King Pekah of the Northern Kingdom (2 Kgs 15:32), who ruled for twenty years (2 Kgs 15:27) and of whom we know that he was the predecessor of Hoshea, who (see above) became king of Israel about 731 BC.

So Pekah reigned 751–731 BC and his second year was 750 BC. Jotham thus became codominant due to his father's illness in 750 BC until his father died in 740 BC and he became sole ruler. Now the Bible tells us that Jotham reigned for a total of sixteen years (2 Kgs 15:33), so that his reign must have ended around 735 BC (counting the accession year).

Let us recapitulate our second interim result:

(Please read now from bottom to top)

735 BC	Jotham's government ends
740 BC	Jotham takes over the sole reign
740 BC	Azariah (Uzziah) dies
750 BC	Jotham comes into the coregency
750 BC	Azariah (Uzziah) becomes leprous and goes into seclusion
767 BC	Azariah (Uzziah) takes over the sole reign
767 BC	Amaziah dies
789 BC	Azariah (Uzziah) comes into the coregency
789 BC	Amaziah gets into captivity
796 BC	Amaziah takes over the sole rule over Judah
...	
931 BC	**Solomon dies, Israel is divided**

And now we want to put our two results together.

We will try to combine both tables, that is, the table that leads us backwards from the assured date of Manasseh's death to the date of Ahaz's assumption of sole rule, and the table just derived, which leads us from the division of Israel in 931 BC to the beginning and end of the government of Jotham, Ahaz's father.

We have omitted the kings from Solomon to Amaziah in our presentation for the sake of simplicity, as they are not relevant here.

587 BC	Destruction of Jerusalem, Babylonian captivity
...	
642 BC	Manasseh dies
687 BC	Manasseh takes over the sole reign
687 BC	Hezekiah dies
697 BC	Manasseh comes into the coreign (with twelve to thirteen years)
709 BC	Manasseh is born
716 BC	Hezekiah takes over the sole reign
716 BC	Ahaz dies
728 BC	Hezekiah comes to the co-regency (with twelve to thirteen years)
732 BC	Ahaz takes over the sole reign
?	
735 BC	Jotham's government ends
740 BC	Jotham takes over the sole reign
740 BC	Azariah (Uzziah) dies
750 BC	Jotham comes into the coregency
750 BC	Azariah (Uzziah) becomes leprous and goes into seclusion
767 BC	Azariah (Uzziah) takes over the sole reign
767 BC	Amaziah dies
789 BC	Azariah (Uzziah) comes into the coregency
789 BC	Amaziah gets into captivity
796 BC	Amaziah takes over the sole reign
...	
931 BC	**Solomon dies, Israel is divided**

Here now the real problem becomes visible: There is a gap of three years between the apparent relinquishment of the rule of Jotham and the taking over of the rule by Ahaz. How can this be explained?

The date 735 BC is remarkable in that it marks the beginning of the so-called Syrian-Ephraimite War. In this war, the leader of the Arameans (Syria) Rezin of Damascus and Pekah, who was ruling the Northern Kingdom of Israel at that time, allied themselves to form an alliance against the Assyrians, from whom they (apparently rightly) felt threatened. Rezin and Pekah urged Judah to join this coalition with considerable pressure. The kingdom of Judah, however, rejected this, so that Aram and Israel went to war against Judah to install a new king, the son of an Aramean

THE LIFE OF HEZEKIAH IN A HISTORICAL CONTEXT 159

named Tabeel, who would then complete the alliance against Assyria. We find this in extrabiblical reports, but the Bible also tells us a lot about it. Let us therefore first read 2 Kgs 15:32–37:

> In the second year of Pekah the son of Remaliah king of Israel began Jotham the son of Uzziah king of Judah to reign. Five and twenty years old was he when he began to reign, and he reigned sixteen years in Jerusalem. And his mother's name was Jerusha, the daughter of Zadok. And he did that which was right in the sight of the LORD: he did according to all that his father Uzziah had done. Howbeit the high places were not removed: the people sacrificed and burned incense still in the high places. He built the higher gate of the house of the LORD. Now the rest of the acts of Jotham, and all that he did, are they not written in the book of the chronicles of the kings of Judah?
>
> In those days the LORD began to send against Judah Rezin the king of Syria, and Pekah the son of Remalia.

So, we read here relatively clearly about God's approval of the attack of Rezin and Pekah against Judah, but we also learn from this that this attack must have begun in the <u>time of Jotham</u>, Ahaz's father. But let us now read one chapter further on in 2 Kgs 16:5–6:

> At that time Rezin, king of Aram and Pekah son of Remaliah king of Israel went up to Jerusalem to fight; and they besieged Ahaz but could not fight against him. At that time Rezin king of Syria brought Elath back to Syria and drove the Jews out of Elath; and Edomites came to Elath, and they have dwelt there until this day. (2 Kgs 16:5–6)

Well, here it is now reported that Rezin and Pekah fought <u>against Ahaz</u> and laid siege to Jerusalem. Against whom then, Jotham or Ahaz?

What facts do we have? The <u>Syrian-Ephraimite War</u> apparently began after 2 Kgs 15 in 735 BC with the attack of Rezin of Aram and Pekah of Israel against Judah <u>under its then king Jotham</u>. And then? Further details about this war are described in 2 Chr 28:5–8.

> Therefore the Lord his God delivered him into the hand of the king of Syria. They defeated him and carried away a great multitude of them as captives, and brought them to Damascus. Then he was also delivered into the hand of the king of Israel, who defeated him with a great slaughter. For Pekah the son of Remaliah killed one hundred and twenty thousand in Judah in one day, all valiant men, because they had forsaken the Lord God of their fathers.

> *Zichri, a mighty man of Ephraim, killed Maaseiah the king's son, Azrikam the officer over the house, and Elkanah who was second to the king. And the children of Israel carried away captive of their brethren two hundred thousand women, sons, and daughters; and they also took away much spoil from them and brought the spoil to Samaria. (2 Chr 28:5–8)*

Here we are told of two lost battles. The first defeat was against Aram under its king Rezin, after which many prisoners were brought to Damascus. Then we read about another defeat against the Northern Kingdom of Israel under Pekah, in which 120,000 men died, including the "son of the king" named Maaseiah, and two hundred thousand prisoners were taken to Samaria (who were subsequently released and sent home through the intervention of the prophet Oded). The attack of Aram and Israel penetrated to Jerusalem according to 2 Kgs 16:5 but did not lead to its capture. Edwin R. Thiele now tries to give the following explanation.

Explanation Attempt after Edwin R. Thiele[9]

The Syrian-Ephraimite War began in 735 BC under Jotham. Severe defeats led to Jotham's son Ahaz urging his father to seek help from the Assyrians, but the latter refused. Ahaz then seized power by a coup d'état, deposed his father and took over the rule of Judah. Ahaz left his father alive for three more years before he either died or was executed. Ahaz would thus be a formal coruler from 735 BC, since the legitimate king Jotham was still alive, while he finally gained sole rule in 732 BC after the death of his father. Thus, the apparent gap between Jotham and Ahaz would be explained by the assumption of rule by Ahaz in 735 BC.

This interpretation has some weaknesses that we will not go into now. Instead, we dare to make our own attempt at explanation.

Explanation Attempt: Jotham Gets into Aramaic Captivity

Some imagination is now required from the inclined reader. The author would like to emphasize at this point that the following descriptions are only a further attempt at explanation, which does not claim to have found

---

9. Thiele, *The Mysterious Numbers of the Hebrew Kings*.

the truth. But we find it quite interesting. Though let the reader decide for himself.

King Jotham of Judah resisted the pressure of Aram and Israel to join an alliance against the Assyrians. As a result, Rezin of Aram and Pekah of Israel moved as allies against Judah to exchange its king for an obedient Aramean. In this difficult situation Jotham appointed his son (Ahaz was about twenty years old), who had grown up in the meantime, as coregent. Possibly Jotham and Ahaz then even had to wage a two-front war, and not for nothing—the Bible mentions here in 2 Chr 28:5–8 two separate disputes, one against Aram and one against Israel, both of which were lost. So let us assume, then, that Ahaz was appointed coruler over Judah by his father Jotham in 735 BC, perhaps because of the onset of war. Let us assume as well that Jotham and Ahaz went to this war together. This would close the three-year gap between Jotham and Ahaz. And it would also be explained why the Syrian-Ephraimite War is mentioned both in 2 Kgs 15 under Jotham and in 2 Kgs 16 under Ahaz.

But what happened to Jotham? Why did he not appear again after the beginning of the war against Aram and Israel? And why did Ahaz not become sole ruler until three years later in 732 BC?

Let us imagine Jotham and Ahaz fighting against Aram and Israel. Let us imagine that Jotham fights against Aram under Rezin and Ahaz against Israel under Pekah. Now Jotham loses his fight against Rezin and after 2 Chr 28:5 many prisoners are taken away to Damascus. <u>Let us now imagine that Jotham was also among these prisoners who were led away to Damascus</u>! Perhaps it was also the case that Jotham and Ahaz fought together against Aram under Rezin, whereby Jotham was then taken prisoner with the others, but Ahaz could withdraw, in order to later fight alone against Israel under Pekah. Whether they fought directly separately on two fronts or together at the beginning, the end result is that Jotham is in Aramaic (Syrian) captivity in Damascus in 735/734 BC and Ahaz now had to fight this war alone. So, Ahaz fought alone against Israel and was defeated devastatingly, whereby two hundred thousand captives were led to Samaria and the "son of the king" named <u>Maaseiah</u> was killed by Zichri, a "hero of Ephraim." This son Maaseiah is often cited to allegedly prove that the dates of the kings in the Bible simply cannot be correct. For if Maaseiah was killed by Zichri here in the battle against Aram, then he must have been an adult by then—and then Ahaz cannot have become a coregent in 735 BC according to 2 Kgs 16:2 at the age of twenty, since he had to have an adult son, Maasseiah, by then, which is simply impossible at the age of twenty. A nice side effect of our attempt to explain is that we no longer must assume that Maaseiah was the son of Ahaz, which would be very difficult to explain. In fact, the Bible does not speak of Maaseiah literally as the son of Ahaz, but rather (and certainly with caution!) as the son of the king!

> *Zichri, a mighty man of Ephraim, killed Maaseiah the king's son . . .* (2 Chr 28:7)

Let's just imagine that Jotham had not only taken his firstborn son Ahaz with him into battle, but another, younger son as well! Maaseiah is not the adult son of Ahaz, who has caused many historians headaches, but simply another son of Jotham.

Now imagine Ahaz's situation. He has just become a coregent, then a little later his father is captured after a heavy defeat against the Aramaeans in Damascus. Soon after, Ahaz himself is defeated at least as hard against Israel and its king Pekah, in which his brother dies. In addition, Jerusalem falls under a siege, which fortunately does not lead to conquest. Since Ahaz does not want to listen to God's words, which were transmitted by the prophet Isaiah and which urge him to keep quiet, he gathers all the treasures of Jerusalem, including those found in the temple, and bribes the then king of the Assyrians, Tiglath-Pileser, to take up arms against Aram and Israel. Perhaps he does this, among other things, to have his father freed in Damascus?

> *So Ahaz sent messengers to Tiglath-Pileser king of Assyria, saying, "I am your servant and your son. Come up and save me from the hand of the king of Syria and from the hand of the king of Israel, who rise up against me." And Ahaz took the silver and gold that was found in the house of the Lord, and in the treasuries of the king's house, and sent it as a present to the king of Assyria. So the king of Assyria heeded him; for the king of Assyria went up against Damascus and took it, carried its people captive to Kir, and killed Rezin.* (2 Kgs 16:7–9)

The Assyrians under Tiglath-Pileser moved against Damascus in 733 BC and conquered it in 732 BC. This date can be proved quite well from the Assyrian sources. Now imagine King Jotham, Ahaz's father in captivity in Damascus, is killed in the Assyrian attack on the city. This means that Jotham would have died in 732 BC at the age of about forty-three years, and Ahaz would have become the sole ruler of Judah that same year.

Still not quite convinced? Have you ever wondered why Ahaz traveled there immediately after taking Damascus, toward Tiglath-Pileser? Probably not, but he actually did.

> Now **King Ahaz went to Damascus** to meet Tiglath-Pileser king of Assyria, and saw an altar that was at Damascus; and King Ahaz sent to Urijah the priest the design of the altar and its pattern, according to all its workmanship. Then Urijah the priest built an altar according to all that King Ahaz had sent from Damascus. So Urijah the priest made it before King Ahaz came back from Damascus. And when the king came back from Damascus, the king saw the altar; and the king approached the altar and made offerings on it. (2 Kgs 16:10–12)

From Damascus, Ahaz brought a beautiful new altar of sacrifice to idols with him, or he had the one he had seen there built in Jerusalem. It is extremely interesting to take a closer look at the first verses in 2 Kgs 16. Here Ahaz is always referred to as "Ahaz," except in his introduction at the beginning to verse 9. Only in verse 10, when Damascus has fallen and Ahaz travels there, is he called "King Ahaz" for the first time and also in the following text always called king (and only like that!). This change in the naming occurs exactly after the capture of Damascus at the time when his father had died, and he became the sole ruler of Judah. Why did Ahaz travel to Damascus? Perhaps he simply wanted to bring his dead father home and bury him? At least this is a very obvious reason and cannot be dismissed.

Let us first list again what we know or can deduce with relative certainty:

The Syrian-Ephraimite War takes place between the Southern Kingdom of Judah and an alliance of Aram and the Northern Kingdom of Israel around 735–734 BC. Israel and Aram want to form an alliance against the Assyrians and force Judah to join. But since King Jotham of Judah refuses, Aram and Israel start a war against Judah, in which they want to depose Jotham in order to install an Aramaic ("the son of Tabeel") as king over Judah, who is supposed to lead it into the coalition against Assyria. The king of Aram at that time is Rezin, and the king of Israel is Pekah. In the Bible, both King Jotham (2 Kgs 15) and his son Ahaz (2 Kgs 16) are mentioned in this war as leaders of the people of Judah.

Judah loses (at least) one battle against Aram under its king Rezin, in which many prisoners are taken to Damascus.

King Jotham's reign over Judah ends in 735 BC.

Judah loses (at least) one battle against Israel and its king Pekah, in which 120,000 fighters die and two hundred thousand people from the population are led into captivity in Samaria but are immediately released again because of the admonishing words of the prophet Oded, who is working there. In this battle, "Maaseiah the son of the king" is also killed by a soldier of the army of Israel named Zichri. Aram and Israel advance against Jerusalem, but there is no capture or prolonged siege of the city.

The battles lost by Judah against Aram and Israel must thus also have taken place in 735/734 BC.

Ahaz now bribes the Assyrians with a considerable sum of gold and silver to start a war against Aram, against the urgent warning of the prophet Isaiah. Incited by Ahaz, the Assyrians under Tiglath-Pileser III attack Aram in 733 BC and take the capital Damascus in 732 BC. Rezin of Aram is killed, Tiglath-Pileser III occupies the city.

Ahaz's sole reign begins in 732 BC.

King Ahaz travels to the occupied city of Damascus to visit Tiglath-Pileser III. King Ahaz brings the model of an Aramaic idol sacrificial altar from Damascus and has a copy made in the temple in Jerusalem.

And now we tell the whole story again and add the assumptions of our attempt to interpret and explain it (our additions always in *italics*):

The Syrian-Ephraimite War takes place between an alliance of Aram and the Northern Kingdom of Israel and the Southern Kingdom of Judah about 735–734 BC *Israel and Aram want to form an alliance against the Assyrians and force Judah to join. But since King Jotham of Judah refuses, Aram and Israel start a war against Judah, in which they want to depose Jotham in order to install an Aramaic ("the son of Tabeel") as king over Judah, who is supposed to lead it into the coalition against Assyria.* King of Aram at that time is Rezin, king of Israel is Pekah. According to the Bible, both King Jotham (2 Kgs 15) and his son Ahaz (2 Kgs 16) are mentioned in this war as leaders of the people of Judah, *because King Jotham appointed his son Ahaz as co-ruler over Judah in 735 BC.*

Judah loses (at least) one battle against Aram under its king Rezin, in which many prisoners are taken to Damascus.

King Jotham also gets into Aramaic captivity.

King Jotham's reign over Judah *therefore* ends in 735 BC.

Judah loses (at least) one battle against Israel and its king Pekah, in which 120,000 fighters die and two hundred thousand people from the population are led into captivity in Samaria but are immediately released again because of the admonishing words of the prophet Oded, who is working there. In this battle, "Maaseiah, the son of King *Jotham*" is also killed by a soldier of the army of Israel named Zichri. Aram and Israel advance against Jerusalem, but there is no capture or prolonged siege of the city.

The battles lost by Judah against Aram and Israel must thus also have taken place in 735/734 BC.

Ahaz now bribes the Assyrians by paying a considerable sum of gold and silver to start a war against Aram, against the urgent warning of the prophet Isaiah.

Incited by Ahaz, the Assyrians under Tiglath-Pileser III attack Aram in 733 BC and take the capital Damascus in 732 BC. Tiglath-Pileser III occupies the city, Rezin of Aram is killed. *King Jotham of Judah also dies during the siege and attack on the city.*

Ahaz's <u>sole reign</u> therefore begins in 732 BC.

King Ahaz travels to the occupied city of Damascus to visit Tiglath-Pileser III *and to bring his deceased father home and bury him there.*

King Ahaz brings the model of an Aramaic altar of sacrifice to idols from Damascus and has a copy made in the temple in Jerusalem.

Conspicuous Features in the Biblical Introduction of King Ahaz

> **Ahaz** *was twenty years old when he became king, and he reigned sixteen years in Jerusalem; and he did not do what was right in the sight of the Lord his God, as his father David had done. But he walked in the way of the kings of Israel; indeed he made his son pass through the fire, according to the abominations of the nations whom the Lord had cast out from before the children of Israel. And he sacrificed and burned incense on the high places, on the hills, and under every green tree. Then Rezin king of Syria and Pekah the son of Remaliah, king of Israel, came up to Jerusalem to make war; and they besieged* **Ahaz** *but could not overcome him. At that time Rezin king of Syria captured Elath for Syria, and drove the men of Judah from Elath. Then the Edomites went to Elath, and dwell there to this day. So* **Ahaz** *sent messengers to Tiglath-Pileser king of Assyria, saying, "I am your servant and your son. Come up and save me from the hand of the king of Syria and from the hand of the king of Israel, who rise up against me." And* **Ahaz** *took the silver and gold that was found in the house of the Lord, and in the treasuries of the king's house, and sent it as a present to the king of Assyria. So the king of Assyria heeded him; for the king of Assyria*

went up against Damascus and took it, carried its people captive to Kir, and killed Rezin. Now **King Ahaz** went to Damascus to meet Tiglath-Pileser king of Assyria, and saw an altar that was at Damascus; and **King Ahaz** sent to Urijah the priest the design of the altar and its pattern, according to all its workmanship. Then Urijah the priest built an altar according to all that **King Ahaz** had sent from Damascus. So Urijah the priest made it before **King Ahaz** came back from Damascus. And when the king came back from Damascus, the **king** saw the altar; and the **king** approached the altar and made offerings on it. (2 Kgs 16:2–12)

Do you notice the sudden change in the naming? In the first verses, only **Ahaz** is mentioned, but from verse 10 onward, namely exactly when the Assyrians had conquered Damascus (and Ahaz's father King Jotham had died there?), only **King Ahaz** or the **king** is spoken of, and this continues in the verses that follow. You are welcome to read it; from now on, until his death, only **King Ahaz** will be spoken of. Is that not conspicuous? Exactly from then on, 732 BC when the Assyrians conquered Damascus and Ahaz visited Tiglath-Pileser III there, the Bible speaks only of **King Ahaz**, before that it always calls him **Ahaz**.

Could this conspicuousness be an indication for our attempt to explain that Ahaz's father King Jotham died in Aramaic captivity in Damascus when the Assyrians stormed the city and thus began Ahaz's sole rule in 732 BC?

So if our attempt of explanation fits to some extent, then this sequence of events results (please read from bottom to top):

587 BC	Destruction of Jerusalem, Babylonian captivity
...	
642 BC	Manasseh dies
687 BC	Manasseh takes over the sole reign
687 BC	Hezekiah dies
697 BC	Manasseh comes into the coregency (with twelve to thirteen years)
709 BC	Manasseh is born
716 BC	Hezekiah takes over the sole reign
716 BC	Ahaz dies
728 BC	Hezekiah comes to the coregency (with twelve to thirteen years)
732 BC	Ahaz takes over the sole reign
732 BC	Jotham dies during the capture of Damascus by the Assyrians

735 BC	Jotham's government ends through captivity
735 BC	Ahaz is appointed coregent by Jotham
740 BC	Jotham takes over the sole reign
740 BC	Azariah (Uzziah) dies
750 BC	Jotham comes into the coregency
750 BC	Azariah (Uzziah) becomes leprous and goes into seclusion
767 BC	Azariah (Uzziah) takes over the sole reign
767 BC	Amaziah dies
789 BC	Azariah (Uzziah) comes into the coregency
789 BC	Amaziah gets into captivity
796 BC	Amaziah takes over the sole reign
...	
931 BC	**Solomon dies, Israel is divided**

We would now like to leave it to our readers to decide how they judge our attempt at explanation. As beautiful and plausible as it reads and at the same time eliminates the "problem" around Maaseiah, the "son of the king," our solution has a serious disadvantage: the Bible mentions nothing about a captivity of Jotham in Damascus. It leaves us completely in the dark about the fate of the father of Ahaz. It is relatively certain that he must have died between 735 and 732 BC. But why so early, at the age of forty-one to forty-three, and how, we don't know anything about. A coregency of Ahaz parallel to his father King Jotham is meanwhile even considered probable by many Bible-critical scientists.

But maybe the story was even a little bit different.

The "Unsolvable" Problem with 2 Kgs 17:1

Here we now address a topic that Bible-true historians prefer not to address, but that Bible-critical scholars are very happy to argue against the reliability of the biblical data.

> *In the twelfth year of Ahaz king of Judah, Hoshea the son of Elah became king of Israel in Samaria, and he reigned nine years.* (2 Kgs 17:1)

Hoshea was the last king of the Northern Kingdom of Israel, under whom, as we already know, Samaria was besieged by the Assyrians from 724 BC onwards and was taken in 722 BC. Thus, the rule of Hoshea ended in 722 BC and since it lasted nine years, it must have begun in 731 BC. This is also largely undisputed in this respect. In the chronology presented in this book, all biblical and extrabiblical information now fit together harmoniously, and we were also able to explain other "little problems" such as the "son of the king" named Maaseiah satisfactorily. This verse is the very last riddle about the difficulties of dating the Hebrew kings and unfortunately does not fit into the whole chronology that has been built up so far. If Hoshea became king over the Northern Kingdom of Israel in 731 BC, which is relatively certain based on the calibration of his nine-year reign in the year of the conquest of Samaria (which is undisputed)—how does the first part of 2 Kgs 17:1 fit in? Here it says that Hoshea became king over Israel in the twelfth year of Ahaz. Or in other words: 731 BC was the twelfth year of Ahaz the king. But now we have laboriously shown in the previous passages that Ahaz became sole ruler over Judah in 732 BC, and possibly even before that, when his father, Jotham, was taken captive, he became coruler from 735 BC. Then how can 731 BC be the twelfth year of Ahaz? No, that does not fit at all. There are no plausible explanations so far. The problem seemed so great that even the Bible-loyal Edwin R. Thiele assumed that it must be an error in the Holy Scriptures. We would now like to offer an explanation based on what has been discussed so far. If 731 BC is really supposed to have been the twelfth year of Ahaz, when would Ahaz have to have come into royal rule? Logically about 743/742 BC (731 + 12 = 743). We have been able to determine Ahaz's year of birth quite well with 755 BC. How old would he have been if he had actually come to rule in 743/742 BC? Is that where you get your first ideas? Exactly, Ahaz would have been twelve to thirteen years old, because 755 − 12 = 743—exactly the age at which a boy became *gadol* in the tradition of that time! Do we perhaps recognize a pattern here? Ahaz, Hezekiah, and Manasseh are all appointed by their fathers as coregents at the time they become *gadol*, when they are considered adults. Could that not even be true?

Do we have to change our table a little bit?

587 BC	Destruction of Jerusalem, Babylonian captivity
...	
642 BC	Manasseh dies
687 BC	Manasseh takes over the sole reign
687 BC	Hezekiah dies

697 BC	Manasseh comes into the coregency (with twelve to thirteen years)
709 BC	Manasseh is born
716 BC	Hezekiah takes over the sole reign
716 BC	Ahaz dies
728 BC	Hezekiah comes to the coregency (with twelve to thirteen years)
732 BC	Ahaz takes over the sole reign
732 BC	Jotham dies during the capture of Damascus by the Assyrians
735 BC	Ahaz becomes "interim king" due to Jotham's absence
735 BC	Jotham's government ends through captivity
740 BC	Jotham takes over the sole reign
740 BC	Azariah (Uzziah) dies
743 BC	Ahaz also comes into the coregency (with twelve to thirteen years)
750 BC	Jotham comes into the coregency
750 BC	Azariah (Uzziah) becomes leprous and goes into seclusion
767 BC	Azariah (Uzziah) takes over the sole reign
767 BC	Amaziah dies
789 BC	Azariah (Uzziah) comes into the coregency
789 BC	Amaziah gets into captivity
796 BC	Amaziah takes over the sole reign
...	
931 BC	**Solomon dies, Israel is divided**

Obviously, at that time it was a trend to lead his son into coregency when he reached the appropriate age. That is, after a boy became *gadol* according to the Jewish tradition, more precisely the Halacha, the legal part of the later Talmud; i.e., he became self-responsible for his actions and thus was considered an adult. If King Jotham actually did the same with his son Ahaz, then all alleged inconsistencies can be finally resolved!

Ahaz was born in 755 BC, in 743/742 BC his father appointed him coregent at the age of twelve or thirteen. So we have here the unique situation that we have three kings in Judah for some years: <u>Azariah (Uzziah)</u>, who is still alive but is in seclusion because of his leprosy and can no longer take part in the affairs of government, <u>Jotham</u>, who therefore had to take over the affairs of government from his father in 750 BC, and now <u>Ahaz</u>, who was elevated to coregency by his father Jotham in 743/742 BC. In 735 BC Ahaz's father, Jotham, is captured in Damascus and at the age of twenty Ahaz has to lead the affairs of government alone, where he immediately "buys" the Assyrians, who rise up against Damascus and conquer it in 732 BC, whereby Ahaz's father Jotham then dies and Ahaz becomes sole ruler. In 731 BC Hoshea then becomes king of the Northern Kingdom of Israel, in the twelfth year of the (co)rule of Ahaz. After sixteen years of (sole and interim) rule, Ahaz dies at the age of thirty-nine. We have explained the "problem" of 2 Kgs 17:1! Edwin R. Thiele passed away in 1986, but he would certainly have been extremely happy about it!

What triggered this "trend"? Suddenly, three kings—Jotham, Ahaz, and Hezekiah—one after the other appointed their sons as corulers at the moment of their attainment of personal responsibility, of adulthood.

Perhaps Hezekiah's great-great-grandfather Azariah (Uzziah) was the trigger. He had to suddenly, and for him surely very surprising and shockingly, take over the royal rule in 789 BC at the age of only sixteen years, because his father Amaziah had fallen into Israeli captivity. But he apparently did his job really well, because he was very successful and followed the LORD faithfully. Then, unfortunately, the success went to his head and this self-important story happened in which he went to the temple and instead of the priests themselves, he wanted to proceed the smoke offerings. God then beat him with leprosy, and he had to go into a lifelong quarantine, separated and sealed off from the outside world. And again suddenly and unexpectedly a king's son had to take over the government, this time Jotham. He surely hadn't expected this so suddenly either, since his father was extremely successful and highly respected, and there was no war. After Azariah (Uzziah) and then Jotham had to jump into the cold water unprepared and take over the entire affairs of government, it could well be that Jotham (perhaps on his father's advice, since the two of them could probably still talk to each other from a certain safety distance during visits of Jotham in his quarantine accommodation) developed the idea to prepare his son Ahaz for the royal rule better than he and his father had done before. Maybe Ahaz and later Hezekiah simply continued to pursue this concept? Hezekiah even had the concrete reason that by the time Manasseh turned twelve years old, he only had ten of the fifteen added years to live. Azariah (Uzziah) and Jotham had to suddenly, unexpectedly, and unprepared take over the affairs of government—Azariah (Uzziah) even at the age of sixteen. Perhaps both of them, or at least Jotham, developed this concept of taking the firstborn son with them as soon as he was old enough, i.e., at the age of twelve to thirteen, and was considered *gadol* according to Hebrew tradition, self-responsible, and adult, in order to introduce them to royal rule and prepare them for later sole rule.

Makes sense, doesn't it? And it is not an individual case with which we want to "explain away" any problem here, it happened three times in a row with Jotham, Ahaz, and Hezekiah—always at the age of twelve to thirteen years, when they became *gadol*.

And the Bible is right after all! In 2 Kgs 17:1 it is not a mistake. The bible does not contain mistakes. Otherwise, it would not be the word of God. Or do you not trust the almighty creator of the universe, who is not bound by time and space, to protect the people whom he lets write down his holy word from making mistakes? But then we would have a very careless God. No, everything is true! In the very end, God is always right.

In any case, I am very much looking forward to standing before my LORD and meeting all the other believers in the kingdom of heaven, to do a little review of my book here with Hezekiah of Judah. I am very curious.

Timeline of Hezekiah's Life in a Historical Context

As we have shown after some research, intensive consideration, but also always accepting the word of God as reliable, the sequence of events in Hezekiah's life can now indeed be presented in a very well harmonized way between biblical reports and extrabiblical material.

Timetable of Events:

1. (Beginning of Ahaz's coregency [with twelve to thirteen years]?) — 743 BC
2. **Hezekiah's birth** — 741 BC
3. **Aram and the Northern Kingdom of Israel invaded Judah** — 735–734 BC
4. *(Ahaz's father Jotham gets captured in Damascus?)* — 735 BC
5. **Beginning of Ahaz's reign** *(as interim king?)* — 735 BC
6. **Aram's capital Damascus is conquered by the Assyrians** — 733–732 BC
7. *(Ahaz's father Jotham dies in the attack on Damascus?)* — 732 BC
8. **Beginning of Ahaz's sole reign** — 732 BC
9. **Hoshea murders Pekah and becomes king of the Northern Kingdom** — 731 BC

10. Beginning of Hezekiah's co-regency
    (with twelve to thirteen years) — 728 BC
11. Tiglath-Pileser III dies, Shalmaneser V becomes King of Assyria — 726 BC
12. King Hoshea of Israel asks Pharaoh Osorkon IV for help — 725 BC
13. Samaria is besieged and conquered by the Assyrians — 724–722 BC
14. Sargon II becomes king of Assyria — 721 BC
15. Beginning of the sole reign of Hezekiah (death of his father Ahaz) — 716 BC
16. Spiritual reforms

    Comprehensive abolition of idolatry, cleaning of the temple — 716 BC

    Celebration of Passover (fourteenth day of the second month) — 715 BC

    Renewal of the temple service, supply for the priests (third—seventh month) — 715 BC
17. Large construction activities, economic growth — 715–705 BC
18. Victories against the Philistines, land gains for Judah — 715–705 BC
19. Sargon II conquers Ashdod with his tartan — 712 BC
20. Birth of Hezekiah's son Manasseh — 709 BC
21. Sargon II is killed, Sennacherib becomes king of Assyria — 705 BC
22. Hezekiah's resistance against the Assyrians — 705–703 BC
23. Sennacherib's first campaign against the murderers of his father — 705–704 BC
24. Merodach-Baladan appoints himself king of Babel — 703 BC
25. Sennacherib's second campaign against Merodach-Baladan — 703 BC
26. Sennacherib sets Merodach-Baladan down again, he flees — 703–702 BC
27. Sennacherib begins his third campaign against Judah — 702 BC
28. Sennacherib defeats Ashkelon, allied with Judah — 702 BC
29. Hezekiah fortifies Jerusalem and raises an army — 702 BC
30. The disease of Hezekiah and its cure — 702 BC
31. The visit from Babel and the prophecy to Hezekiah — 702 BC
32. Sennacherib penetrates to Lachish and besieges it — 702–701 BC
33. Hezekiah pays tribute to Sennacherib — 701 BC
34. Sennacherib takes Lachish and lays siege to Jerusalem — 701 BC
35. Sennacherib's call to surrender by Rabshakeh — 701 BC

36. Salvation through the intervention of God — 701 BC
37. Sennacherib's departure and return (via Chaldea) — 701 BC
38. Merodach-Baladan must flee from Chaldea into exile — 700 BC
39. Hezekiah appoints Manasseh as coregent
    (aged twelve to thirteen) — 697 BC
40. Merodach-Baladan dies in exile in Elam — 694 BC
41. Hezekiah's death, Manasseh becomes sole ruler — 687 BC
42. Sennacherib's death, Esarhaddon
    becomes king of Assyria — 681 BC

FIGURE 17

Chronological table of the Judaean kings from Azariah (Uzziah) to Manasseh - incl. all biblical references

	Birth	Co-reign	Sole-reign	Age	Duration of reign	Death	Age at Death	2 Kgs	2 Chr	Isa	Further references or derivations
Azariah (Uzziah)	808		792	16	52	740	68				Calculation (792-16=808)
											Beginning of the reign of Zechariah (753) in the 38th year of Azariah (792-38=754/753)
								15:2			Beginning of the reign of Menahem (752) in the 39th year of Azariah (792-39=753/752)
								15:8			
								15:17	26:1		Beginning of the reign of Pekahiah (741) in the 50th year of Azariah (792-52=740/741)
								15:23			
								15:27			Beginning of Pekah's sole rule (740) = 52nd year of Azariah (792-52=740)
				767							27th year of Jerobeam II (793-27=766/767)
								15:2	26,3		Calculation (792-52=740)
											Calculation (808-740=68)
Jotham	775		750	25	16						Calculation (750-25=775)
											750 = leprosy illness of his father
											2nd year co-rule of Pekah (751-2=749/750)
											End of reign: 750-16-734/735 (due to imprisonment in Damascus?)
			740								Azariah's (Uzziah's) death = assumption of sole-reign
											735 = Beginning of the Syrian-Ephraimite war against Judah
								15:32	27:1		Takeover of Ahaz sole rule = Jotham's death
					732/731			15:37			Died during the conquest of Damascus by the Assyrians (732)?
								15:30			20th year of Jotam (750-19=731/732) = 1st year of Hoshea (731)
							43				Calculation (775-732=43)
Ahaz	755	743		12-13							Calculation (735+20=755)
		735	732/731	20	16	716	39	16:1	28:1		Hoshea 1st year = Ahaz 12th year (731+12=743) / Gadol
								16:1	28:1		17th year of Pekah (751-17=734/735) / Jotam in captivity?
								16:1	28:1		Jotham's death = assumption of sole rule
											Calculation (755-716=39)
Hezekiah	741	728	716	12-13	29	687	54	18:2	29:1		Calculation (716+25=741)
				25				18:1			3rd year of Hoshea (731-3=728) / Samaria's siege and fall in the 4th and 6th years of Hezekiah (724 and 722) and the 7th and 9th years of Hoshea (731-7+724) (731-9=722) / Gadol
								18:9			
								18:10		36:1	Attack of Sanherib in the 14th year of Hezekiah (716-14=702)
								18:2	29:1		Calculation (716-29=687)
								20:6		38:5	Calculation: 15 Jahre nach seiner tödlichen Erkrankung (702-15=687)
											Calculation (741-687=54)
Manasseh	709	697	687	12	55	642	67	21:1	33:1		Calculation (697+12=709)
											Gadol
								21:1	33:1		Hezekiah's death = assumption of sole rule
											Calculation (697-55=642)
											Calculation (709-642=67)

We have thus succeeded in placing the entire chronological sequence and all the biblical details without contradiction in the overall historical context, beginning with Hezekiah's great-great-grandfather Amaziah and ending with the fall and destruction of Jerusalem in 587 BC by Nebuchadnezzar. For clarification, however, we would like to emphasize once again that, due to the accession year topic presented in chapter 2, there may be uncertainties of one year for individual dates.

The Time, the Time, and Again and Again the Time . . .

It is amazing how much time plays a role in this period of Hebrew history. Just think of the fifteen years of additional lifetime that God gave to Hezekiah, who was actually terminally ill. Let us just think of the sundial of Ahaz, which suddenly went backwards, let us think of the exact one hundred (10 x 10) years after Hezekiah's death, in which the prophecy was fulfilled that all his treasures and possessions would be taken to Babel. And let us think of the fulfilled prophecy of Ahaz that Ephraim (= the Northern Kingdom of Israel) would no longer be a people in sixty-five years. Again and again, time is the center of attention.

It is really amazing. Let's think about the many time indications the Bible gives us in the sections considered here. Let us think of the great problems that historians have had with the chronological classification of the beginning and end of the reigns of the Hebrew kings. For many centuries there was simply no satisfactory solution. Some of these problems with time have given nonbelieving scientists a great deal of scope to attack the historicity of the Bible and have even made some believing Christians doubt the reliability of the Bible. Honestly, from a human point of view, there was certainly cause for this.

But, as **always**, in the end it is so that he who trusts in God, who believes him, who trusts his word, who is sure that God does not make mistakes and does not allow mistakes in his work that will be right by God. So also here. The word of God is absolutely credible, both in terms of its historical information and its entire content. Believe it! Believe what he has written down for us. It is all true. Therefore, please also believe him that he sent his son to this world to save you from your guilt. Believe him, no, be sure that he has an eternal and wonderful place ready for you in heaven with him . . .

Extrabiblical Testimonies

In the previous chapters we have of course taken most of the information from our three biblical sources, 2 Kings, 2 Chronicles, and Isaiah, but we have also added a great deal of extrabiblical information, especially if it was reliable and secure. There is a multitude of extrabiblical sources, evidence, documents, artifacts, and other materials that move in or deal with the time epoch of our protagonist King Hezekiah. We cannot look at them all and especially at this point discuss them all in detail, this would completely go beyond the scope of the book. Nevertheless, we would like to list some of them in this chapter so that the reader can get an impression of how impressively even the extrabiblical testimonies confirm or at least support the biblical accounts. King Hezekiah was no fantasy product! The story took place as we have worked out and appropriated it in this book. Let us try to sort the extrabiblical information a little bit first. On a first level we can separate them into

- Other scripts
- Archaeological finds

The other nonbiblical writings can be separated into apocryphal books, the Assyrian records, Greek historiography, and Jewish-Roman historiography. Among the archaeological finds, one could distinguish between those that are directly related to King Hezekiah and those that are related to his epoch. So our basic structure, how we want to approach the topic, could be as follows:

- <u>Other scripts</u>
  - Apocryphal books
  - Assyrian records
  - Greek historiography
  - Jewish-Roman historiography
- <u>Archaeological finds</u>
  - In direct connection with Hezekiah
  - In connection with the epoch of Hezekiah's

As mentioned in the beginning, this chapter cannot deal with all these contents in detail. Nevertheless, it should at least provide an overview and ultimately also document the fact that the Scriptures are confirmed here by many other witnesses. We will leave it as far as possible with an enumeration and will neither evaluate nor comment on the now listed evidence with regard to quality or content. This may be done by the inclined reader himself, if he wishes.

The Apocrypha

First of all, we will look at the so-called apocryphal books. These are religious writings of Jewish or Christian origin from the period between about 200 BC and AD 400, which were not included in the biblical canon or about whose affiliation there is disagreement, either for reasons of content or religious policy, because they were only written after the canon was completed or were not generally known at the time of their creation.

Apocryphal books dealing with Hezekiah:

- The Ascension of Isaiah
- The book of Sirach
- The book of Tobit
- The Testament of Hezekiah

We have already reported in detail on the apocryphal book of Tobit in an excursus in chapter 3. Therefore, we only list it here, but do not discuss it in detail.

The alleged Testament of Hezekiah does not really exist, or if it ever existed, the text has not been handed down. However, it is mentioned twice by the Greek historian Georgius Credenus around AD 1100. It is possible that he was also referring to the apocryphal Ascension of Isaiah and simply gave this text a different name.

Believing Christians, who often deal with the word of God, usually recognize very quickly and also quite easily when reading these apocryphal books why they were not included in the biblical canon or why there is disagreement whether they should belong to it. We do not want to write more about this at this point. Even though these writings lack the divine inspiration by the Spirit of God, it is at least interesting that people at that time were concerned with these events and also wrote about them.

The Apocryphal Book of the Ascension of Isaiah

The Ascension of Isaiah, also "Ascension of the Prophet Isaiah," is an originally Jewish, in the version available today, strongly Christian extended New Testament apocryphal scripture from the second to third century AD.

The text around the prophet Isaiah has been handed down in the languages Ethiopian and fragments in Greek, Latin, Coptic, and Slavic.

Chapters 1 to 5 contain the martyrdom of Isaiah under King Manasseh. It tells how the prophet foretold his martyrdom and how he was actually cut in half under King Manasseh. The martyrdom of Isaiah (chapters 1–5) is the oldest part from the first century BC and is originally written in Hebrew; all other parts are written in Greek.

CHAPTER 1:

> *And it came to pass in the twenty-sixth year of the reign of Hezekiah king of Judah that he called Manasseh his son. Now he was his only one.*
>
> *And he called him into the presence of Isaiah the son of Amoz the prophet, and into the presence of Josab the son of Isaiah, in order to deliver unto him the words of righteousness which the king himself had seen:*
>
> *And of the eternal judgments and torments of Gehenna, and of the prince of this world, and of his angels, and his authorities and his powers.*
>
> *And the words of the faith of the Beloved which he himself had seen in the fifteenth year of his reign during his illness.*
>
> *And he delivered unto him the written words which Samnas the scribe had written, and also those which Isaiah, the son of Amoz, had given to him, and also to the prophets, that they might write and store up with him what he himself had seen in the king's house regarding the judgment of the angels, and the destruction of this world, and regarding the garments of the saints and their going forth, and regarding their transformation and the persecution and ascension of the Beloved.*
>
> *In the twentieth year of the reign of Hezekiah, Isaiah had seen the words of this prophecy and had delivered them to Josab his son. And whilst he (Hezekiah) gave commands, Josab the son of Isaiah standing by.*

> Isaiah said to Hezekiah the king, but not in the presence of Manasseh only did he say unto him: "As the Lord liveth, and the Spirit which speaketh in me liveth, all these commands and these words will be made of none effect by Manasseh thy son, and through the agency of his hands I shall depart mid the torture of my body."
>
> And Sammael Malchira will serve Manasseh, and execute all his desire, and he will become a follower of Beliar rather than of me:
>
> And many in Jerusalem and in Judea he will cause to abandon the true faith, and Beliar will dwell in Manasseh, and by his hands I shall be sawn asunder.
>
> And when Hezekiah heard these words he wept very bitterly, and rent his garments, and placed earth upon his head, and fell on his face.
>
> And Isaiah said unto him: "The counsel of Sammael against Manasseh is consummated: nought will avail thee."
>
> And on that day Hezekiah resolved in his heart to slay Manasseh his son.
>
> And Isaiah said to Hezekiah: "The Beloved hath made of none effect thy design, and the purpose of thy heart will not be accomplished, for with this calling have I been called and I shall inherit the heritage of the Beloved."

Chapter 2:1–3:

> And it came to pass after that Hezekiah died and Manasseh became king, that he did not remember the commands of Hezekiah his father, but forgot them, and Sammael abode in Manasseh and clung fast to him.
>
> And Manasseh forsook the service of the God of his father, and he served Satan and his angels and his powers.
>
> And he turned aside the house of his father, which had been before the face of Hezekiah (from) the words of wisdom and from the service of God.[10]

Besides the apostasy of Manasseh, the prediction and then also the execution of the sawing up of Isaiah by Manasseh, it is highly interesting in this text, which apparently dates from the first century BC, that Hezekiah "calls" his son Manasseh in the very first verse. He apparently calls him

---

10. Peter Kirby, ed., "The Ascension of Isaiah," http://www.earlychristianwritings.com/text/ascension.html.

into the reign. But isn't this a very nice indication of our theme of co-regencies? And it is also an indication that Hezekiah had indeed led his son Manasseh into co-rulership during his lifetime! Unfortunately, the mentioned year does not correspond with our chronology. Coptic writings have obviously corrected it by another ten years, and this correction unfortunately does not correspond to our chronology either, but nevertheless we have a clear indication here—at least from the first century BC—that these co-regencies existed, and that Hezekiah actually made Manasseh co-regent during his lifetime.

The Apocryphal Book of Sirach

The book of Sirach (/ˈsaɪræk/) or Ecclesiasticus (/ɪˌkliːziˈæstɪkəs/), is a Jewish work, originally in Hebrew, of ethical teachings, from approximately 200 to 175 BC, written by the Judahite scribe Ben Sira of Jerusalem, on the inspiration of his father, Joshua, son of Sirach, sometimes called Jesus, son of Sirach, or Yeshua ben Eliezer ben Sira.

Chapter 48:17–25:

> *Hezekiah fortified his city*
>   *and brought water into its midst;*
> *he tunneled the rock with iron tools*
>   *and built cisterns for the water.*
> *In his days Sennacherib invaded the country;*
>   *he sent his commander and departed;*
> *he shook his fist against Zion*
>   *and made great boasts in his arrogance.*
> *Then their hearts and hands were shaken,*
>   *and they were in anguish, like women in labor.*
> *But they called upon the Lord who is merciful,*
>   *spreading out their hands toward him.*
> *The Holy One quickly heard them from heaven*
>   *and delivered them through Isaiah.*
> *The Lord struck down the camp of the Assyrians,*
>   *and his angel wiped them out.*
> *For Hezekiah did what was pleasing to the Lord,*
>   *and he kept firmly to the ways of his ancestor David,*
>   *as he was commanded by the prophet Isaiah,*
> *who was great and trustworthy in his visions.*

In Isaiah's days the sun went backward,
and he prolonged the life of the king.
By his dauntless spirit he saw the future
and comforted the mourners in Zion.
He revealed what was to occur to the end of time
and the hidden things before they happened. (NRSV)

CHAPTER 49:4

Except for David and Hezekiah and Josiah,
all of them were great sinners,
for they abandoned the law of the Most High;
the kings of Judah came to an end. (NRSV)

This reads like a very short summary of the royal rule of Hezekiah with all the essential details. Interesting is the mention of the image of the birthing, one would not have expected that. The whole summary seems to agree with those of the three biblical books, except for the small but decisive detail that the victory over the Assyrians is based on a plague and not on an angel of God who worked a miracle.

The Assyrian Records

Sennacherib's Annals

Sennacherib's Annals are the annals of the Assyrian king Sennacherib. They are found inscribed on a number of artifacts, and the final versions were found in three clay prisms inscribed with the same text: the Taylor Prism is in the British Museum, the Oriental Institute Prism in the Oriental Institute of Chicago, and the Jerusalem Prism is in the Israel Museum in Jerusalem. The Taylor Prism is one of the earliest cuneiform artifacts analyzed in modern Assyriology, having been found a few years before the modern deciphering of cuneiform. The annals themselves are notable for describing Sennacherib's siege of Jerusalem during the reign of king Hezekiah. This event is recorded in several books contained in the Bible including Isa 36 and 37; 2 Kgs 18:17; 2 Chr 32:9. The prisms belong to the three documents found so far, which the Assyrian monarch left behind about his campaign against Judah.

The Taylor prism is a 15.2 inches high and 6.5 inches wide, six-sided prism made of fired clay. It was discovered in the Assyrian capital Nineveh in the Tell, now called Nebi Yunus. The British Consul General of Baghdad, Colonel Robert Taylor (1790–1852), acquired it in 1830 and it was named after him when his widow sold it to the British Museum in London in 1855. The Taylor prism has been located there ever since. As one of the first large Assyrian text documents, it also played an important role in the deciphering of cuneiform script.[11]

The Chicago Prism (or: the Oriental Institute of Chicago Prism) is a 15 inches high and 5.5 inches wide clay prism. It was also excavated in the ruins of Nineveh. In the winter of 1919/1920 it was sold in the art trade in Baghdad and is now in the Oriental Institute in Chicago.[12]

They describe the siege of Jerusalem in detail and it is also described how Sennacherib conquered many villages in Judah and carried off many people to Assyria as booty. Although the siege is presented as "fait a compli," there is no clear evidence that Jerusalem was actually conquered. Since not Jerusalem but Lachish was depicted on the walls of Sennacherib's palace in Nineveh as a crowning triumph, there is at least considerable doubt whether Jerusalem was really conquered (archaeologically there is no direct evidence for this either, while the destruction by the Babylonians in 587 BC is clearly demonstrable).

According to the inscription on the Taylor Prism, Sennacherib reports about the events:

> Like a bird in a cage, Hezekiah was locked up in his royal residence. I threw up redoubts against him and made it impossible to leave his city gate.... I drove away 200,150 people, horses, mules, donkeys, camels, countless cattle, large and small.... I handed over his fortified cities to Mitinti of Ashdod, Padi of Ekron and Silli-bel king of Gaza.[13]

As on the wall relief in Sennacherib's royal palace, which will be discussed later, there is clearly no evidence whatsoever—despite full-bodied victory hymns—that Jerusalem has been captured.

---

11. The British Museum, https://www.britishmuseum.org/collection/object/W_1855-1003-1.

12. The University of Chicago, https://isac-idb.uchicago.edu/id/19b0b883-e842-4a54-9739-a5136d82702e.

13. "Sennacherib's Annals."

THE LIFE OF HEZEKIAH IN A HISTORICAL CONTEXT 183

FIGURE 18

The Taylor Prism

Greek Historiography

Herodotus (Ancient Greek: Ἡρόδοτος, romanized: Hēródotos; c. 484—c. 425 BC) was a Greek historian and geographer from the Greek city of Halicarnassus, part of the Persian Empire (now Bodrum, Turkey) and a later citizen of Thurii in modern Calabria, Italy. He is known for having written the Histories—a detailed account of the Greco-Persian Wars. Herodotus was the first writer to perform systematic investigation of historical events. He is referred to as "The Father of History," a title conferred on him by the ancient Roman orator Cicero.

The Histories primarily cover the lives of prominent kings and famous battles such as Marathon, Thermopylae, Artemisium, Salamis, Plataea, and Mycale. His work deviates from the main topics to provide a cultural, ethnographical, geographical, and

> *historiographical background that forms an essential part of the narrative and provides readers with a wellspring of additional information.*[14]

In his history books, Herodotus explicitly mentions the Assyrian Empire, all the people and events involved, and also that Sennacherib fought against the Egyptians, from whom Herodotus obviously also obtained his information. However, as already discussed, he justified the defeat of the Assyrians with a severe plague of mice, in which the mice tore up everything made of leather and thus incapacitated the Assyrian military so that they had to withdraw.

Although the mouse story seems quite far-fetched, it was told relatively early after the actual events. People who did not want to believe in God or a divine miracle obviously needed a natural explanation, no matter how ridiculous it might be.

We must not forget that Herodotus lived in the fifth century BC, which means that his records were written at the same time or even a little before the chronicles and only one hundred or two hundred years after the Kings books and Isaiah's records. So here we have an extrabiblical reporter who is very close in time, which again clearly underlines the credibility of the biblical account (with the exception of the story of the mouse).

Jewish-Roman Historiography

> *Flavius Josephus (/dʒoʊˈsiːfəs/; Greek: Ἰώσηπος, Iṓsēpos; c. AD 37—c. 100) was a Roman–Jewish historian and military leader. Best known for writing* The Jewish War, *he was born in Jerusalem—then part of the Roman province of Judea—to a father of priestly descent and a mother who claimed royal ancestry.*
>
> *He initially fought against the Roman Empire during the First Jewish–Roman War as general of the Jewish forces in Galilee, until surrendering in AD 67 to the Roman army led by military commander Vespasian after the six-week siege of Yodfat. Josephus claimed the Jewish messianic prophecies that initiated the First Jewish–Roman War made reference to Vespasian becoming Roman emperor. In response, Vespasian decided to keep Josephus as a slave and presumably interpreter. After Vespasian became emperor in AD 69, he granted Josephus his freedom, at which time Josephus assumed the Emperor's family name of Flavius.*

---

14. Wikipedia, "Herodotus," https://en.wikipedia.org/wiki/Herodotus.

Flavius Josephus fully defected to the Roman side and was granted Roman citizenship. He became an advisor and friend of Vespasian's son Titus, serving as his translator when Titus led the siege of Jerusalem in 70 AD. Since the siege proved ineffective at stopping the Jewish revolt, the city's pillaging and the looting and destruction of Herod's Temple (the Second Temple) soon followed.

Josephus recorded the Great Jewish Revolt (AD 66–70), including the siege of Masada. His most important works were The Jewish War (c. 75) and Antiquities of the Jews (c. 94). The Jewish War recounts the Jewish revolt against Roman occupation. Antiquities of the Jews recounts the history of the world from a Jewish perspective for an ostensibly Greek and Roman audience. These works provide valuable insight into first-century Judaism and the background of Early Christianity. Josephus's works are the chief source next to the Bible for the history and antiquity of ancient Israel, and provide a significant and independent extra-Biblical account of such figures as Pontius Pilate, Herod the Great, John the Baptist, James, brother of Jesus, and possibly Jesus of Nazareth.[15]

Tacitus and Herodotus top the "hit list" of ancient historians today, depending on how well known they are. People educated in the humanities are more likely to name Thucydides, Xenophon, Polybios, Livy, and Suetonius; the name Flavius Josephus would undoubtedly appear less frequently among them. However, Flavius Josephus was the most widely read historian of antiquity until well into the nineteenth century.

Josephus's account of the events of the time corresponds fairly closely to the biblical reports. Although he also mentions a plague of mice or an epidemic as a possible explanation for the defeat of the Assyrians before Jerusalem, the events and descriptions otherwise fit very well. Since he himself was obviously somewhat uncomfortable with the plague of mice as an explanation, he also states that he took it from his Babylonian predecessor Berossos. So he only quotes Berossos.

Berossos (rarely Berosos, Akkadian Bêl-re'ušunu, latinized Berossus) was a Babylonian priest of the god Marduk who lived in the late fourth century BC and was one of the most important priest-astronomers of the ancient world. He is known as the author of a historical work in ancient Greek, of which unfortunately only a few fragments have survived. Several other ancient historians quote from it, including Josephus.

Flavius Josephus's historiography clearly confirms the biblical accounts.

15. Wikipedia, "Josephus," https://en.wikipedia.org/wiki/Josephus.

Archaeological Finds

Of course, the two Sennacherib prisms already mentioned are also archaeological finds. But since they actually contain historical records, we have classified them there.

Now let's have a look at what else the archaeologists have to offer us.

Archaeological Finds in Direct Connection with Hezekiah

THE HEZEKIAH TUNNEL

This gigantic testimony to the work of King Hezekiah of Judah is still almost perfectly preserved and can be visited today. We have looked at more details about this building in chapter 3 above.

Until the year 2003, there were doubts about the age of the Hezekiah Tunnel due to its good state of preservation—until, in the summer of 2003, researchers from the Hebrew University of Jerusalem were able to determine the age of the tunnel using the C14 radiocarbon method and stalactites and other plant material found in the tunnel. It fit perfectly into the reign of King Hezekiah. Since then, this accusation about the authenticity of the tunnel and Hezekiah's construction team has never been heard again. There is now finally clarity about this.

FIGURE 19

The inscription in the Hezekiah Tunnel

THE LIFE OF HEZEKIAH IN A HISTORICAL CONTEXT 187

FIGURE 20

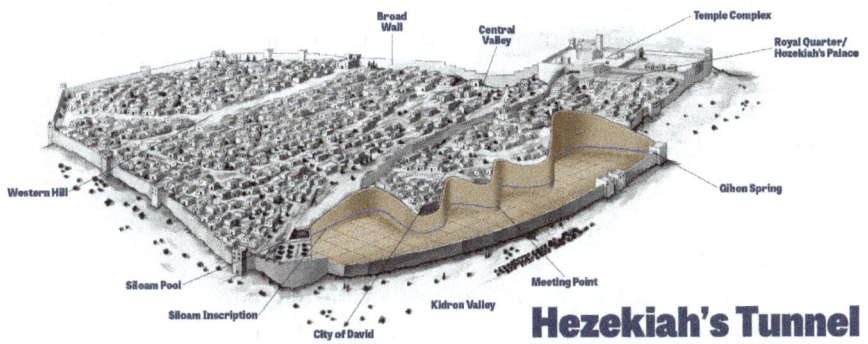

Hezekiah's Tunnel

FIGURE 21

Hezekiah's Tunnel—interior view

The Hezekiah Seal

In Jerusalem, in 2009, archaeologists discovered a 2,700-year-old 0.51 by 0.47 inches seal imprint bearing the name of King Hezekiah. The discovery during excavations in the former royal area of Jerusalem south of the foot of the Temple Mount is said to be the first seal impression of an Israelite or Judean king ever found during a scientific excavation. The significance of this artifact did not become clear until 2015, when students at the Jerusalem College were able to read "Hezekiah (son of) Ahaz, King of Judah" on the seal.

Since the mid-1990s, various seals with the name Hezekiah have appeared on the antiques market, but none of them came from secured archaeological excavations. This find now also confirms the authenticity of the other seals. The archaeologists are completely enthusiastic about this and call this find the "closest as ever that we can get to something that was most likely held by King Hezekiah himself."[16]

FIGURE 22

Hezekiah's Seal

Archaeological Finds in Connection with the Period of Hezekiah

The Wall Relief in Sennacherib's Palace in Nineveh

Here the facts speak for themselves.

---

16. Ben Zion, Ilan. "Seal Bearing Name of Judean king Found in Jerusalem" (Dec 15, 2015, https://www.timesofisrael.com/seal-bearing-name-of-judean-king-found-in-jerusalem/), para. 3.

The relief of Lachish is an alabaster relief that the Assyrian king Sennacherib had made for the southwest palace of Nineveh. It depicts the conquest of the Judean city of Lachish under this king in 701 BC. It was almost 9 feet high and 68 feet wide and covered the interior walls of Hall XXXVI of the palace, a central room of the main reception hall. A total of 12 panels of the relief were found by Austen Henry Layard during his excavations in 1849, along with other reliefs of Sennacherib, Esarhaddon and Assurbanipal. These are now in the collection of the British Museum in London.

The relief, consisting of twelve panels, depicts the conquest of the Judean city of Lachish in 701 BC in a coherent narrative scene. The narrative begins to the left of the entrance to the room with a depiction of the attacking Assyrian army. In the center of the relief, the attack on the city is depicted, from whose gates the people (later) fled and were taken prisoner. The neighboring area shows the deported Jews. King Sennacherib is depicted on the right wall, but his face was obliterated by the Medes or Babylonians when they conquered Nineveh. This is followed by the royal tent and the royal chariots. The last scene is a depiction of a military camp on the right-hand side of the entrance.

The first scene is on the left-hand side of the relief and shows slingers, archers and spears moving towards the besieged city in a landscape full of trees and bushes (top edge of the picture). The Assyrians are attacking the city walls with a siege tower.

The second scene shows the attack on the city, which is well equipped and fortified with a high and mighty wall. The soldiers attack an outer gate and parts of the city fortifications with battering rams or a kind of siege tower, behind which the troops advance with shields. The mighty siege ramp, which has stood the test of time and can still be seen today, is particularly noteworthy. Torches are thrown from the city walls onto the siege weapons. Some of the defenders flee the city.

The third scene shows the conquerors removing the booty, which consists of cultic implements and great treasures. The booty also includes children, women and men who are taken prisoner and are sometimes depicted with a two-wheeled chariot. Some men are killed.

The fourth scene depicts King Sennacherib sitting on his throne. All the figures in the entire relief are centered on him. The Jews kneel before him and beg him for their lives, while his soldiers pay homage to him.

The fifth scene depicts the camp of the Assyrian army, with the figures facing in opposite directions, which corresponds to scene 4. The camp has an oval ground plan and a resting place for the soldiers. The camp has an oval ground plan and is protected by towers and a rampart. Inside the camp are tents and sacrificial priests. There are more soldiers in front of the camp.[17]

The reliefs were discovered by the then twenty-eight-year-old Austen Henry Layard during excavations in 1845–1847. Layard wrote:

> Here, therefore, was the actual picture of the taking of Lachish, the city as we know from the Bible, besieged by Sennacherib, when he sent his generals to demand tribute of Hezekiah, and which he had captured before their return; evidence of the most remarkable character to confirm the interpretation of the inscriptions, and to identify the king who caused them to be engraved with the Sennacherib of Scripture. This highly interesting series of bas-reliefs contained, moreover, an undoubted representation of a king, a city, and a people, with whose names we are acquainted, and of an event described in Holy Scripture.[18]

For biblical archaeology, the relief of Lachish, together with the prisms of Sennacherib, represents an extremely important extrabiblical source for the biblical account of the conquest of Lachish (2 Kgs 18:13–15).

FIGURE 23

17. Wikipedia, "Lachisch-Relief," https://de.wikipedia.org/wiki/Lachisch-Relief. Author's translation.

18. Austen Henry Layard, *Discoveries among the Ruins of Nineveh and Babylon* (London: Murray, 1853), 128.

FIGURE 24

The Original Siege Ramp from Lachish

This artifact is little known and yet so highly interesting. After a very short Internet search you will find the following:

> Siege ramps are ramps that were piled up in ancient times to place siege machines against elevated fortresses on mountains, rocks or hills. Heavy battering rams or siege towers could thus be brought directly up to the fortress gates or walls. . . . <u>The oldest siege ramp to date was found in **Lachish**</u>, where it was piled up by the Assyrians under King Sennacherib in 701 BC. <u>It is the only known example of an ancient siege ramp from pre-Greek and pre-Roman times</u>. A special feature is also that a contemporary image of this siege ramp with the Lachish relief of Nineveh exists. Remains of the ramp can still be seen today.[19]

Unbelievable, right? Not only is the <u>only</u> siege ramp ever found from that time the one from Lachish, no, it is also the one that Sennacherib had depicted on his wall relief. So, we have the same proof twice: once the image by the Assyrians and once the real artifact. Unbelievable. God wants us to know that we can believe his word. We only have to make a little effort to gain this knowledge and always trust him. We will, like the author on this subject, never get out of amazement.

---

19. Wikipedia, "Belagerungsrampe," https://de.wikipedia.org/wiki/Belagerungsrampe. Author's translation.

The Grave of Azariah (Uzziah)?

In 1931, a find that, according to its inscription, represented "Uzziah's grave plate" caused a sensation. The content of the inscription is accompanied by a warning which explicitly states that the tomb must not be opened. It is a tomb slab which closed a second grave and was dated by historians to the first half of the first century AD. Professor Eleazar Lipa Sukenik of the Hebrew University of Jerusalem, the father of the famous archaeologist Yigael Yadin, discovered this slab. It is clearly not the original tomb slab from the eighth century BC—which would have been written in ancient Hebrew script—but a later inscription from the first century BC. Here it says in Aramaic, literally translated:

> *Here were brought*
> *the bones of Uzziah,*
> *the king of Judah.*
> *Do not open.*[20]

FIGURE 25

Let us remember that Azariah (Uzziah) is suspected to be suffering from leprosy and had to live in isolation for many years. And after

---

20. Bryan Windle, "King Uzziah: An Archaeological Biography" (Aug 7, 2020, https://biblearchaeologyreport.com/2020/08/07/king-uzziah-an-archaeological-biography/), para. 6.

2 Chr 26:23 he was buried in a field. So, it is very possible that he was buried under a tomb slab with a warning against infection. If the plate is authentic, it is obvious that the bones of Azariah (Uzziah) were reburied at some point. Since 1865, this grave plate has been in the possession of a small museum belonging to the Greek Orthodox Eleona Church (today: Paternoster Church) on the Mount of Olives.

The Assyrian Kings

About the Assyrian kings we find a lot of artifacts that prove their existence and reigns. And even in our days there are new discoveries, such as the underground tunnel of Assurbanipal, discovered by the ISIS in 2017 after the reconquest of Mosul, which leads to a hitherto unknown treasure chamber. Unfortunately, this was already looted by the ISIS. The interested reader may want to take a closer look at it; the author can only recommend it highly.

The Second Outer Wall of Jerusalem

Hezekiah had this outer wall built when he fortified the city against the approaching Assyrians. We have already considered this in this book and it can be read in chapter 3.

Where Even the Absence of Records Is a Testimony

The Assyrians have always been known for their will to conquer, their aggressiveness, and their brutality. They are also known for boasting these qualities and for recording them in detail and decoratively. The Assyrian rulers always tried to surpass their predecessors in everything and so the whole Assyrian records read like martial penny dreadful novels. Strangely enough, however, in the history of the Neo-Assyrian Empire there is a period of three successive royal reigns, in which this was not the case at all. These three kings were

- Shalmaneser IV   (782–772 BC)
- Assur-dan III   (772–755 BC)
- Assur-nirari V   (755–745 BC)

Interestingly, these three Assyrian kings report very little about their reign. No great campaigns, rarely conquests, no brutalities, no strict regime with the surrounding countries. We hear almost nothing from these three. How could it have come to such a quiet phase with the Assyrian rulers? That is highly unusual and difficult for historians to understand even today. Even the subsequent Assyrian kings were suspicious of this, and they derogatorily described these three of their predecessors as weak and insignificant.

Whoever reads the Bible might come up with a possible explanation. Do you have an idea?

Who does not know the story of Jonah the prophet, who did not want to fulfill the mission of God, runs away from God, goes on a ship that was supposed to take him to the other end of the then known world, only not to the place where God had actually sent him? We know the rest of the story too, the ship is caught in a terrible storm, the captain then has Jonah thrown overboard. Jonah is on the verge of drowning until a huge fish swallows him, in whose belly he can then survive and repent. After the fish spits him out on land again after three days, Jonah carries out God's mission and goes to the place where God had sent him. And where had God sent Jonah? To Nineveh! To the metropolis of the Assyrians! (Jon 1:2)

But do we know when Jonah lived and when he went to Nineveh? This is not easy to determine, since there is unfortunately no reliable extrabiblical evidence for this. But its dating can be reasonably well deduced.

> The main figure Jonah is Jonah Ben Amittai, who, according to 2 Kings 14:25, predicted the restoration of the ancient Israelite northern border by King Jeroboam II (781–742 BC). According to the biblical calendar, the time of Jonah must therefore be before or during the reign of Jeroboam II, who became king of Israel in the fifteenth year of the reign of his brother Amaziah.[21]

We now add here that Amaziah became king of Judah in 796 BC according to our chronology, so that Jeroboam II of Israel must actually have become king over the Northern Kingdom of Israel in 796 − 15 = 781 BC. **Jonah must therefore have worked as a prophet in Israel around 780 BC.**

---

21. Wikipedia, "Jona," https://de.wikipedia.org/wiki/Jona. Author's translation.

Are we beginning to understand the connections? What mission did Jonah have from God, which he then fulfilled after his detour through the fish?

> Now the word of the Lord came to Jonah the son of Amittai, saying, "Arise, go to Nineveh, that great city, and cry out against it; for their wickedness has come up before Me." (Jon 1:1–2)

And when he finally comes to Nineveh, the metropolis of the so much feared Assyrians, and, as instructed by God, announces judgment to them, what happens then?

> Now the word of the Lord came to Jonah the second time, saying, "Arise, go to Nineveh, that great city, and preach to it the message that I tell you." So Jonah arose and went to Nineveh, according to the word of the Lord. Now Nineveh was an exceedingly great city, a three-day journey in extent. And Jonah began to enter the city on the first day's walk. Then he cried out and said, "Yet forty days, and Nineveh shall be overthrown!" So the people of Nineveh believed God, proclaimed a fast, and put on sackcloth, from the greatest to the least of them. Then word came to the king of Nineveh; and he arose from his throne and laid aside his robe, covered himself with sackcloth and sat in ashes. And he caused it to be proclaimed and published throughout Nineveh by the decree of the king and his nobles, saying, Let neither man nor beast, herd nor flock, taste anything; do not let them eat, or drink water. But let man and beast be covered with sackcloth, and cry mightily to God; yes, let everyone turn from his evil way and from the violence that is in his hands. Who can tell if God will turn and relent, and turn away from His fierce anger, so that we may not perish? Then God saw their works, that they turned from their evil way; and God relented from the disaster that He had said He would bring upon them, and He did not do it. (Jon 3)

The Assyrians in Nineveh come to repentance! They recognize their malicious actions, and they convert to God! First of all, the king of the Assyrians, who obviously was in Nineveh, which was already an important city at that time but not yet the Assyrian capital. And now we can come back to our dating:

When did Jonah live and preach?

As we have just deduced, about 780 BC.

When did the three Assyrian kings live and rule, with whom it was so conspicuously quiet? No conquests and brutalities, none of the usual martial records to be found. Let us read again above. These three reigned from 782 BC to 745 BC!

Is there anything else to explain?

Is it not interesting to discover and recognize such connections? We just have to believe what the Bible tells us! Jonah was in Nineveh and by divine mandate preached the judgment of God and the Assyrians came to repentance. We can now deduce that it was their king Shalmaneser IV who wrapped himself in sackcloth and ordered his people to repent. The Assyrians were peaceful through the preaching of the Israelite prophet Jonah for about thirty-five years and three successive reigns of kings. Only with Tiglath-Pileser III does this change again in 745 BC, the "Jonah effect" unfortunately does not last any longer and the Assyrian rulers fall back into old patterns. By the way, it was Tiglath-Pileser III who was bribed by Hezekiah's ungodly father Ahaz to go to war against the Arameans and the Northern Kingdom of Israel.

And here we actually have the case where the obvious, unexpected absence of Assyrian records is a testimony, and what a huge testimony!

Afterword

When I began writing the first lines of this book, I had just turned fifty-four years old. I soon realized that this is exactly the age at which King Hezekiah of Judah died, including the fifteen years that God gave him after he was cured of the deadly ulcer. This hit me very hard. What had this King of Judah experienced and achieved—especially through his amazing trust in God? And what had I, now also fifty-four years old, achieved? For God? Relatively little, I had to admit. I really have no idea what drove me to write this book, since I have never done anything like this before (except for a "work" about a special defense in chess, which the world certainly didn't need). And then a spiritual, biblical theme? Actually, I had been thinking about a career as a novelist from time to time. In such dreams you sit somewhere on a sunny beach with crystal clear blue water, a cocktail next to you, and a laptop in front of you, on which you are writing your next bestseller. Wonderful! Now things have turned out quite differently. I still have to make my living with very exhausting and challenging office work, and I wrote this theological book. Well, I'm not going to get rich with it, that's for sure, but something has fascinated me for many years about this Hezekiah. Again and again, I was led to this topic, as well as to the story about the bronze snake. Then I actually began to write this book, at the age of fifty-four. It was not so easy; I can assure you. Very often plagued by distractions, doubts, or crises of meaning, life and faith, this book always progressed step-by-step, often with major interruptions. But perhaps that was just what was needed. Perhaps my LORD wanted me to live through all this so that he could reach his goal with me, his child, just as he did with Hezekiah in the end. Unfortunately, like so many of us, I don't know what the LORD has planned for me and the rest of my life on earth, but I ask him for this insight.

Well, you probably won't believe this, but when I am writing this epilogue and the book will be finished soon, I have actually noticed an ulcer on me that has grown menacingly in just a few days. I don't want to read too much into it now, but it makes me think again. What have I achieved for the LORD so far? Still not really much. The job, which can quickly drown us men in vanities, has eaten up most of my time, the rest of my time I have done mostly nonsensical or unholy things. May the LORD forgive me! I am such a weak and unhelpful child of God. Please pray for me.

I hope that this book, if you have read it, could give you something. At least my earthly existence might have borne some fruit for God. I, for one, am very much looking forward to meeting King Hezekiah of Judah sometime in heaven with my God and to having a very detailed conversation with him. I am very curious to hear what he will say about my book about him. I don't know if it will be quite soon or not until fifteen years from now or whenever the LORD calls me from the earth—but I am very much looking forward to this conversation.

Possibly this book is also another example of what the main theme of God is in his work with Hezekiah, but actually also with all his children:

God is Strong in the Weak!

If you are plagued by doubts or weaknesses yourself, always remember that! God does not need the strong and beautiful and rich and super smart people! God and the Lord Jesus make themselves great in the weak and simple! There are countless examples of this over and over again. King Hezekiah is only one of them. But one from which we may learn, because here God has really led his child to the extreme dependence on him—only when there was no way out according to human judgement, Hezekiah could be very close to God, trust him completely—entrust himself to *him* completely, and thus also the fate of the whole people of Judah. God had promised Hezekiah the salvation from the Assyrians long before, yes: <u>promised</u>. Hezekiah only had to <u>believe</u> and trust. And so it is no different today. If only we would trust God and his Son Jesus Christ. In the New Covenant, in the New Testament, they bought us salvation, freed us from our inner bonds and promised us so many things; if we would only believe them. Hezekiah knew nothing about all this, because the Lord Jesus was born seven hundred years later. How much easier it is for us today, who know all that the Lord did for us, what he promised us, and what the apostles recorded for us in the Bible on his instructions.

Perhaps you will take a little more time to read the Scriptures in the future? It is the message of God to you! If you ignore it, then you ignore him! I can assure you that I have been infinitely blessed in my study of the Scriptures for this book. The word of God is so alive, so current, so fresh and life-giving. I can really only ask you: read the Bible, read what God has written down for *you*.

You will experience wonder after wonder. You will discover which deep, living, and still highly topical thoughts God wants to open up to you through his word.

This he did with me. You cannot imagine how much I have been blessed by God and our Lord Jesus Christ in studying his word. How much joy and blessing I was able to experience by writing this book. I very much hope that something similar will happen to you. Please read the word of God! As often as you can. It is the Lord to whom you pay attention . . . it is the Lord Jesus Christ who is waiting to have fellowship with you. His arms are spread out, they are wide open and waiting for *you*. You only have to let yourself fall into his arms. Close your eyes, trust in God, as King Hezekiah did, and let yourself fall into the arms of our Lord Jesus Christ.

> *For the word of God is living and powerful, and sharper than any two-edged sword, piercing even to the division of soul and spirit . . .* (Heb 4:12)

> *"And God will wipe away every tear from their eyes; there shall be no more death, nor sorrow, nor crying. There shall be no more pain, for the former things have passed away." Then He who sat on the throne said, "Behold, I make all things new."* (Rev 21:4–5)

May the Lord bless you!

> *Then one of the criminals who were hanged blasphemed Him, saying,*
> *"If You are the Christ, save Yourself and us."*
> *But the other, answering, rebuked him, saying,*
> *"Do you not even fear God, seeing you are under the same condemnation?*
> *And we indeed justly, for we receive the due reward of our deeds; but this Man has done nothing wrong."*
> *Then he said to Jesus,*
> *"Lord, remember me when You come into Your kingdom."*
> *And Jesus said to him,*
> *"Assuredly, I say to you, today you will be with Me in Paradise."*
> (Luke 23:39–43)

www.ingramcontent.com/pod-product-compliance
Lightning Source LLC
Chambersburg PA
CBHW052341230426
43664CB00041B/2578